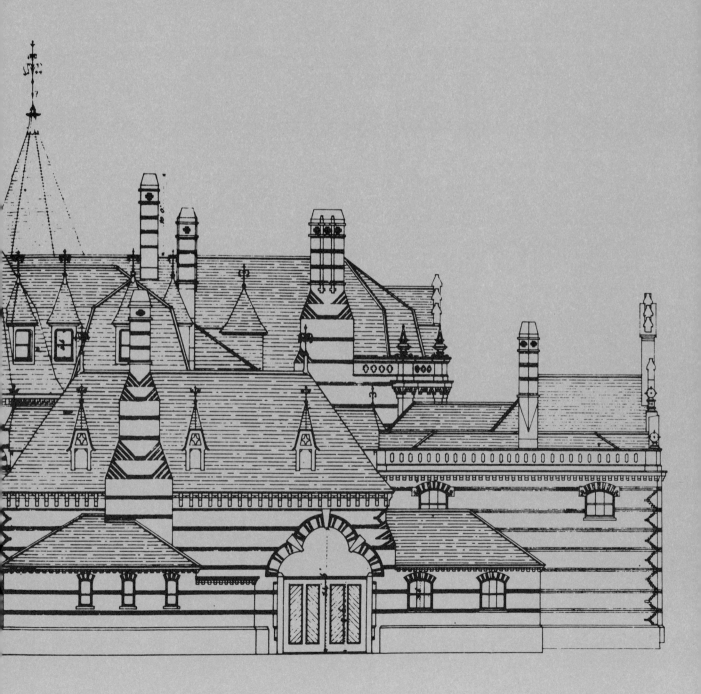

The Architectural Outsiders

THE ARCHITECTURAL OUTSIDERS

INTRODUCTION BY KERRY DOWNES
EDITED BY RODERICK BROWN

WATERSTONE · LONDON

First published in Great Britain by Waterstone and Company Limited 1985

Published 1985 in Great Britain by Waterstone and Company Ltd., London.

Designed by Nancy Slonims and James Beveridge

Distributed by Thames and Hudson Ltd (except in the USA)

Manufactured in Singapore by Imago Productions (F.E.) Pte Ltd

ISBN 0 947752 04 8 hardback

EDITOR'S PREFACE

The aim of this book is simple: to present a diverse group of architects characterised by their talent and its undue neglect; architects who are outsiders in the sense of being outside the body of designers who have been adequately studied. Beyond that, they are outsiders for various reasons: Teulon flouted contemporary sensibility; Vardy was denied the fruits of high office; Keene had a consistent problem fitting in with the taste of the day, and so on. All had skills, all made important contributions to the development of British architecture. This is true of many other architects and indeed many others were considered. The final selection was made with the intention of presenting many facets of British architecture over the last three centuries which have yet to be fully covered. The Hiorns, for example, are not only worthy of study in themselves, but also in the light they shed on provincial practice as a whole; Leoni not merely for his buildings, but for his being an Italian architect in England at a time when such a man could expect to be lionised; Hopper for representing in his diversity both the energy and the rootlessness of the Eclectic movement.

Such a collection must stand on its own. But it is hoped that this volume will prove a spur to further discoveries of architects and buildings in need of reappraisal. Wren, Adams and Lutyens were exceptional, but also fortunate. While it would be idle to suggest that these outsiders were all Wrens, constrained by ill fortune, the point must be made that an architect's reputation, both in his lifetime and subsequent eras, depends on much more than talent alone. Proper critical appreciation will, we hope, establish the reputations of ten architects who have not always had the luck of a Lutyens about them.

The authors have made their individual acknowledgements elsewhere, but everyone concerned with this study is indebted to many helpful and courteous archives throughout the country and in particular to Stephen Croad and the staff of the National Monuments Record. My personal thanks go to Bridget Sleddon and Celia Van Oss. Vital, too, has been Howard Colvin's *Biographical Dictionary of English Architects 1600–1840,* without which many more architects would be outsiders still.

Roderick Brown *1984*

CONTENTS

INTRODUCTION
Kerry Downes

WHAT IS AN architectural outsider? Is he a dreamer who, like Baudelaire's grounded albatross, finds his feet encumbered by the wings on which he should soar? Is he like the flower 'born to blush unseen', unknown and unpatronised? Or is he the one whose public presentation perhaps involves an act of faith on the part of the publisher? This less romantic category is perhaps the only one that embraces all the subjects of the pages that follow. The existence of such a category, and the idea that strength rather than safety lies in numbers, are sufficient justification for the attempt to bring together a group of such figures, each presented by a scholar with special knowledge and special enthusiasm for his subject.

The result is doubly welcome because the field is large. Each of the architects presented here is worthy of the attention he receives, and many others come swiftly to mind. Without leaving Britain, another dozen might easily be Webb, William Samwell and Hugh May from the seventeenth century, Wakefield, George Clarke, Flitcroft, the elder Dance, and Carr of York from the eighteenth, Somers Clarke, Herbert Gribble and James Colling from the nineteenth, and Owen Williams from the twentieth. All would be welcome, though not all are equally feasible. Much of Samwell's and May's work, like Pratt's, has gone, and of May hardly anything on paper survives except his will and his flamboyant signature. Pratt is fortunate not only in the preservation of his notebooks but also (unlike May, who died a year earlier) in his receipt here of a tercentenary tribute. There are certainly good reasons for choosing some architects and not others. Some are unstudied; of others, like Webb and Carr, too much is known for the space available. Yet of the chosen ten, Pratt has virtually no extant works, Hopper, Vardy and Rhind virtually no personal documents.

On the other hand six thousand words is as long as you make it. It is longer than the thin quarto Benn monographs of the mid-1920s, illustrated with F.R. Yerbury's photographs, which were notable for their time although conspicuous for the lack of an adequate wide-angle lens. Students of my generation used them — around 1950 when the longer but minuscule *Art and Technics* series came out — because there was little else: the *Pelican History of Art* was still just a twinkle in Allen Lane's eye. I paid five shillings for Birnstingl's *Soane* then, but Goodhart-Rendel's *Hawksmoor* had become a collector's piece before I had my own copy. Goodhart-Rendel's spirited essay contained a number of insights but only fourteen dates, and I dwell on this not because Hawksmoor is now a redeemed outsider with whom I have been intimately connected, but because in 1950 none of that was predictable. After presenting an interminable and tendentious if equally spirited essay on my new hero, I remember asking my tutor if there was 'enough on Hawksmoor for a thesis' and receiving the considered reply that there *might* be, because there were quite a lot of drawings.

Hawksmoor would have attained Parnassus even if my tutor had said 'No', not because anything in history is inevitable but because he belongs up there. My own good fortune lay in timing, hunch, obsession and obstinacy, the moral support of fellow students and the example and encouragement of elders and teachers. The rest is now history, but important questions arise: what makes an architect studiable, what makes him worth studying, and can he be over-studied?

Hiring an architect is not like hiring a bricklayer or a plumber; essentially and initially it means saying to him, 'Think a building for me'. The architect needs, as the Roman writer Vitruvius says, both *fabrica* and *ratiocinatio* (practice and theory), or the application of the world of the mind to that of workmanship. Thus an architect may be studiable who never built anything but whose designs, uncommissioned or unrealized, survive on paper; books have recently been devoted to unbuilt schemes in London and Oxford. On the other hand he will not be studied without someone's enthusiasm. There is also the question of quality.

William Benson's chief claim to fame is as the usurper of the Surveyorship of Works from Wren in 1718; he was patently incompetent in that office, and only a little study shows that as an architect, rather than a patron or a manipulator, he was at best a plagiarist. Nevertheless the story of his life is eventful and interesting, and further study may make it more so. Indeed an hour in any social gathering will confirm that, because it reflects our own humanity, any life-story is interesting; yet history is more than the compilation of mirror-like anecdotes.

Different kinds of historian apply different criteria to their material, and there is a range even within the history of architecture. It may be the study of building types, of styles, of structures, or of social or other external influences. The medievalist is limited to such options: the succession of William of Sens by William the Englishman at Canterbury Cathedral was chronicled because the former was disabled in a building accident, not because the stamp of either's personality on the building was originally considered significant. It was the Renaissance that gave the Artist a capital letter and introduced the concept of the monograph that underlies the present volume. And the monograph involves, with a necessity from which other historical studies are free, if not a hero at least a question of quality.

I hasten to repeat that all the architects presented in this book are of a quality deserving study. None is a household name, and three have escaped the *Dictionary of National Biography,* but none is quite unknown and some of their works are of great significance. The growth of architectural studies since the Second World War has been remarkable, and even thirty years ago none of these small monographs could have been presented with the range of scholarship, judgement, experience and documentation that informs this volume. History shows us how, if not always why, we came to be where we are now, and the landscape as we look back contains landmarks and features of many shapes, sizes and kinds. Every study of this nature clarifies a part of the landscape, and so alters and enhances our appraisal of the whole.

SIR ROGER PRATT 1620–1685

The Ingenious Gentleman Architect

Nigel Silcox-Crowe

IN 1673, SIR ROGER PRATT wrote a review of his estate and a history of what had befallen it since he had inherited in 1640 from his father. It reveals vital facts about his early adulthood:

> In this verry nick of time comes on the Civill Warre … to avoide wch storme and give myselfe some convenient education, I then went out of England about April Anno 1643 and continued travelling in France, Itally, Flanders, Holland etc. till Aug: 1649, viz about six yeares and a halfe, at wch time I againe returned after ye ende of ye warre, and ye death of ye King etc.[1]

During the war years many educated and financially solvent Englishmen crossed the channel to avoid the turmoil. Ralph Symonds, John Evelyn, Andrew Marvell, Robert Boyle, Sir Ralph Verney, Nicholas Stone the younger, Hugh May, all travelled abroad at some stage during the war. Pratt possibly found himself taking a tour which he had never intended to make, at least not one so exhaustive and protracted. Any diaries or journal which he may have kept on his travels — and he was a prolific recorder of detail — have been lost, but he later wrote about the architecture he had studied abroad as a young man. There is no reason to believe that he took an interest in buildings before he left England in 1643, and it is feasible that had the war not broken out, Pratt might not have gone abroad and would probably not have become an architect.

The Pratt family had been settled at Ryston, near Downham Market, Norfolk, since the mid-sixteenth century. Roger, the only son of Gregory Pratt of Ryston, was educated at Magdalen College, Oxford, matriculating in 1637, and at the Inner Temple, entering at the age of nineteen in 1639. Pratt remained in residence for longer than the two years or so typical for non-professional students, and bought a chamber at the Inner Temple which he kept until 1672. His accounts for the late 1650s show that he kept commons at the Inner Temple and indeed he lived in London for most of the time until 1668. Thus the indications are that Roger Pratt was at first seriously interested in taking up the study of the law, but the coming of war put an end to his studies.

Pratt's first experience of continental architecture, apart from books he may have looked at, occurred in 1643 when he made his way down through France, no doubt in the company of other English gentlemen, to Italy, to perform the *giro d'Italia*. Although he visited the Low Countries and possibly Switzerland, he would have avoided Germany, which was embroiled in the Thirty Years War. He later wrote

1. Sir Roger Pratt, portrait, School of Lely.

that the 'most beautifull Buildings of these times are cheifely to bee seene'[2] in France and Italy. In Italy he remarked upon the churches and the palazzi of Rome, Venice and Genoa. He was in Rome during the winter of 1644–45, and Evelyn later recorded that he and Pratt had been 'cohabitant and contemporarie'[3] there, although it is not clear whether they shared lodgings.

In January 1645 Pratt was in Padua; he signed himself at the University there as 'Rogerus Prat'. Evelyn was at Padua later in the year. How much time Evelyn and Pratt spent together abroad is difficult to decide, but it is not unlikely that they travelled in each other's company and perhaps toured the sights of Rome together. On 14th July 1655 Evelyn invited Pratt to dinner and referred to him as 'my old acquaintance at Rome etc.'[4] To begin with, Evelyn's learning and enthusiasm for art, architecture and gardens perhaps bore a certain influence upon Pratt's own intellectual direction. Evelyn may have been instrumental in helping along Pratt's career as an architect; he was on friendly terms with Lord Clarendon, for whom Pratt built Clarendon House, and he later wrote patronizingly of both the house and its architect to Lord Cornbury, Clarendon's son.

The impact which continental architecture made upon Pratt during the 1640s is revealed in the notes which he later made upon the subject. An educated gentleman with some talent for design and a good eye could put together a classical style house merely from study of the right books and instructing his craftsmen, but the results were likely to remain provincial and unsatisfactory. Baulms House, Hackney, London (c. 1635), Raynham Hall, Norfolk (c. 1630s), Lees Court, Kent (c. 1640), Wimborne St Giles, Dorset (c. 1650), Wisbech Castle, Cambridgeshire (1655–7), exemplify various stages of the mannered classicism which could be achieved at home, and which reached its high point with Thorpe Hall, Peterborough (1653–6).

But if a real classical house was desired, instead of an interesting, but eccentric compromise — and Pratt was insistent in his advice — then travel and study abroad were essential. Reading the right books could not guarantee authenticity, and although an aspiring builder could receive some help 'upon a most diligent studdy from those excellent, and most exact designes of Palladio, Freart, Scamozzi, and some few others,' Pratt remarked that 'yett never haveing seene anything in its full proportions, it is not to bee thought yt hee can conceive of them as hee ought …'[5]. For those who were unable or unwilling to make a continental tour and yet wanted a modern house, Pratt advised them to 'gett some Ingenious Gentelman who hath seene much of yt kinde abroad and bin some what versed in ye best authors of Archt: viz Pallad. Scamozzi, Serlio etc to doe it for you.'[6] There is self-advertisement in this advice, written at the time when Pratt was only beginning his career as an architect. Nonethcless he had recognised that architecture in England 'hath not as yett received those advantages which it hath in other partes it continuing allmost still as rude heere as it was at ye verry first.'[7]

The houses Pratt designed during the Restoration period were both innovatory and influential. Pratt built five known houses betwcen the late 1650s and 1675: Coleshill House, Oxfordshire (c. 1650s–c. 1662), Horseheath Hall, Cambridgeshire (1663–65), Kingston Lacy, Dorset (1663–65), Clarendon House, Piccadilly (1664–67) and Ryston Hall, Norfolk (1669–72). There is some evidence to show that he may have built other buildings, although no definite proof. His notes reveal that he also designed buildings which are known not to have been executed, such as plans for palaces on the Thames, which like Jones's vision of a new Whitehall, never reached fruition.

Until this century, when the study of architectural history began in earnest, Pratt's achievements, with those of his contemporaries and followers Hugh May, Robert Hooke, William Samwell, William Winde and Henry Bell, were obscured by the supposed feats of Jones and Wren. The publication in 1928 of an edition of many of Pratt's notes by R.T. Gunther, *The Architecture of Sir Roger Pratt,* to some extent disqualified previous misattributions of Pratt's work. But Gunther would not dismiss the notion that Jones and Pratt were at Coleshill together as co-architects, and he was mistaken in assuming that Pratt worked in 'an advisory capacity' at Raynham Hall.[8]

The frequency of confused attribution existed because architectural literature from the seventeenth century is rare in England. Of those who wrote concerning architecture: Bacon, Gerbier, Wotton, Evelyn, Pratt and North, the last two were the most prolific and extensive in their coverage of the subject, and are most relevant with regard to what is known of contemporary English building practice. Pratt's work is of particular importance but much of our knowledge of the careers of

3

seventeenth-century architects relies on supposition.

Pratt's architectural notes form part of a substantial collection of manuscript material which is still kept in the house which Pratt built for himself, Ryston Hall. The collection consists of nine notebooks and five bundles of loose papers. Pratt's personal accounts from 1657 until his death in 1684/5 survive, along with building notes, directions, and memoranda, copies of contracts with craftsmen, building specifications and accounts of expenditure upon materials and wages. After 1668, there are many detailed notes upon farming and land management, interspersed with notes concerned with fen drainage and the construction of his own house. Other papers deal with litigation, history and the history of architecture and with Pratt's observations and directions when he acted as an adviser to the Commission for the repair of St Paul's Cathedral, London in 1666 and as a Royal Commissioner for the Rebuilding of London in 1666–7.

Two extended essays upon building and architecture, both written in 1660, may have been intended for publication as a treatise.[9] 'Certaine Heades to bee largely treated of concerning ye undertakeing of any buildeing' was written in July 1660 and dealt with practical aspects of construction and design. This was followed in November 1660 by 'Certaine short noates concerning Architecture,' which, in conjunction with the earlier essay, gave advice upon designing on paper and model-making, and dealt with the 'formes' or types of buildings and plans for houses. Pratt, unlike Roger North, found the 'Dubble Pile' plan to be the most useful and best suited to a gentleman of modest fortune. Single pile plans were inconvenienced by weather and a lack of privacy, and courtyard plan houses, Pratt remarked, were 'without all doubt, fitt onely for a large famely, and a greate purse.'[10] He also discussed continental architecture in this essay: palazzi in Italy, châteaux in France and modern churches, usually with domes, or cupolas, in both countries. He does mention English buildings in both essays; Wimpole Hall, Chevening, Wisbech Castle, Wilton House, the Queen's House, Greenwich, the Banqueting House, Whitehall, the portico of Old St Paul's Cathedral and Covent Garden piazza. The only English architect whose work Pratt found to be 'remarkeable' was Inigo Jones.

Pratt's Coleshill House, Oxfordshire is referred to frequently in these notes about architecture, and his later houses, although all were in detail quite different, depended heavily upon its example. All Pratt's ideas about architecture are comprehended in his two 1660 essays and a later selection of advice written in 1665, 'Certaine generall rules concerning building.'[11] His later embarrassment over the building of Clarendon House, however, meant that any plans he had for publishing a treatise had to be postponed indefinitely.

It is difficult to decide whence Pratt's architecture derived its influences. He was an eclectic architect. Double-pile plans, rooftop platforms and cupolas, half-sunk basements, backstairs, dormered attic storeys, and symmetrically placed apartments had all been used before, although not so much in England as abroad in France, Italy and Holland. Pratt's achievement was to bring all these features together in a house to maximise their effectiveness, in order to gain a 'demonstrable harmony of parts'[12]; the aim of classical architecture. This formula, pioneered by Pratt and his near contemporaries, enabled English architecture to develop its own insular classical language during the second half of the seventeenth century. The type introduced, modified and popularised by the work of Pratt, May and later architects found

2. Coleshill House; Oxfordshire started c. 1657–8; the west front before destruction in 1952.

acceptance across a far wider spectrum of English middle and upper class society in the seventeenth and eighteenth centuries than the over-refined Italianism of Jones was able to do.

In November 1660 Pratt wrote, 'I conceive Architecture to bee an art teacheing us to build as wee ought, both in regard of ye person, for whom ye building is made; as alsoe for ye ende, for which it is cheifely intended.'[13]

The person for whom Pratt was building in that year was his cousin Sir George Pratt of Coleshill. The events surrounding the building of Coleshill House are not entirely clear. Between c.1645–c.1662 there appear to have been three consecutive houses begun on different sites at Coleshill. In 1645 Sir Henry Pratt, a Royalist, was either making additions to an old medieval house, or building a new one, since he made his will that year commanding his executors to collect any debts outstanding in order to finish 'my building in Colcell if I shall leave any part thereof unfinished at my decease.'[14] He died in 1647 and according to Sir Mark Pleydell (1692–1768), a later owner of Coleshill, the house he was building burnt down 'soon after' the wedding of his son, Sir George Pratt, also in 1647.[15] Pleydell does not say how soon after 1647 this occurred and he refers to the house as 'the old house,' which it hardly can have been if it was still being built in 1645.

This house, Coleshill I, was replaced by Coleshill II, which was begun, according to Pleydell, 'in ye Cucumber Garden,' and was already advanced 'one storey' when 'Pratt & Jones arriving caused it to be pulled down and rebuilt where it now stands,' as Coleshill III. In 1746 Pleydell and friends apparently found 'ye remains of ye walls

5

in ye Cucumber Garden.' Pleydell's account is unreliable however, and it may be that Coleshill I and II were the same house. Further complication arises from the fact that John Webb made drawings for Sir George Pratt in the 'Book of Capitols.' Coleshill III was astylar, and its architect had little time for the work of Webb. John Bold suggests that Webb's designs were for Coleshill II.[16] The existence of such designs need not however mean that they were executed.

A date of c. 1649–50 has usually been given to the house begun at Coleshill by Roger Pratt. This allows Jones to remain in the story, but there is no evidence for such a starting date. Sir George Pratt, although accused of Royalist sympathies, was active in supporting the Commonwealth Government; during the 1650s he sat on the Committee for Berkshire and he was a J.P. and a sheriff of the County. He avoided paying the Decimation Tax because of his friendship with Major-General Goffe. He lent £2,000 to Sir Henry Marten, the regicide, and in 1652 bought the Manor of Becket near Shrivenham from him. The nature of his sympathies meant that he had to be pardoned in 1662 by Charles II.

Jones does not appear to have been very active in the late 1640s. He had been taken prisoner at Basing House in 1645, but although afterwards pardoned, died in Somerset House in 1652, a building guarded by soldiers and usually reserved for state servants and perhaps people like Jones, whose existence was a sensitive issue and whose behaviour was monitored. John Aubrey reveals that in 1649 Jones had been too ill and old to travel down to Wilton House, so he sent Webb instead. In these circumstances, he is not likely to have been at Coleshill in 1650. The evidence suggests that the ultra-Royalist Jones, whose megalomaniac visions of a new Whitehall Palace had been swept aside during the war, would not have accompanied an unknown young man to Coleshill in c. 1649–50 to design a modest house for a country knight whose sole purpose at the time was collaboration with the new rulers of England. Sir George Pratt was a different man to his father; his republican sympathies were probably quite genuine.

During the early 1650s Pratt was living in London although he had acquired property and land of his own in East Anglia. He may have lived in Tuddenham Hall, Suffolk for a while after his return to England — he was involved in litigation proceedings against tenants there after 1652. There is no mention of any collaboration with Jones, no suggestion anywhere in Pratt's notes that he and Jones ever met. Had they known each other, or even worked together, then Pratt would certainly have said so and he does not. In 1660 Pratt wrote in 'Certaine short noates,' that builders of houses should 'lett theire undertakeings bee noe more, than what they can buye materialls for ye first yeare, build ye second, finish ye third, and at most furnish ye fourth one …'[17]

When he wrote this Coleshill was still incomplete; in January 1661/2 Pratt entertained Sir George and his wife to dinner in London and four months later in May 1662 Richard Cleare (or Cleere) the carver, sent in his bill for interior decorative work. The house was probably finished by the end of 1662. Pratt wrote his 'Certaine short noates …' with Coleshill and his experience there in mind. His accounts for the years before 1657 do not survive but he made journeys down to Coleshill in 1659 and in 1662 and possibly on other occasions. A note made in August 1660 reveals that the windows had not yet been fitted at Coleshill. When these facts are considered together with Pratt's comment about four years being the optimum time to build a house, a starting date of c.1657–58 seems more plausible for the Coleshill House built by Pratt, which survived until it was burnt in 1952.

Coleshill was a double-pile house with symmetrically placed rooms in its two main storeys. The most important rooms — the double height entrance hall and great parlour, with the dining room above — were placed in the centre of the house, with rooms of diminishing size and importance on either side. The house was

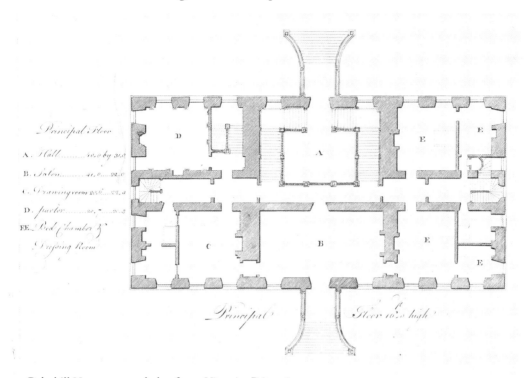

3. Coleshill House; ground plan from *Vitruvius Britannicus*.

bisected in all four of its storeys by a north-south running corridor, at either end of which were backstairs. The ceilings of hall, parlour and dining room were sumptuous and were inspired by Jones's work at the Queen's House and in the Banqueting House, where Pratt sent John Grove the elder to measure Jones's ceiling. Grove may have worked at Coleshill; he certainly worked later for Pratt at Clarendon House. There was some similarity between ceilings at Coleshill and those at Thorpe Hall which Pratt visited in May 1659. The busts of Roman emperors in roundels placed in the hall between windows and doorways were repeated at Coleshill on the pair of gate piers which survive. These piers in turn repeated the appearance of the large chimneys which gave the house its extraordinary silhouette. The busts in their niches, and the double branched staircase with its balcony-landing were Italianate. By placing such a grand staircase in the large hall at Coleshill, Pratt broke with the traditional usage of the hall as servants' eating-place and placed the servants in the half-sunk basement instead. Backstairs and corridors ensured greater privacy for the family, and the circulation patterns which a member of the household could enjoy at Coleshill were unparalleled in England in 1660. PLATE I

Half-sunk basements occur at Longleat House, Wiltshire (1570s), Condover Hall, Shropshire (1590s) and Raynham Hall, Norfolk (1630s). At Coleshill they were an

4. Coleshill House; the staircase, now destroyed.

important feature; the two main storeys, given equal treatment, sat upon the rusticated basement storey; the main entrance of the house was reached by a short sweep of steps. There was no attempt to hide the basement storey. Its rustication continued up to the eaves cornice of the roof in the angle quoining and found a subtle echo in the chunky modillions of the cornice. Compared to the interior, the external appearance of Coleshill was subdued. The nine bay east and west fronts had their centres emphasised by a wider spacing of the central trio of windows than occurred in the three bays on either side. Similar, although less subtle, fenestration rhythms were used at Old Somerset House (1540s) and at Thorney Abbey, Cambridgeshire (c. 1660). Pratt used this effect differently on the south front of Kingston Lacy, Dorset, where he grouped the central three windows slightly closer together than those on either side. The window surrounds at Coleshill were plain Palladian mouldings; those on the upper storey had bracketed architraves. The attic storey windows had alternately triangular and segmental pediments, repeating the segmen-

8

tal pediment above the entrance on the east front and the triangular above the west front doorway, both of which intruded into the plain string course dividing upper and lower storeys.

The marked horizontal emphasis of Coleshill, implied in the leisurely rhythm of windows, string courses and roof top balustrade, complied with an English preference for length instead of height, when enough space was available. The tall chimneys, like vestigial giant orders rising through the roof, gave the house an unexpected vertical counter-emphasis. Pratt had to make the chimneys tall in order to carry smoke away from the balustraded platform where people would walk, but he made a virtue of necessity by giving the chimneys cornices of their own and raised panels, like those of the great gate piers. French influence can be discerned in these chimneys, although tall chimneys had long been a tradition in English architecture. Centrally placed upon the leaded roof, between the innermost chimneys was the 'cupilow or large lanthorn,' as Celia Fiennes called it.[18] Again, such a feature appears on earlier houses: Longleat, Worksop Manor, Nottinghamshire, Doddington Hall, Lincolnshire and later at Thorpe Hall and Wisbech Castle. At

5. Coleshill House; the cupola, now destroyed.

Coleshill it was the final decorative emphasis at the centre of the house. Roger North thought cupolas were unnecessary and expensive, but following the fresh impetus given to such a feature by Pratt's work, they caught on rapidly and appeared all over the country in the late seventeenth century from Ashdown House in Oxfordshire (c.1660s) Sudbury Hall, Derbyshire (c.1670s) and Belton House, Lincolnshire (1680s), to Eagle House, Surrey (c.1700).

Celia Fiennes found Coleshill to be 'exact and very uniform', in other words a classical house. With it Pratt established a style which found immediate success. Coleshill was only just completed when he received commissions to build three more houses in quick succession.

Kingston Lacy was built for Sir Ralph Bankes to replace the Bankes's residence at Corfe Castle, destroyed during the Civil War. The house was of two main storeys above a half-sunk basement, with a hipped roof carrying an attic storey with dormers, rising to a balustraded platform with symmetrically placed cupola and chimneys. The north front, for which a seventeenth-century drawing survives, was given a pedimented centrepiece, which projected slightly forward. This feature was not repeated on the south front. Kingston Lacy was a nine bay house, built of red brick with Chilmark and Portland stone dressings used for the window and door

6. A seventeenth-century drawing of the north front to Kingston Lacy, Dorset, 1663–65.

surrounds, angle quoining and string courses. At some stage during the late eighteenth century or early nineteenth century, extensive alterations were made to the house, and between 1835–46 it was entirely remodelled and encased in Caen stone by Sir Charles Barry so that the house today is an almost wholly nineteenth-century one.

Recent archaeological investigation at Kingston Lacy has made it possible to reconstruct Pratt's original plan of the house. It was a double-pile house but, unlike Coleshill, had no corridors. The plan produced a tripartite division of the house, the centre of the building again occupied by a double height 'Great Anteroom' and 'Great Parlour' (hall and saloon), axially aligned north–south. Above the 'Great Dining Room', two large staircases, the 'Great Stairs' and the 'Great Backstairs', were placed on either side of the large Anteroom, where at first floor level a 'Pergolo' running across the rear wall linked both sides of the house. The corners of the house in both main storeys each had a smaller room accompanied by two closets, as at Coleshill.

In the most important room of the house, the 'Great Anteroom', was the balcony, or 'Pergolo' as Pratt refers to it, which no longer exists. Not only did this pergola link the two large staircases, but it also gave access into the dining room whose doorway was placed immediately above that which linked the two large rooms below. The pergola was either free-standing against the wall, in the manner of the balcony/landing at Coleshill, or else was supported upon columns, of brick in the basement storey, of timber in the principal storey. If the column support system was used, then this could at the same time have supported the cupola, part of the weight

7. Kingston Lacy as it is today, after nineteenth-century alterations.

of which would devolve through the attic floor onto the columns of the pergola below. The column system of supporting the pergola would have created an arched, quasi screens-passage in the 'Great Anteroom' below. Eaton Hall, Cheshire (1675–83) had a similar arrangement and at Ragley Hall, Warwickshire (c.1678–83) the columns also served as support for the cupola. Belton House had a gallery in its chapel, supported on columns, as did Horseheath Hall, Cambridgeshire, with its own staircase.

The principal contractor for the work at Kingston Lacy was 'Thomas Fitts of

Farnham … Bricklayer'. He was Sir Thomas Fitch (1637–1688), an important figure in the London building trade, who built himself a Pratt-influenced house in the City. The 'Articles of Agreement'[19] he made with Bankes in April 1663 are the earliest evidence of his activities so far discovered. Pratt made his own copy of Fitch's contract, which gives full directions concerning the work to be carried out, how it was to be performed and the date by which it would be completed and subsequently paid for. The whole work had to be completed 'at ye latter ende of August next insueing, at ye farthest' or else a 'penaltie of £100' would be levied.

Fitch had to provide his own labourers, mortar and scaffolding. The bricks were made on or near the building site. As the most important master-craftsman on the site, Fitch must have enjoyed the trust of the architect; he was Pratt's 'Capo Maestro' at Kingston Lacy. John Fitch, Thomas's younger brother, may also have worked at the house. In 1691 he bought High Hall nearby, built about twenty years before. Pevsner refers to it as 'a Kingston Lacy in Little.'[20]

The master-mason at Kingston Lacy was Mr Goodfellow who kept an office throughout his contract in a room in the north west corner of the basement storey. Giles Hinde, a stone cutter from London and Joseph Godfrey, a freemason from Sherborne, were brought to Kingston Lacy. Godfrey was no doubt competent in working the local Oolitic and Liassic limestones from the Isle of Purbeck. The master carpenter and master joiner were respectively Mr Taylor and Mr Allnut. Allnut worked again for Pratt at Clarendon House. Edmund Smith, the locksmith at Kingston Lacy, worked at Clarendon House and Ryston Hall. Pratt had a talent for selecting good craftsmen to work for him; Edward Pearce, who became one of the most celebrated craftsmen of the post Restoration period, seems to have found his first important commission working for Pratt at Horseheath.

Horseheath Hall, Cambridgeshire, which was demolished from 1777 onwards, was built for William, the third Lord Alington. Like Pratt and Evelyn, Alington had travelled abroad; he was living in Rome in 1652. After the Restoration he wanted a modern classical style house built, having, as Pratt recommended, 'seene much of yt kinde' abroad. Horseheath was the largest house Pratt had so far designed. It was eleven bays by seven, of two main storeys above a half-sunk basement and with the usual roofline of dormers, cupola, balustrade and chimneys. On either side of the house were symmetrical ancillary ranges, producing a compositional hierarchy of descending size and corresponding importance, from the tall main block through the two storey courtyard ranges to the final one storey ranges, all united by low walls and gateways. The south courtyard ranges contained the kitchens and related offices. On the north side were the stables.

Essentially the plan of Horseheath was similar to that of Kingston Lacy, except that the corner rooms at Horseheath were larger and the backstairs did not occupy as much space on the plan as they did in the smaller house. The circulation pattern of both plans is almost the same; no corridors, rooms arranged *en enfilade* and with the most important rooms placed centrally on axis. At Horseheath a chapel occupied the north-west corner of the principal storey, effectively interrupting circulation through this side of the house; Kingston Lacy had no such feature. The chapel took up three of the four bays in its corner at Horseheath, leaving an oddly proportioned one bay room beyond it with which Pratt himself was not happy since he noted that if the chapel was felt to be too small, then it might be enlarged 'by takeing away ye

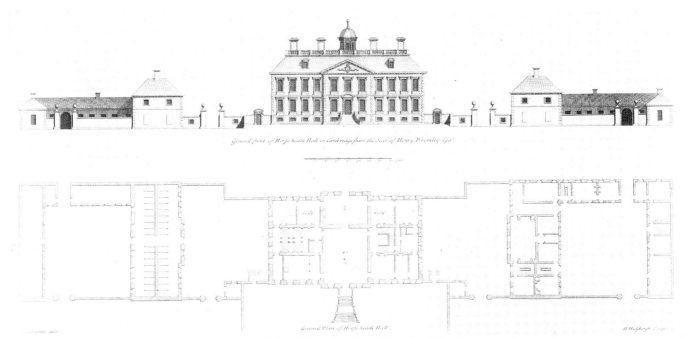

8. Horseheath Hall, Cambridgeshire, 1663–1665, plan and elevation from *Vitruvius Britannicus;* now destroyed.

partition'[21] which separated it from the end room. Roger North remarked that one consequence of the double pile plan with its constant height rooms was 'that if you have any great rooms with fitt height your lesser rooms are all like steeples.'[22] The one bay rooms at Horseheath beyond the chapel and in the south west corner of the principal storey, would have invoked criticism from North for their attenuated dimensions.

Like Kingston Lacy, the great hall at Horseheath had a 'pergolo' although in the larger house the hall was, according to North 'balconed round,'[23] on all four sides. This balcony was free standing, cantilevered out upon large wooden modillion brackets carved by Edward Pearce and his workmen. An eighteenth-century visitor to the house noted that the ceiling in the great hall was similar to that of the Banqueting House.[24] John Evelyn, who visited Horseheath in 1670 wrote that it had been an expensive house to build, costing, 'I believe little less than 20,000 pounds.'[25] He did not like it as much as Clarendon House, begun in 1664.

Clarendon House was Pratt's largest commission. It only stood for sixteen years but its location in Piccadilly and its appearance as one of the first grand classical London mansions made it the centre of attention while it was being built and an influential example after its demolition in 1683. Pepys and Evelyn were both eye-witnesses to its construction and visited the house often. Evelyn referred to it as 'my L. Chancellor's new Palace.'[26] It impressed him more than Audley End, the most magnificent of the Jacobean palaces near London.

No plan exists of Clarendon House. Several engravings provide an idea of its appearance. Ogilby and Morgan's map of London and North's comments reveal that it was H-shaped. North wrote that the house 'had a double midle frontoned and four grand pavilions'[27] but that it lacked grand 'rooms of parade,' such as the two storey hall common to Coleshill, Kingston Lacy and Horseheath. In appearance

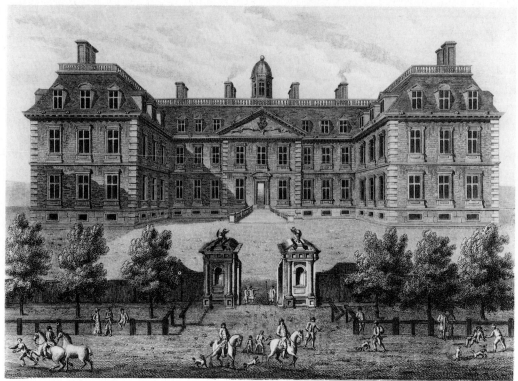

9. Clarendon House, Piccadilly, 1664–1667, destroyed 1683.

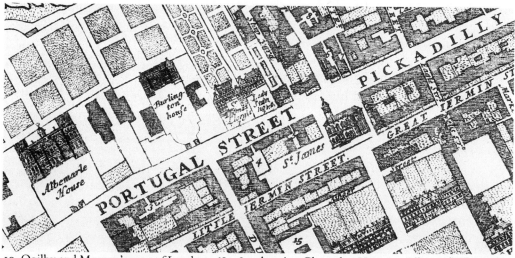

10. Ogilby and Morgan's map of London 1681–82, showing Clarendon House as Albemarle House.

Clarendon House looked almost exactly like Horseheath, except that it had wings. Its double pile centre was nine bays wide, the wings three bays each, making an impressive fifteen bay elevation.

Clarendon House had a dual function; it was the Lord Chancellor's private town house but it was also, as Pratt's notes and Pepys's diary entries reveal, the office of an important Crown servant. Amongst the list of rooms wainscotted by the joiners Kinward and Allnut appear such designations as 'The Room of Audience,' 'The

Lawyer's Lobby,' and 'The Room of Causes.' On 9th May 1667 Pepys attended a committee for Tangier at Clarendon House. In spite of its in-built capacity for continuous use as an office, Pratt stuck to his formula for a private residence with rooms of an official nature allied to those of the purely domestic scheme. There was probably no space for unnecessary 'rooms of parade,' and North's remark that no excuse would do for not having such rooms, overlooks Pratt's achievement in cramming all he could behind the impressive but not oversized façade of Clarendon House.

The craftsmen employed on the house were London men of proven ability. Robert Streeter, serjeant-painter to the King, worked on decorative paintwork. Hugh May, who was building Berkeley House next door to Clarendon House at this time, supervised some interior decoration in the latter building; he certified 'Mr Cleere' the carver's bill. Cleare had already worked for Pratt at Coleshill. Thomas Kinward, who worked with Allnut, was master joiner while John Grove the elder was master plasterer in the Office of Works. Mr Sowersby, the 'measurer' had worked at Horseheath and Mr Switzer, the Isle of Purbeck quarry mason had supplied stone for Kingston Lacy.

In spite of the employment of good craftsmen and administrators, building operations at Clarendon House, after a vigorous start, rapidly fell foul of politics, pestilence and war. Opposition to Lord Clarendon had been mounting in the mid 1660s; the large modern house he was building at London became a symbol of its owner's arrogance, power and supposedly ill-gotten wealth. Clarendon was blamed for the demolition of Cromwell's Scottish forts, the sale of Dunkirk and Tangier to the French and the disastrous consequences of the Second Anglo-Dutch War. In 1664 some stone originally intended for the repair of St Paul's was bought up by Clarendon's agent, Mr Clutterbuck, and transported to the Piccadilly building site. This event and accusations of bribery, extortion and the diversion of timber from Navy yards to Clarendon House during the war aroused popular resentment against the Chancellor. His house became known as 'Dunkirk House' and 'Tangier Hall'. In 1667 mobs smashed windows and uprooted trees there and Andrew Marvell satirised the building in 'Clarindon's House Warming'[28] in which he names Pratt as the architect and complains that the great house, which had grown 'like a vegetable', had cost the nation dear.

Between 1665–67, Pratt as architect had had to contend with the Plague which carried off many of his workmen and the war which increased the cost of timber so much that the master carpenter threw up his contract and had to be persuaded 'by faire words and promises' to continue, as well as a series of disasters on the site itself. These were listed in a letter Pratt wrote to Clarendon in February 1665/6 and included time and expense wasted in filling in an old pond, upon which the chapel pavilion was being built; rebuilding walls damaged by severe frost; adding a foot more to the height of the first floor rooms (the result of interference by Lord Cornbury) and the necessity of buying bricks from the entrepreneur Sir Nicholas Crisp, after attempts at making them on site failed, the master bricklayers and their workmen having died of Plague. Pratt was forced to admit that he had chronically miscalculated the cost of building the house. The original estimate was £18,000. When the house was finished in 1667 it had cost £50,000 to build. Castle Howard, Yorkshire, built at the end of the seventeenth century only cost c. £35,000.

Clarendon House, 'that rash enterprise'[29], was inhabited by its owner for no more than a few months. Clarendon moved there in March or April 1667. At the end of November that year he fled abroad to France.

Before this, however, Pratt took part in the decisions of two Commissions, the first for the repair of Old St Paul's Cathedral,[30] the second for the rebuilding of London in 1666–7. The Commission for the repair of Old St Paul's was constituted in 1663; Lord Clarendon was one of the Commissioners, with Sir John Denham and Henry Chicheley. Wren, Evelyn, Pratt and May are not listed, although they met at St Paul's in August 1666, as Evelyn described, and Pratt made two sets of proposals concerning repairs earlier in 1666. Pratt's initial advice was to do as little as possible in the way of repairs to the Cathedral. In May 1666 following Pratt's 'first Directions,' Wren submitted his 'Proposals' to the Commission. He wanted to remove the steeple and replace it with a dome. This idea was followed by Pratt's 'second paper,' in which he made it clear that he disagreed with Wren's suggestions, which would look incongruous, and that he believed that, if the church had to be repaired, then it should follow Jones's alterations of the 1630s. He was really against spending any money upon the church; he and Wren had disagreed over the necessity of repairs in the first place. The differences of opinion crystallized at a meeting on August 27th, attended by Evelyn, Wren, Pratt, May, Thomas Chicheley, Henry Slingsby, some clergy and workmen. According to Evelyn, Pratt and Chicheley disagreed with himself and Wren about the state of the nave walls, which they incorrectly assumed leaned outwards towards the top 'for an effect in perspective,'[31] rather than as a result of the weight of the tower and roof, as Evelyn and Wren supposed. Pratt and Chicheley disagreed over proposed alterations also; they wanted to reinforce the steeple on its old foundations. Evelyn and Wren wanted to provide new foundations and replace the steeple with a dome; they promised to bring a plan and an estimate of their proposed scheme to the next meeting. The next meeting never took place. A week later, on 2nd September, at about 10 o'clock at night 'began that deplorable fire neere Fish Streete in London'[32].

On 13th September 1666 a Royal Proclamation announced that the City of London would be rebuilt of brick and stone, that it would have wider streets, that a survey of the damaged area would be carried out and a new plan for the City made. Six Commissioners were chosen; Wren, Pratt and May acting on behalf of the King in Council; Hooke, Jerman and Mills, the architect of Thorpe Hall, on behalf of the City. The Commissioners had two duties; to survey the burnt area and to present proposals for rebuilding legislation. Their recommendations were the foundation of the first *Act for Rebuilding the City of London* (1667).

Pratt provides some details of the meetings held in October 1666. His notes describe the new dimensions which were decided upon for streets and alleys. They reveal also that the proposed survey proved impossible to carry out and that it proved unfeasible to impose a more radical plan on London. The schemes which Wren, Evelyn, Hooke and others had rushed to the King after the Fire were laid aside. Pratt, pragmatically, does not appear to have drawn up a grand design of his own. He was more concerned with the far more essential problems of stockpiling building materials and finding places in which to store them and from which to distribute them. The Commission took little further part in the rebuilding work after the Act of 1667 was passed.

Pratt's brief appearance as a Royal Commissioner, and the completion of Clarendon House in 1667, marked the end of his career as a successful architect. The knighthood he received in 1668 was a timely honouring of his services. That year Pratt wisely chose to remove himself from London.

In 1667 Pratt had inherited his family's Norfolk estates. A year later, knighted and married to Ann Monins, the young daughter of a Kent baronet, he went to Norfolk and began, in the following year, to build a new house for himself at Ryston. Ryston Hall was a modest building; nine bays wide but of unusual appearance, a hybrid of French and English classical styles. The house was originally of one principal storey above the familiar basement but with only an upper storey in the three bay central projection, crowned by a large segmental pediment on top of which perched a small cupola, or lantern bell turret, a whimsical addition of Pratt's own choosing. The

11. A contemporary view of Ryston Hall, Norfolk, 1669–72, artist unknown.

lower three bays on either side of the central projection had hipped roofs and dormers with alternately triangular and segmental pediments. The roof rose to a flat area, with no balustrade, where the chimneys were grouped symmetrically on either side. Pevsner refers to the segmental pediment as a 'solecism of French origin.'[33] In his own way Pratt was keeping up with the progression of styles and the change of emphasis which was taking place between the 1670s and 1690s. Although showing French influence in its central attention and roof line, Ryston remained a house whose style was fundamentally rooted in that form of English classical architecture which Pratt had pioneered in its early progress. Ryston was a compromise building but so were the equally Gallicized Euston Hall, Suffolk (1660s), Bedlam Hospital (1670s), and Ragley Hall, Warwickshire (1680s). The large seventeenth-century painting which hangs in Ryston Hall provides some idea of what the house and its environs looked like soon after its completion. Pratt's accounts reveal that it cost £2,880 to build, and that almost all the craftsmen he employed upon it were local East Anglians, from Kings Lynn, Wisbech, Ely, Swaffham, Horseheath, Bury St Edmunds and Downham Market.

After he built Ryston Hall, Pratt turned his enthusiasm towards farming and managing his lands in Norfolk. His notes concerning this aspect of his life are equally prolific. But he still continued to make occasional notes about buildings referring back to his earlier travels in his essay 'The new way of Architecture for ye outside of Churches'[34] and writing about Old St Paul's after it was burnt. He made notes for a Thames-side 'Princes Palace,' and he remarks upon his plans for 'Greenwich'[35] which, no doubt along with other plans and essays by Pratt, are missing.

History has made Pratt appear as an outsider. During the early 1660s he was probably the most important architect in London. Pratt transformed ideas which were current about architecture and design into a far more complete statement about domestic buildings than had hitherto been achieved. His houses were extremely influential, both in the City and in the provinces. He may well have built more than

12. Ashdown House, Oxfordshire, mid 1660s, showing the influence of Pratt's style.

has been assumed: Warwick House (c.1660s) could have been designed by Pratt; there are notes of work carried out by Pratt's workmen for Sir Philip Warwick, and a copy of a lease of land to Warwick in London exists amongst the non-estate papers of the Pratt collection. A bill for work done at Lord Alington's house in Blooms-bury exists in the collection and it does not seem unlikely that Pratt could have supervised other, perhaps earlier work for Alington in London. A small garden pavilion in the grounds of Beckett Hall, Shrivenham, owned by Sir George Pratt during the 1650s, might have been designed by Pratt as an early exercise before he went on to build Coleshill.

PLATE II

The type of symmetrical double-pile formal house exemplified in Coleshill bore an influence upon such houses as Ashdown, Oxfordshire (similar in appearance to Warwick House), Tredegar Park, Gwent (1660s), Ramsbury Manor, Wiltshire (c.1680s), Kinross House, Scotland (1680s), and Eagle House, Mitcham, Surrey (c.1700). Kingston Lacy and Horseheath both influenced houses in their regions. In Dorset, High Hall, Pamphill (c.1670), Stepleton House (1670s) and more importantly The Grange, Hampshire (1660s) and later Antony House, Cornwall (1720s), owe a debt to Pratt's work. In Cambridgeshire, Horseheath probably inspired additions to Chicheley's Wimpole Hall (1640s and later) and later houses like Hatley Park (c.1700). The Bishop's Hostel, Trinity College and additions to the Bishop's Palace, Ely (both early 1670s) identify with the Restoration classicism expounded by Pratt and May. Clarendon House, however, produced the greatest influence upon late seventeenth-century domestic architecture. Buildings which owe a debt to Pratt's London mansion are Holme Lacy, Hereford and Worcester, (1670s), Eaton Hall, Cheshire (1670s), Belton House, Lincolnshire (1680s), Combe Abbey, Warwickshire (1680s), Stanford Hall, Leicestershire (1690s), Stowe, Cornwall (c.1680s) and Hanbury Hall, Hereford and Worcester, (1700s). In Scotland, Hopetoun House, Lothian (1690s), carried the influence north. Of the houses which can be interpreted as having been influenced by Clarendon House, Belton House is the one remaining building which most closely imitated Pratt's work.

Sir Roger Pratt did not form or leave a school of architecture behind him. Other architects working at the same time or later than he, May, Samwell, Winde and Hooke, were influenced to some extent by Pratt's work, as were a host of other master craftsmen and builders whose names have been lost. Pratt's achievement was to build houses which for a time epitomised the needs and aspirations of his own class, the gentry. Chronologically, the Restoration type of house should begin with the Prince's Lodging at Newmarket by Inigo Jones, but in spite of the claims made

13. Belton House, Lincolnshire, 1684–86.

for this building, Pratt never once mentions it in his notes or essays; if he knew of it, and it seems impossible that he could not have done, then its importance and relevance for him was not as great as they have been for historians. Pratt admired Jones as an architect but he was wise enough not to copy his work.

The compactness of Pratt's double pile plans, the undemonstrative, symmetrical, uncluttered appearance of his elevations, the choice of good craftsmen, enthusiastic clients and the speed with which Pratt's house were built, all contributed to his success as an architect. After 1660, the cosmopolitanism, the newness (remarked by contemporaries) of Pratt's style would disappear rapidly into the consciousness of a nation as it spread across the country; eclecticism would emerge as Englishness. Double pile houses with axially aligned central rooms, basement offices and corridors, two principal storeys given equal treatment and hipped roofs, which gradually lost cupola, balustrade and sometimes dormers, became the norm until well into the eighteenth century.

After 1669 Sir Roger Pratt in a sense outgrew his career as an architect. In that year he moved upwards to become one of that fabled élite towards whose lifestyle and ranks he had for so long aspired, the Country Gentry. Pratt's own notes provide the best epitaph for his life and work. Describing the state of Ryston Hall, which he had owned for about eight years, he wrote in 1675:

> Besides yt ye outward face of all thinges is now soe
> exceedingly changed for the better; yt of a most deformed
> and doubtelesse an unholsome hole as it was formerly
> deemed by most men; its now accounted by them for its
> extente, to farre exceede ye most seates, and to bee
> comparable to ye best in this county of Norfolk, both for
> beauty and pleasure; it beeing much likewise advanced in
> its annual income. Laus Deo in aeternum. [36]

2

JAMES LEONI c. 1686–1746
An Anglicized Venetian

Richard Hewlings

L EONI WAS NOT an outsider, but he remains critically misplaced. He has never been quite forgotten, because he published a book which has been useful to English-reading classical architects to this day. This was his edition of Palladio, the first complete and illustrated edition in English, with Palladio's illustrations redrawn clearer and larger.[1] A damning article by Wittkower in 1954, reproducing as its only pair of illustrations Palladio's and Leoni's versions of the one elevation which Leoni transformed, has continued to give Leoni's edition a bad name.[2] It was Wittkower's belief that Leoni gave 'Palladio's designs a Baroque flavour'. Yet of the fourteen plates which Leoni altered, only six changes can be said to have been gratuitous embellishments (of which three consist of no more than the addition of window architraves). Another three are rash interpretations rather than gratuitous improvements. A further two follow the buildings as executed, rather than Palladio's plates. Two more correct Palladio's mistakes. The illustration of the Villa Valmarana is the only one which Leoni really transformed, and even that may be a rectification of what Leoni saw as an unworkable proposal on Palladio's part.[3] Leoni's alterations are of a more archaeological nature than Wittkower gave him credit for.[4]

Nonetheless a mind with an almost nineteenth-century appreciation of the value of history and of untampered evidence found Leoni's adjustments historically offensive. Such a mind animated Lord Burlington, who commissioned Isaac Ware to produce what remains the definitive version on copper of Palladio's woodcut illustrations, in 1738, no more than eighteen years after Leoni.[5] Leoni's *Palladio* bears the date 1715, but actually appeared in four instalments between 1716 and 1720, a second edition following in 1721. Despite Ware's rival version, demand was evidently enough for Leoni to produce a third edition in 1742, with some of Inigo Jones's annotations obtained from his copy of the 1601 edition.[6] Ware's, by contrast, was not reprinted. Nor was Ware paid the compliment of a pirated edition. Leoni, however, was — by Benjamin Cole and Edward Hoppus, whose *Andrea Palladio's Architecture, in Four Books* ... came out in 1735, using Leoni's plates reversed.[7] The demand for architectural illustration in eighteenth-century England was evidently enough to keep both Ware and Leoni on library shelves, Leoni in more demand than Ware. Enough also for Leoni to produce a translation of Alberti in 1726, illustrated by himself, and with some of his own designs appended.[8]

In the nineteenth century, Palladio's book was no longer the best source book of classical architecture, although Palladio's architecture was still a subject of respectful curiosity. By then, too, Palladio's translators were becoming the subject of antiquarian curiosity in themselves. Among them, Leoni acquired a privileged position just by virtue of preceding Ware. The earliest historians of English architecture made little distinction between its Baroque and its Palladian phases. Chapters beginning with Wren continue to Robert Adam.[9] In so far as the Palladian group were a hiatus of any kind for Blomfield, for Belcher and MacCartney, or for Nathaniel Lloyd, they were

> ... devoid of creative powers, often ignorant, ... content
> to adapt and copy. Wren absorbed everything and
> produced new creations. The Palladians designed ...
> slavishly.[10]

For all of these writers, Leoni was a prominent member of this servile bunch. Nathaniel Lloyd regarded its ringleaders as Leoni, Campbell and Gibbs; Blomfield chose Burlington, Campbell and Leoni. Lloyd described Leoni's monumental Lyme Park as 'a very indifferent composition', but the modest Argyll House, Chelsea, as 'domestic and cosy'.

With the change of taste in the inter-war period, from cosy picturesqueness to austere elegance, the Palladians found new champions. John Summerson, writing in 1953, expressed the revised point of view, with the Palladian revolution ushering in an entire new phase of English architecture. Leoni retained his prominence in the new order, as in the old. With Shaftesbury as its expatriate godfather, the pioneer group now comprised Campbell, Leoni, Dubois, and William Benson.[11]

Today's viewpoint only differs in details from the Summerson thesis, but one of those details would be Leoni. By the mid-1970s it was suggested that Leoni, despite his publications, was not really a Palladian at all. In 1975 Timothy Hudson wrote that Leoni

> had none of the dogmatic purism [of Colen Campbell and
> Lord Burlington], and he stood aloof from them and their
> followers.[12]

Gervase Jackson-Stops, publishing some important newly discovered Leoni drawings in 1976, described Leoni as 'rarely Palladian in the Burlingtonian sense'.[13] Summarising recent scholarship, Howard Colvin, writing in 1978, describes Leoni as

> hardly an orthodox Palladian of the Burlington school. ...
> he was prepared to introduce features of Baroque origin,
> especially in the interiors of his buildings. ... his work ...
> has more in common with that of Gibbs.[14]

In view of the high reputation now (more than ever) enjoyed by the Palladian group of architects, Leoni's separation from them is an implicit critical demotion. Leoni's critical descent is partly relative, and scarely the result of much attention on him. For in the years since 1953 research on Lord Burlington has proliferated;[15] so has research on Campbell.[16]

Meanwhile research on Leoni has produced more new commissions than have been found for Burlington or Campbell. Leoni's works have increased by nine (from 17 to 26), Campbell's by eight (from 21 to 29), Burlington's by six (from 23 to 29). Yet these new commissions have still not produced enough information to fuel a re-assessment such as Burlington and Campbell have benefitted from. In the last thirty years it has been discovered that Leoni was the architect of three London town

I Sir Roger Pratt; Coleshill House, Oxfordshire, gatepiers.

II A garden pavilion at Beckett Hall, Shrivenham, Oxfordshire, attributed to Sir Roger Pratt.

III James Leoni; Clandon Park, Surrey c. 1731–3.

IV James Leoni; Lyme Park, Cheshire, 1725–40.

v James Leoni; Lyme Park, the staircase.

VI William and David Hiorn; Foremarke Hall, Derbyshire, the entrance front, 1759–61.

houses, all rather anonymous, only known from distant or oblique photographs of their exteriors, and all three demolished. It has been discovered that Leoni was the author of a spectacular re-modelling of Thorndon Hall, Essex, but his work is only known in plan. Two very fine proposals for rebuilding a country house have been located, in a volume of drawings at Cliveden, but they may not have been for Cliveden itself, and they do not appear to have been executed. Two country houses

14. Lathom House, Lancashire, c. 1740, destroyed 1929. Central attic storey added 1862.

in the north (Alkrington and Wortley Halls) now turn out to be Leoni's work; Alkrington is rather an anonymous effort, and Wortley only survives as a facade, the interior rebuilt by William Burn. In the course of research for this article, it has emerged that Leoni worked at Wycombe House, Buckinghamshire, for the Earl of Shelburne, but, true to form, no other information about this commission has yet emerged, and, since it was rebuilt by James Wyatt, its appearance is only known from a distant and oblique eighteenth-century view.

Even with these additional works, only four Leoni interiors are known to us. Lyme Park is the work of several periods, and not many interiors are Leoni's. Clandon Park is dominated by plaster ceilings in the manner of Artari and Bagutti who worked, perhaps for Leoni, at Moor Park, and these display motifs common to Artari and Bagutti ceilings in houses designed by other architects; probably Leoni's interior decoration at Clandon was confined to the joinery, especially chimneypieces and doors. 21, Arlington Street was altered by Chambers, and evidently again c.1820, but at least retains a Leoni staircase and three distinctive chimneypieces. Alkrington Park has been divided into flats, but only by flimsy partitions; so it is the least substantially altered.

Again, despite a reasonable number of known works, few are properly documented. Three (Queensberry House, Argyll House, Carshalton Park) are only known to be Leoni's because Leoni published drawings of them in his edition of *Alberti*. Eight (Bold Hall, Clandon Park, Bath House, Alkrington Hall, Burton Park, Lathom House, Wycombe House, and the gateways at Stowe) are only known from single references by contemporaries. Five (Wrest Park, Thorndon Hall,

15. Leoni's side elevation of a country house, probably for Cliveden, 1727.

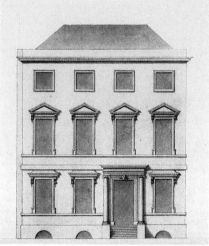

16. Leoni's design for 21, Arlington Street, London, 1738.

Cliveden House, Arlington Street, and Wortley Hall) are known from drawings without supporting documentation. Three (Shardeloes House, The Mansion House, and 4, Whitehall Yard) are known from payments for drawings which have not been seen since. For only two of Leoni's commissions are building accounts known to survive, for Moulsham Hall and Lyme Park. Very little is therefore known about Leoni's relationships with craftsmen and with patrons, about the way commissions were obtained, or work executed.

Almost the only thing which is known about the manner in which Leoni organised his career is that it was not very successful. On 8 June 1746 his patron at Moulsham Hall, Earl Fitzwalter, wrote in his account book, 'Mr. Leoni, my Italian architect, died this day. Sent him during his illness, which lasted about one month, *par charité*, £8.8s.od.'[17] But fully twelve years earlier Leoni was already in trouble. On 17 June 1734 Lord Fitzwalter wrote, 'Advanced Mr. James Leoni, £25, on account of the building I am [to] go on with next year, being in distress, £25.os.od.'[18]

It seems to have been assumed that Leoni was a Papist, although the evidence is rather slight. Nothing is known about his Venetian origins, and he was buried in St Pancras churchyard.[19] But he witnessed a Catholic marriage, together with the Venetian painters Sleter and Amigoni, in the Portuguese Embassy Chapel, in 1734.[20] On the other hand, he seems not to have compensated for this disability, as

Gibbs did, by building up a Catholic clientèle. He is only known to have had two Catholic patrons, Lord Petre, of Thorndon Hall, and Richard Biddulph, of Burton Park.

In 1726 the ratebooks reveal that he lived in the aristocratic Charles Street, St James's.[21] From 1731 to 1742 he was in Vine Street; from 1744 to 1746 in Poland Street[22]; both are in Soho, then still partly occupied by the lodgings and town houses

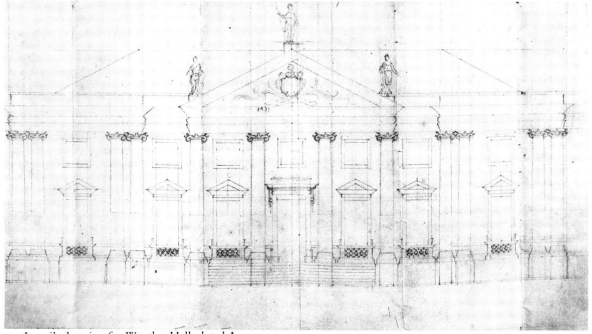

17. Leoni's drawing for Wortley Hall, dated Apr. 1743.

of the gentry, although gradually being deserted for the broader streets and larger houses of Mayfair. The larger part of Soho's ratepayers were fashionable tradesmen such as himself. It was not quite the craftsmen's casbah of St Martin's Lane, but it was within a few minutes' walk. Doubtless most architects would have acted as agents for this community in their dealings with clients, but Leoni may have acted as intermediary for, in particular, foreign craftsmen. When Lord Fitzwalter paid Andrea Soldi for paintings of his stepson the Earl of Holderness, and his grandson the Earl of Ancram, it was on both occasions 'by the hands of Signor Leoni'.[23] Whether his foreign-ness helped or hindered his social advancement is open to question.

Edward Wortley-Montagu wrote on the back of his drawing of Wortley Hall 'Rough Draught of the Upright of Wortley by Sigr. Leoni, Apr. 1743'[24], after Leoni had lived in England for nearly thirty years. Lord Fitzwalter referred to him as 'Mr.' at least fourteen times, but 'Signor' twice, both times in connection with buying pictures from a fellow Italian.[25] It seems as if 'Signor' was a compliment, recognition of his status as a *virtuoso,* and thus an early instance of social advancement consequent on the possession of a rarified sensibility. Yet he certainly made some attempt to naturalise himself. His written English was as good as most of his professional rivals, his continental origins only being revealed by occasional attempts to make adjectives agree with nouns.[26] On the five occasions when Lord

25

Fitzwalter used his christian name it was 'Mr. James Leoni.'[27] His twelve surviving autograph signatures are either 'J. Leoni' (seven times), or 'James Leoni' (five times).[28] The title page of his *Alberti* is signed 'James Leoni, Venetian architect.'[29] A subscription ticket, dated 29 March 1740, for a projected *Treatise of Architecture* advertises the author as 'J. Leoni.'[30] On only one occasion did he style himself Giacomo, and that was on the title page of his *Palladio*.[31]

His patrons do not reveal any particular social or political pattern, although there is some metropolitan bias. With the exception of the Lancashire group, all his commissions were in London or the home counties. Five were in Buckinghamshire, and this group may have a geographical rationale. For instance, John Pigott of Doddershall, who commissioned the monument at Quainton, inherited in 1735 from the widow of a distant cousin.[32] He had no previous connections with Leoni, and was perhaps introduced to him by his new neighbours.

The Lancashire patrons were so isolated and so close to each other that they must surely have formed a group. Peter Bold of Bold, Sir Darcy Lever of Alkrington, and Sir Thomas Bootle of Lathom were probably introduced to Leoni by Peter Legh of Lyme, for he was the first among them to employ Leoni, and his correspondence reveals that he introduced his architect to other gentry neighbours. Wortley Hall, although in Yorkshire, must also be regarded as part of this group, for it is less than 25 miles across the Pennines. Edward Wortley-Montagu originally engaged George Platt, whose family had been masons at Lyme for generations. But Platt died almost immediately, and it may be that his widow, who carried on his business, recommended Leoni in his place.[33] Strangely for Lancashire, none of this group were Papists. If Legh was the means of introduction to them, Leoni may perhaps have been introduced to Legh by Thomas Scawen of Carshalton. In three of Leoni's letters to Legh he presented Scawen's service or respects, in one told the Leghs that Mrs Scawen was delivered of a son, and in another he explained that Scawen was taking him to York, whence he hoped 'to make an escape for fews days to Lyme to see the progress of your Building.'[34]

If Scawen was not their means of introduction, Legh did have two contacts in the circles where Leoni might have been found. One was his first cousin, Sir Andrew Fountaine,[35] the connoisseur and architect, whose house at Narford was admired by Colen Campbell.[36] The other was the fourth Earl of Barrymore, like Legh one of the ten constituent members of the Cheshire Club,[37] whose wife was aunt to the Earl of Burlington.[38]

A further four patrons were kinsmen of Lord Burlington, and a fifth was related to one of them. Charles Douglas, third Duke of Queensberry, who built 7, Burlington Gardens, was Lord Burlington's first cousin.[39] Henry Petty, first Earl of Shelburne (of the first creation) was his uncle by marriage.[40] It may be that his employment of Leoni at Wycombe House introduced him to the Buckinghamshire group. Richard Boyle, second Viscount Shannon, who built 21, Arlington Street, was Lord Burlington's second cousin twice removed.[41] Lord George Hamilton, first Earl of Orkney, owner of Cliveden, was the father-in-law of Lord Burlington's first cousin three times removed, John Boyle, fifth Earl of Orrery, who in 1728 married Lord Orkney's daughter Henrietta. The relationship may sound distant, but on Lord Burlington's death in 1753, it was Lord Orrery who inherited his Irish peerage, becoming fifth Earl of Cork.[42] The fifth patron was not related to Lord Burlington, but was related to one of the others. This was Henry Worsley, Governor of Barbados, builder of 4, New Burlington Street, who was Lord Orkney's second cousin three times removed. Again the relationship may sound distant, but it was cemented in the next generation by the marriage in 1749 of Sir Thomas Worsley, Governor Worsley's cousin, to Lady Elizabeth Boyle, Lord Orkney's grand-daughter.[43]

The Boyle family was a large one, but its senior member was Lord Burlington, and it seems likely that he effected the introduction of Leoni to his cousins, and they to theirs. For we do know that, at least in the first few years after his arrival, Leoni enjoyed Lord Burlington's favour. It was signalled by his choice, in 1721, as architect of 7, Burlington Gardens.[44] This was the largest and most lavish of the houses on the Burlington estate in Piccadilly, the only one to face the rear elevation of Burlington House itself, and to overlook and be overlooked by his lordship's garden. Leoni was at pains to point out that Lord Burlington had approved the design for this very reason, and that Lord Burlington had himself designed the courtyard entrance, built on the Old Burlington Street elevation.[45]

Any Venetian architect could expect to be lionised in Augustan England, especially one who had published the first English edition of Palladio. Leoni must have had an automatic *entrée* to any architectural circles of his choice, at least until Lord Burlington signalled his disapproval of Leoni's *Palladio* by commissioning an improved version from Isaac Ware. Before then Burlington's evident approval indicates that some sort of understanding existed between them, and such a relationship must surely have included access by Leoni to Lord Burlington's collection of architectural drawings. The pride of this collection was the acquisition from John Talman in 1720–1 of a large part of the surviving drawings of Inigo Jones,[46] and it is therefore a reasonable assumption that Leoni saw these drawings at this moment.

Most of Jones's drawings which were not acquired by Lord Burlington had been bought c.1713 by Dr George Clarke of All Soul's College, Oxford,[47] and it happens that Leoni had a professional relationship with him also. Jointly they intended to publish the annotations made by Jones to his 1601 Venetian edition of Palladio, a scheme which Leoni only realised, and in part, after Clarke's death, by adding some of them to the third (1742) edition of his *Palladio*.[48] It is therefore another reasonable assumption that Leoni saw this collection of Jones's drawings also.

These last relationships, therefore, have consequences beyond the question of patronage, and must have significantly affected the appearance of his designs. Judged by an evolutionary ethic, Leoni performs indifferently. No motifs seem to be of his own invention.[49] Italy may have provided him with one. Germany may have provided him with five, although for four of them there are English alternatives. An English source can be found for all his remaining motifs, suggesting that English architecture would probably have developed in a similar way without him. But his continental experience was not wholly without consequence.

Leoni's chief lien on Palladio was his self-styled appellation on the title pages of both his *Palladio* and his *Alberti* as 'Venetian Architect'. Although no record of his existence in the Venetian Republic has yet been found, his claim may not have been purely promotional. For he also claimed to have measured Palladio's buildings anew, and his edition does in some particulars correct Palladio's illustrations from his buildings. In addition *Compendious Directions ...* describes in detail only familiar

18. Sansovino's Villa Garzoni, Pontecasale.

to a native how Venetian foundations were laid, walls were plastered, beams were prevented from rotting, and other local building practices.[50]

It is therefore surprising to find that his architecture does not exploit the advan-

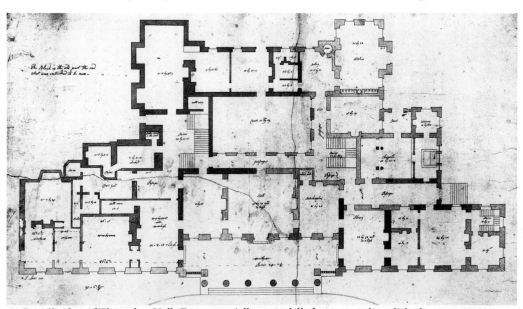

19. Leoni's plan of Thorndon Hall, Essex, partially remodelled 1733–42, demolished 1763.

tages of his birth by introducing motifs unfamiliar to the English. In a few instances a resemblance to a Venetian building can be traced. Clandon can be seen as a Palladian version of a huge *cinquecento* block by Sansovino, the Villa Garzoni at Pontecasale, near Padua.[51] Among specific features there is but one which, for lack of English prototypes, Leoni might have been obliged to introduce from the Veneto. This is the colonnade at Thorndon (only known in plan) which breaks

PLATE III

28

20. The Villa Barbarigo Rezzonico, at Noventa Vicentina, near Vicenza.

forward in the centre. The stupendous effect can be seen at one of its probable sources, the seventeenth-century Villa Barbarigo Rezzonico, at Noventa Vicentina, near Vicenza, which now makes a suitably stagey town hall.[52]

This building was not designed by Palladio. It is surprising to find that Leoni used not one motif of undisputably Palladian origin which had not previously been introduced to England by other architects. Most of the motifs he used were indigenous by the time of his arrival.

Like the painter Pellegrini, Leoni came to England from the Italophile court of the Elector Johann–Wilhelm of the Palatinate at Düsseldorf. We know this from the title-page of his *Palladio,* where he described himself as 'Architect to his most Serene Highness the Elector Palatine'.[53] This he was apparently not, for the Elector's Italian secretary, Giorgio-Maria Raparini, left biographies of all the architects and artists working on the Elector's hunting lodge, Schloss Bensberg, where Leoni, in a manuscript treatise called *Compendious Directions for Builders,* claimed to have had 'the honour to be assisting'. Raparini did not mention him.[54] But, perhaps in an inferior capacity, he undoubtedly visited the Palatinate before coming to England. We know this from another manuscript, *Li Cinque Ordini dell' Architettura,* which is signed 'Scrite e Desegnate da me Giacomo Leoni 1708 Düsseldorff'.[55]

Johann-Wilhelm's court architect was a Venetian, Count Matteo d'Alberti, but it was not Venetian Baroque architecture which Alberti introduced to Düsseldorf.[56] Alberti was widely travelled in northern Europe. In England, where he stayed from 1682 to 1684, he had taken particular interest in the work of Inigo Jones, and had seen Wren's Winchester Palace, under construction from 1683. The English experience, relatively brief though it was, was evidently the decisive one, for Alberti's architecture scarcely looks Italian at all, not even Palladian; rather it looks Jonesian. For instance Alberti's Neue Haus at Schloss Malberg, Eifel (1711–2), is a version of Jones's Prince's House, Newmarket. Leoni must have come into contact with Alberti (indeed Alberti's biographer makes the assumption that Leoni was his pupil), and, if Leoni worked at Bensberg, he did so under Alberti's direction, for Alberti was its architect. It is a reasonable assumption that Alberti's anglophilia communicated itself to Leoni, and that Leoni's devotion to Jones, apparent in his subsequent work, was acquired from this early influence.

In addition, Leoni may have learned some of Alberti's own motifs. Schloss Bensberg has a U-plan of the Versailles variety, although based more closely on the Winchester Palace variant of that plan. Its garden front, however, breaks forward in two stages towards the centre. Now this was Leoni's most idiosyncratic method of dividing up a long facade (see note 49, no. 12), and unbuilt in England on his arrival.

It is not possible to demonstrate beyond doubt that Leoni learned this motif from Alberti, for there are also Venetian examples, though not Palladian ones.[57] Nor are they typical. The commonest Venetian method of dividing a long facade was, in the seventeenth century the same as in the sixteenth, spacing the windows irregularly in a quite flat wall plane.[58] But this observation can fuel two contradictory arguments; that the double break forward motif was too rare in Venice for Leoni to have learned it there, or that its rarity, coupled with its appearance in the years just before Leoni's departure, could have drawn it to his attention. The idea certainly seems to have been in the air around the time of his departure, for his more famous contemporary

Muttoni used it in the Villa da Porto, 'La Favorita', at Monticello di Fara, built in 1714, by which time Leoni was in England.[59] However, since nothing at all is known of Leoni's life in Venice, it would be perverse to insist that he learned the motif from Italian buildings which we cannot be certain he saw, when it also occurs on a German building on which he claimed to have worked.

There is a further complication. Although no elevation with this treatment had been built in England before Leoni's arrival, John Webb had designed two. Kent published them (as Inigo Jones's work) in his *Designs of Inigo Jones* (1727).[60] For designs after 1727, Leoni could have got the motif from Kent's book. For earlier designs Leoni could well have seen Webb's original drawings, then belonging to Lord Burlington. Matteo d'Alberti could also have seen Webb's drawings, which in 1682–4 were probably owned by John Oliver, Master Mason to the Board of Works, and one of the surveyors appointed to rebuild the City after the Fire.[61] If this is the case it would furnish a particular example of how Leoni acquired a taste for Inigo Jones from a Venetian architect domiciled in Germany.

The double break forward is one of Leoni's most distinctive motifs. Even more idiosyncratic in its English context is the panelled pediment of Clandon (see note 49, no. 68). It is not quite unique, for Gibbs designed the same feature for the east end of All Saints', Derby, built in 1723–5.[62] From 1728 Leoni could have seen the latter illustrated in Gibbs's *Book of Architecture*.[63] Leoni almost certainly saw the actual building two years before Gibbs published it, because a letter to his patron, Peter Legh of Lyme Park, dated 5th April 1726, reveals that his habit was to travel to Lyme by the public coach as far as Derby, where he rested before being met by Legh's 'chair'.[64]

However, All Saints', Derby may not have been Leoni's source, for he was almost certainly acquainted with the motif earlier, from Matteo d'Alberti's Ursulinenkirche in Cologne, built in 1709–11.[65] It is perfectly possible that Leoni may have had a still earlier sighting of this motif, and this may have provided a common source for both him and Alberti. For the panelled pediment has a Venetian pedigree. Its earliest use appears to be by Sansovino, in 1532 on the Scuola Grande della Misericordia,[66] and again, in 1557, on San Geminiano, both in Venice.[67] The next generation refined it out of their vocabulary, and it did not recur until a giddier age dawned. That was in 1649 and its employer was Giuseppe Sardi, on the Venetian churches of San Lazzaro dei Mendicanti,[68] and San Salvatore, and on the Scuola Grande di San Teodoro, adjoining this last.[69] The succeeding generation, who were far from giddy, evidently found it suited their suaver purpose as well, and the motif recurs in 1706 on Andrea Tirali's San Nicolo da Tolentino,[70] in 1709 on Domenico Rossi's San Stae,[71] and, after Leoni's departure, in 1726 on Giorgio Massari's Santa Maria del Rosario.[72] So, like the double break forward, the motif was evidently in the air around the time of Leoni's departure from Venice. But, as with the former motif, there is nothing to prove that he saw panelled pediments in Italy, whereas he is known to have worked under the designer of a German example.

It is unlikely that Gibbs's use of the motif would have encouraged him, were it not for the existence of alleged Palladian authority. Palladio did not use it; but he was asked to complete Sansovino's Scuola Grande della Misericordia, and Lord Burlington acquired a drawing for its completion, in the belief that it was by Palladio.[73] Leoni, who may have had access to Burlington's drawings, may have seen this drawing (which is more probably Sansovino's), believed it to be Palladio's, observed that it contained a panelled pediment, and felt this to be sufficient authority for the use of a motif which he had probably first seen in Germany.

PLATE IV The final feature which Leoni may have learned from Alberti is more a compositional device than a motif. At Carshalton and at Lyme the elevations end pictorially where the order ends, but structurally they are continued by a foot or two of completely astylar wall recessed a little from the main elevational plane. It is as if the design were executed in shallow relief and applied over plain structural masonry. The intention at Lyme is to effect a junction between two quite different elevations by interposing a completely still *caesura*. Indeed a letter from Leoni to Peter Legh counters criticism of differences in the south and west elevations by pointing out

21. The Pigott Monument in Quainton Church,
Buckinghamshire, after 1735.

that, as complete uniformity was impossible, he had not attempted anything more than uniform floor levels.[74] Lyme was an old house being re-cased. But Carshalton was built anew, and there the device seems to have been employed for the pleasure of it. I argue below that it follows closely a design of Colen Campbell's. But there is an earlier precedent. Matteo d'Alberti's Hospital St Anna at Heidelberg treats its corners in the same manner.[75] It was built between 1714 and 1715, by which time Leoni was in England. But he may well have known it at the design stage, or his contact with Alberti may have familiarised him with the device. It is logical to assume that the earlier building provides the source, but, since at Carshalton the details are taken from Campbell's design, the device was evidently perfected by comparison to the later building.

In general compositional matters, Leoni adopted native practice in preference to Venetian, although he also used compositional rhythms of his own. His most frequently used type of elevation had a rhythm of nine bays, divided into three groups of three (ie 3.3.3) He used it six times (18%) [76]. A survey of Venetian villas, [77] reveals that this rhythm occurs only three times in a sample of 80 (4%). By contrast, a sample taken from Gibbs's *Book of Architecture* and the three volumes of Colen Campbell's *Vitruvius Britannicus* shows its relative popularity in Britain [78]: it is found thirteen times (seven instances in *Vitruvius Britannicus* alone) in a survey of 110 designs (12%).

With longer facades, Leoni's preferred rhythm was 1.1.3.1.1, used by him three times (9%) but only once in the Venetian sample of eighty (1.25%) and not at all in the English sample of one hundred and ten. With still longer facades, Leoni's preferred rhythm was 1.2.1.3.1.2.1, used twice by him (6%), but only twice out of eighty examples in the Veneto (2.5%), and, again, not at all in the English sample.

On the other hand the two most popular rhythms in both samples he scarcely used. 2.3.2 occurs twenty two times in the Venetian sample (28%) and fifteen in the English (14%). Leoni used it twice (6%). 1.3.1. occurs fourteen times in both samples (18% of the Venetian sample, and 13% of the English one). Leoni used that once (3%). 3.5.3 occurs six times in the Venetian sample (8%) Leoni used that once. Apart from 1.5.1, Leoni's favoured rhythms only occur one or two times in the Veneto.

The elevation with projecting wings at either end is almost unknown in the Veneto. In England Pratt designed a classicised version at Clarendon House by reducing the wings to slight breaks forward, more like French *pavillons* than anything Italian, [79] and Pratt's version became a standard Anglo-Baroque type. Leoni used it seven times, nearly as often as the elevation with two breaks forward towards the centre. But it may be a sign more of his anglicisation than of his interest in Baroque architecture.

Of this last there is scant evidence, confined almost entirely to a few borrowings from Gibbs's *Book of Architecture*. Leoni's two signed monuments are of a Gibbsian character. Both are sumptuous yet austere objects. The Pigott monument at Quainton, Buckinghamshire, has a black marble sarcophagus with lions' feet, a variant on the various designs published by Gibbs, set against a simple Ionic tabernacle of exotically veined marble. The monument to Daniel Pulteney in Westminster Abbey cloisters has a reading figure, carved by Rysbrack, reclining on another black marble sarcophagus of Gibbsian character. [80]

The designs for Temples at Cliveden appear to have a Gibbsian character. Temple C has a plan identical to one published by Gibbs. [81] On the other hand, the elevational treatment of both Leoni's and Gibbs's centrally planned garden temples appears to be taken from the cupolas of Jones's Whitehall Palace, of which detailed designs were published by William Kent the year before the publication date of Gibbs's book. [82]

The above are scattered gatherings, and do not remotely amount to an affinity with Gibbs's style. In common with most of his contemporaries, Leoni could hardly help being influenced in the choice of ornamental detail by Gibbs's lavish and comprehensive book. But there is one further motif which Leoni and Gibbs had in common, and that is the giant portico *in antis*. The earliest are Palladio's, who certainly did two, the Villa Badoer, at Fratta Polesine, and the Villa Emo at Fanzolo. He might have done a third, the Villa Arsiero, at Vicenza.[83] Leoni probably designed his because of Palladio's example, especially as the motif was largely a Palladian invention. But meanwhile a respectable English pedigree had accrued. Webb had designed one for Whitehall Palace in the 1660s.[84] The first to be built, surprisingly, were Archer's; one partially *in antis* at Heythrop (1699), and another at St John's, Smith Square (1713).[85] Hawksmoor built a *serliana in antis* at St Alfege, Greenwich, in 1712.[86] Thornhill built one at Luxborough House, Chigwell, c.1716–20.[87] Galilei built one at Kimbolton c.1719.[88] But Gibbs designed three, at Sudbrook (1715), Witham (c.1716) and (probably) Adderbury (1717), of which the first two were published.[89] In all Gibbs published three giant porticos *in antis* in his *Book of Architecture*,[90] and has some claim to be the *portico in antis* man of Leoni's day. Leoni must have been aware of this, however sanctioned by Palladian precedent were his own versions.

Random gleanings from Gibbs's influential book and one important motif in common do not give Leoni and Gibbs a sustainable stylistic affinity. Leoni's chief debt was to Inigo Jones. The media were principally publications, but, as argued above, he may also have had access to Jones's drawings, including those then believed to be Jones's, but which we now know to be by John Webb.

Among motifs which can only have come from the drawings is the striking plan for rebuilding Wrest Park, with a hall bisecting a great internal courtyard, approached on the long axis, and leading into a saloon whose long axis is at right angles to that of the hall, similar to John Webb's proposal for Durham House.[91] Vanbrugh designed a similar conjunction of rooms for Seaton Delaval, but this was in 1720,[92] whereas the Wrest design is Leoni's earliest known work in England, dating from 1715. Either Durham House was their common source, or Vanbrugh, untypically, was Leoni's debtor.

Another drawing must be the source for a Leoni chimneypiece. Most of Leoni's overmantels, for instance five out of six at Clandon, are variations on motifs found in Jones's numerous chimneypiece designs.[93] The only one known at Lathom has a more specific source. Its overmantel has the two flanking parts of a swan's neck pediment framing the central section of a triangular pediment. It is identical to the overmantel in the Whistlejacket Room at Wentworth Woodhouse, designed by Flitcroft, and probably carved by Henry Watson in 1748.[94] Documentation being unavailable for Lathom, it is not known who carved this example. But one evidently copied the other, neither had a published source, and both appear to be a finished version of a sketch by Webb, then in the possession of Lord Burlington.[95]

On the other hand, two major publications provided Leoni with a generous quantity of Jones's motifs. The most specific was Kent's *Designs of Inigo Jones,* though only for Leoni's work after 1727, its publication date. There, if he had not already seen it among Jones's drawings, Leoni would have seen the idiosyncratic elevation with two breaks forward. The probable source for this was Alberti's Schloss Bensburg. But the belief that Jones used it may have encouraged Leoni to do so. Kent's book also illustrates a Jones portico *in antis* (now known to be by Webb).[96] And Kent illustrates[97] a detailed design for cupolas in Jones's Whitehall Palace proposals, which, taken in isolation, look like prototypes not just for the

34

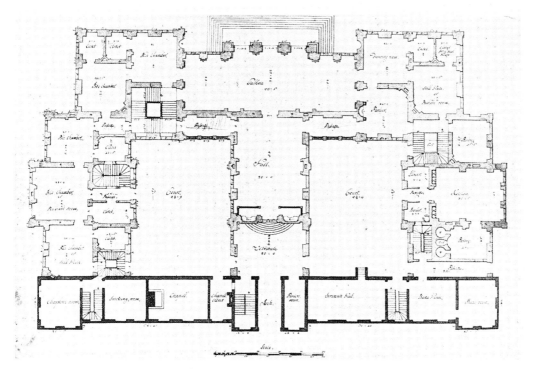

22. Wrest Park, Bedfordshire. Leoni's unexecuted plan, 1715.

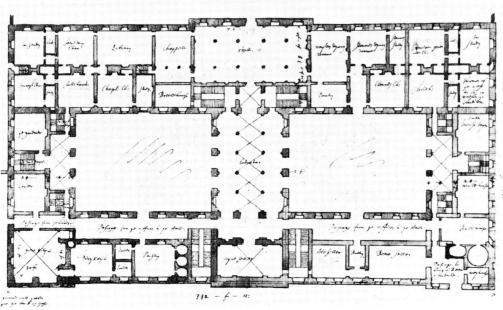

23. John Webb's proposal for Durham House, London.

Cliveden Temple designs, but for Gibbs's own circular and octagonal garden
buildings also. Despite the title of Leoni's 'Country Seat in Imitation of the Stile of
Inigo Jones', published as plate 16 of his *Alberti,* the octagonal hall and oval saloon
look more French or Piedmontese than Jonesian. Yet the source for both is in Kent's
book, the oval room from the pavilions of Whitehall Palace[98] and the octagonal one

35

from a 'Building with four distinct Apartments' (also now known to be by Webb).[99] Leoni's closest adaptation from Kent's book is actually not a Jones design, but one by Lord Burlington for William Pulteney (plate 12 of Vol. I), which Leoni made simpler and more monumental in a 'Design of a House in Town', plate 24 of his *Alberti*. Leoni's version is the better of the two, and it is perhaps not surprising that William Pulteney employed him, not Lord Burlington, to design the house he eventually built at 82, Piccadilly in 1735, although to a yet different design.

The other publication, in three volumes between 1715 and 1727, thus earlier than Kent's, was Campbell's *Vitruvius Britannicus*. It had fewer unexecuted Jones designs, but all Jones's famous executed buildings, and was thus arguably the more influential. A single building illustrated by Campbell may have decisively influenced Leoni in favour of single storey orders. Giant orders were sufficiently familiar in England as in Italy that a search for the source of the fourteen designs (note 49 no. 2) in which Leoni used one is hardly meaningful. It is single storey orders which were rarer, and their use by Leoni on nine occasions (note 49 no. 8) looks more like a conscious pose. Whether the pose was made in imitation of Palladio's Basilica or Jones's Banqueting House may have been as unanswerable for the architect as for ourselves. But a parallel argument suggests that Jones was the model. The list of Leoni's motifs (note 49) shows twelve rusticated ground floors or basements, and nine elevations of two equal storeys. Six members of these two groups are the same; that is to say, six of the nine elevations with two equal storeys have the ground floor rusticated, for

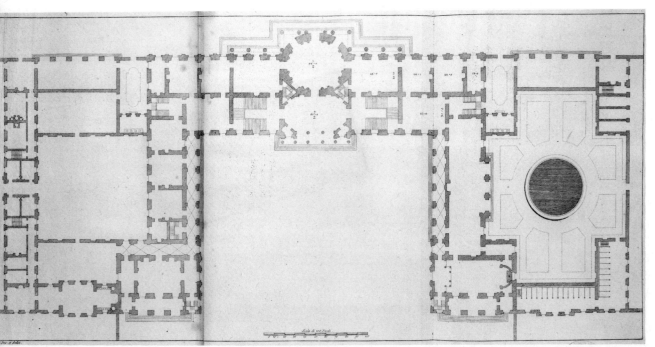

24. Leoni's design for 'A Country Seat in imitation of the stile of Inigo Jones', from his *Alberti*.

which the model was Jones's Queen's House, Greenwich, made available to Leoni in *Vitruvius Britannicus* I, plate 15.

Vitruvius Britannicus introduces a complication. Where Leoni used a motif of Jones's he may not have taken it directly from Jones's drawings, published works or buildings, but from other architects who had quarried Jones first, notably Colen Campbell. For instance, the rusticated piers at Lyme which Leoni could have adapted from the Wilton Loggio (probably designed by Isaac de Caux, but thought then to be by Jones) (*Vitruvius Britannicus* II, plate 65), he may equally have adapted from the same motif used by Campbell on the office wings at Houghton, or in a variant form on the Stables at Studley Royal.[100]

Again, although Jones supplied precedents for single-storey orders, Campbell supplied even more striking examples, of which the most conspicuous was at Burlington House. There were also Campbell's design dedicated to Lord Percival in *Vitruvius Britannicus* I, plates 96–7, and his design 'in the Theatrical Style', dedicated to Paul Methuen in *Vitruvius Britannicus* II, plate 90.

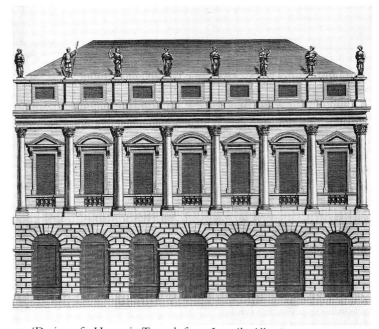

25. 'Design of a House in Town', from Leoni's *Alberti*.

So the elevations of two equal storeys, with the ground floor rusticated, could have come fron Campbell's own work, as easily as from Jones's Queen's House. Campbell published three designs of this type in *Vitruvius Britannicus* I,[101] two more in *Vitruvius Britannicus* II,[102] and one more in *Vitruvius Britannicus* III.[103] There are three more such elevations among Campbell's drawings in the RIBA, one for a town house, and two for country houses.[104] One of these is strikingly similar to Bold Hall, though two bays longer, and without Bold's attic storey.

There are even instances where it looks as if Leoni may have used motifs which were invented by Palladio, but in the form given to them by Colen Campbell. For instance, Carshalton was intended to have a pediment which was clear above the eaves line, instead of backing onto an attic or a sloping roof, in the manner of Jones's Prince's Lodging, Newmarket (note 49, no. 35). Lyme had such a pediment until Wyatt added what looks like a giant scenery bay behind it. Proper temple fronts like this, with the pediment clear of the adjacent roof line, were a Palladian invention. Palladio built two, at the Villa Barbaro, Maser, and the Villa Thiene, Quinto

Vicentino, and intended others.[105] Campbell built none, but designed two, the design dedicated to Sir Robert Walpole in *Vitruvius Britannicus* II, plates 83–4, and the 'New Design of my own Invention' in *Vitruvius Britannicus* III, plates 98–9. These two pediments and Palladio's two crowned free-standing blocks. But Campbell also applied pediments above the eaves line to the frontispieces of flat-fronted blocks in two designs in the RIBA[106], which is also what he did at Wanstead, although there the effect is blurred by the high parapets which run into the pediment on either side. Campbell's debt is obviously to Palladio. But Leoni's debt is to Campbell, rather than to Palladio direct, since, when he designed pediments above eaves level, they were not for free-standing blocks, but for the frontispieces of flat-fronted elevations.

The same argument applies to the elevation of Carshalton. Carshalton had a variant version of Palladio's Palazzo Valmarana elevation. But Campbell also did a version of the Palazzo Valmarana, the design dedicated to General Stanhope in *Vitruvius Britannicus* II, plate 86. His was a much more slavish version than Leoni's, and among the few differences are these two. First, Campbell's pilasters do not stand on individual tall pedestals as do Palladio's, but on a continuous plinth proud of the wall face, and this plinth has semi-basement windows set into it. Secondly, Palladio's facade ends where the order ends, but Campbell's is continued another foot or two. Leoni's version has a number of differences from the Palladio prototype, but

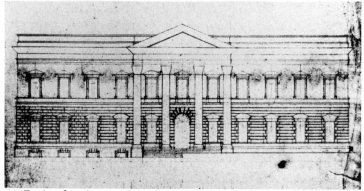

26. Design for a house of eleven bays by Colen Campbell.

these differences include Campbell's differences, to which he adhered precisely. It is evident that Carshalton is not a version of the Palazzo Valmarana, but a version of Campbell's version of it.

This dependence on Colen Campbell is rather unexpected. It is confirmed by internal detail which Leoni could have obtained from Palladio's buildings at first-hand. Enough of Palladio's chimneypieces exist for Leoni to have introduced truly Palladian chimneypieces to English architects who knew nothing about them. Jones had used French models for his chimneypieces, and Palladio's remain uncopied to this day.[107] However, Leoni used Jones's chimneypieces for ornament; and for the structure of the chimneybreast, on which Jones did not pronounce, Leoni followed Campbell. Campbell, for instance at Mereworth,[108] and his assistant Roger Morris, at Marble Hill,[109] Combe Bank and Adderbury,[110] designed distinctive chimneypieces with which the chimneybreast corresponded. The chimneybreast, instead of being continued up to ceiling height, broke back to the wall plane at the top of the

27. Bold Hall, Merseyside, 1731–8, demolished 1901.

overmantel, leaving a broad shelf for a rather old-fashioned *garniture de cheminée*. Leoni followed this in all his surviving chimneypieces (note 49, no. 9), save the one in the saloon at Clandon, which is so different from the others that it looks as if it might have been designed by the stuccadors.

Exactly the same goes for the staircases. Leoni was in a position to introduce truly Palladian stair types to break the dominance of the Baroque stone stair with wrought iron balustrade which had prevailed since the days of Wren. At 21, Arlington Street his stair is of exactly this pattern. But at Lyme and at Clandon they are of wood with PLATE V huge, square, panelled newels and fat vase-shaped balusters. Doubtless they were intended to look seventeenth-century and Jonesian; but where intention is indistinct owing to the shortage of Jonesian models, what it clearly does resemble are Campbell's stairs at Houghton,[111] Morris's at Marble Hill,[112] and Campbell's follower James Moyser's at Nostell.[113]

In fact, Leoni and Campbell had more in common than similarity of style. Both arrived in London around the same time. Leoni was definitely in Düsseldorf in 1708,[114] Campbell definitely in Edinburgh in the same year.[115] Leoni was in England at least by 1714, Campbell slightly earlier, by 1710.[117] Both produced seminal publications beginning in 1715. Probably as a result both enjoyed Lord Burlington's favour in the immediately ensuing years, Leoni's signalled by his employment at Queensberry House, as mentioned above. Equally, both were later supplanted in his lordship's favour.

Accounts for Leoni's buildings are unusually scarce, so only 48 of the craftsmen he engaged are known to us, 25 from Moulsham alone, and a further 14 from Lyme.[118] Some, like Artari and Bagutti the plasterers, Amigoni and Sleter the painters, and

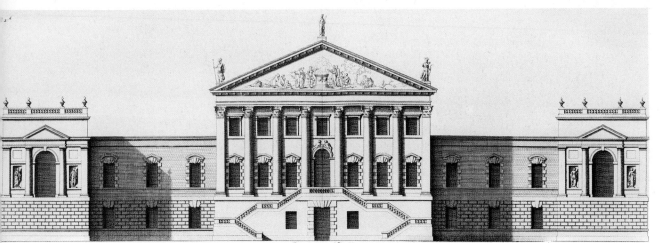

28. Colen Campbell's design for a house dedicated to Sir Robert Walpole, from *Vitruvius Britannicus, II.*

James Richards the carver, were so much at the top of their trades that they were engaged by too many architects to draw any meaningful conclusions. Of the rest, only 6 are known to have worked at any other commissions, one, the otherwise unheard of plasterer Francis Consiglio, at the otherwise unknown Euxton Park, Lancashire,[119] another, the otherwise unheard of plasterer Polfreman or Panfroyman, at Chatsworth, engaged by Paine in 1756, and again in 1775.[120] The remaining

29. An elevation for a country house by Colen Campbell, now in the RIBA.

four worked on houses designed by architects associated with Campbell. John Boson was the carver at Moulsham;[121] his only other known commissions were at 4, St James Square, designed by the Campbell-influenced architect Edward Shepherd,[122] and Culverthorpe Hall, Lincolnshire, probably designed by Campbell's assistant Roger Morris.[123] Robert Sparke, brazier and smith at 7, Burlington Gardens, and James Slater, plumber at the same place,[124] also worked at 4, St James's Square,[125] while James Richards, who executed further carved work at Moulsham,[126] may also have worked at Culverthorpe[27] and John Gardom of Eden-

40

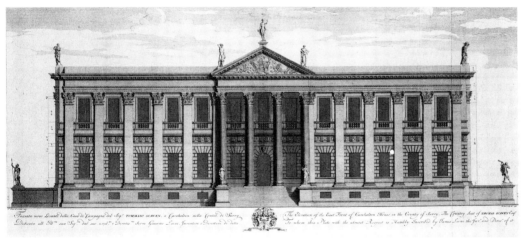

30. Leoni's scheme for Carshalton Park, Surrey, 1723, from his edition of *Alberti*.

sor, smith at Lyme Park,[128] had worked under Campbell himself at Newby Park.[129]

These are very frail links, but there is one slightly more robust. Leoni's son Joseph worked at Mereworth.[130] As his presence there is only recorded in 1739 it may not have been in Campbell's lifetime, but in that of Roger Morris, Campbell's assistant, and his successor as architect of Mereworth. And it may be that he was not directly engaged by Morris, but by the Venetian painter Francesco Sleter, on whose behalf he signed a receipt.[131] It would be unconvincing to propose that Leoni and Campbell were partners, friends or even in general professional contact on the basis of these uncertain connections, but, on the other hand, there are no other known connections between Leoni and any other English architect at all. Taken with the clear stylistic similarities described above, there is evidently a much better case for suggesting a liaison between Leoni and Campbell than there is between Leoni and Gibbs.

Leoni's ability as a designer cannot just be judged by the introduction (or failure to introduce) of motifs. The variations he developed on the inventions of others are of less interest to an evolutionary historian, but are as good an index of the quality of his work. At first his design for an arch in Hyde Park seems only a variation on the arch designed by Palladio for the Venetian entry of Henry III of France in 1574,[132] and an even slighter variation on the arches designed by Inigo Jones in Lord Burlington's collection.[133] But the circular plan of the arch's interior is Leoni's own contribution, obviously one of innumerable variants of an idea first stated in Bramante's and Sangallo's proposals for St Peter's. It is an idea which exercised students of the Beaux Arts in nineteenth-century France and twentieth-century America. Had it been designed by an English contemporary of Lutyens it would be treated with respect as architecture of some inventive flair. It would therefore be unwise to think the worse of it because it apparently found no imitators in eighteenth-century England.

Again, his designs for Carshalton are inventive enough to be intriguing, and generous enough to be dramatic, even though the individual motifs would have been familiar to his English contemporaries. This is the sort of language we usually reserve for William Kent. Kent is indisputably important, and for doing the same sort of thing. But the difference is this. When Leoni is inventive, his work looks like

31. Palladio's Palazzo Valmarana, elevation.

an accomplished, highly educated Mannerist of 1530 or 1540. When Kent is inventive his work looks Rococo. It may be that a dose of Mannerist erudition and suavity was a contributory ingredient of Rococo art in its English form. The spirit of Hawksmoor's designs, for instance, always erudite and suave despite their *terribilita,* is ancestor to the spirit of Kent's designs, although Hawksmoor's forms are not. If that is the case, Leoni has some historical importance. But his importance is lesser than Kent's, for Kent's Rococo was both the mood of the moment and a sizeable contribution to the Romantic classical architecture which followed it.

These are, however, only a few designs. Most of Leoni's designs are Palladian, of the English variety, and share the virtues as well as the vices of that architectural

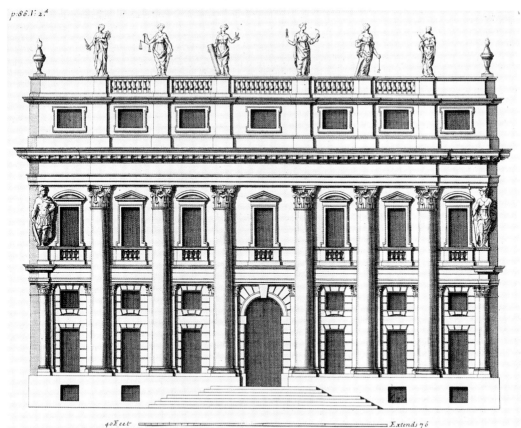

p:86.V.2.ª

40Feet *Extends 76*

This new Design of my Invention is most humbly Inscrib'd to the R.ᵗ Hon.ᵇˡᵉ James Stanhope Esq.ʳ principal Secretary of State &c :
Elevation D'un Nouveau Dessein de mon Invention .

32. Campbell's design for a house, dedicated to General Stanhope.

style. (The simple grandeur of Bold Hall, for example, deserves recognition in its own right). Historically Carshalton is less remarkable for its stylistic independence than for its dependence upon Colen Campbell, even though the former makes it better architecture. What Leoni's surprising debt to Campbell illustrates is the influence of the English Palladian architects. Apparently a Venetian architect could come to a country where anything Venetian was greatly in demand, fail to exert any apparent influence on native practitioners who were more than ready to learn, and instead produce a corpus of design almost exclusively of native type. The story of Alessandro Galilei, whose façade of St John Lateran reflects his Anglo-Palladian experiences, makes the same point.[134] So does that of Servandoni and the façade of St Sulpice.[135] That point is that in the 1720s the balance of trade in architectural motifs shifted decisively in England's favour. Irrespective of his merits as an architect, Leoni's historical importance is that he illustrates it.

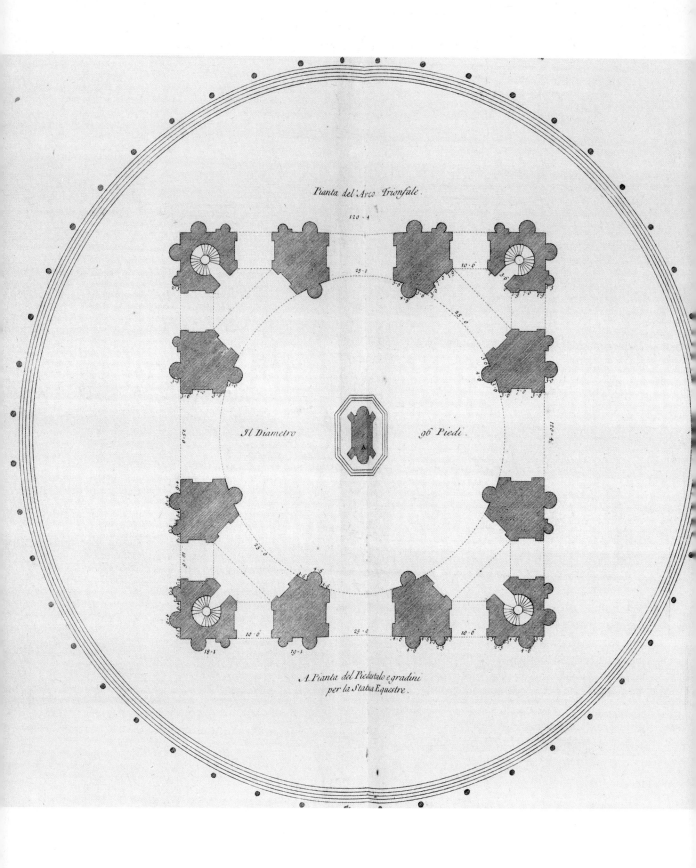

Pianta del'Arco Trionfale.

Il Diametro   96 Piedi.

A. Pianta del Piedestalo e gradini
per la Statua Equestre.

33. Leoni's design for a triumphal arch in Hyde Park, never executed, from his *Alberti*.

3

WILLIAM & DAVID HIORN
1712–1776; ?–1758
The Elegance of Provincial Craftsmanship

Andor Gomme

'THE MISTAKE might easily arise, as he was a local man who has been described as an architect.' Thus the editors of correspondence to Sanderson Miller safeguard Miller's claim to the authorship of the Shire Hall in Warwick and sweep aside suggestions that William or David Hiorn was the real architect ghosting for the gifted amateur. The Shire Hall is the best-known building in which the Hiorns took a prominent part, and Mr Anthony Wood has subsequently given good reasons for confirming that in all essential points the design was indeed Miller's. Now that foundations have been laid for re-establishing Miller's place as an architect, there is a danger that the Hiorn brothers will be considered no more than decent craftsmen carrying out the ideas or designs of others.[1] This would both belittle them unjustly and misrepresent the place of such men in the architectural history of eighteenth-century England.

Certainly they were trained as craftsmen; and the craftsman's skill and familiarity with building materials and techniques was and remained an essential element in their careers. William and David Hiorn emerged in their own right in the very middle of the eighteenth century at a moment when, as Sir John Summerson wrote, 'most provincial centres … had one leading figure, usually a mason who had 'left off his apron', who led the way in design, who designed and built the bigger houses … and whose manner was copied by lesser men'.[2] Summerson would very likely count the Hiorns among these lesser men, for they never left off their aprons (although William twice assumed mayoral robes). But there was no-one else in their province to lead them: they had to make their own way. They followed their masters, Francis and William Smith (though within a more modest geographical and social range) in being fundamentally master-builders who, through talent and the assiduous study of the best models (by then widely available in pattern-books), made themselves into architects. Their designs were never less than competent, occasionally something more, and had the inestimable advantage of being practical, made by those who had the knowledge and experience to ensure their structural soundness and an interest in their functioning commodiously.

The Hiorn family came from north Oxfordshire, where William and David's grandfather John was a mason of Great Tew.[3] Their father, another John, can be assumed to be the John Hyron who was the foreman of Francis Smith's masons at Ditchley in 1723 and was the only person outside Smith's family to be remembered in his will.[4] William, who was born in 1711 or 1712, was evidently trained as a mason and David his younger brother[5] as carpenter and joiner, without doubt within the Smith firm. Payments to them both start in William Smith's bank account as soon as he takes it over on his father's death in 1738 and are very heavy

45

34. Lee Place, Charlbury, Oxfordshire c. 1752.

from 1742 onwards when William Hiorn appears to have acted as Smith's clerk of works at Kirtlington.[6] David's work there as a carpenter is confirmed in the detailed schedule of charges included in a notebook kept, it seems, by William Smith:[7] these relate to the building of the two pavilions in 1744–5 and show David as working over the whole range of house carpentry, from the framing of floors, roofs and staircases to such small details as mouldings on doors and window-frames. It is likely, though so far no documentary evidence has turned up, that the two brothers worked on other buildings of William Smith's: perhaps including Thame Park, Barrington Park and Stanford Hall, and there is every reason to believe that by the time of his death in 1747 they were fully equipped to take over not only his place as the leading Midlands master-builder but the Smith practice itself. This may in fact not have happened immediately, for though David Hiorn's name appears for the first time in Sir James Dashwood's accounts late in 1747 (for the sort of amount 'in full of all demands' which had previously been paid direct to Smith), in those for 1749–50 there are substantial payments to Richard Smith (presumably William's rather shadowy younger brother) and almost nothing to the Hiorns.

The early 1750s must have been taken up in completing projects left unfinished at William Smith's early death. At Stoneleigh Abbey William Hiorn evidently took over immediately (he came back many years later to continue the almost never-ending decoration of the house).[8] Elsewhere, as at Charlecote, where David Hiorn designed and built a bridge in 1755 and William made internal alterations in the 1760s, or at Stanford Hall, Leicestershire, where a proposal for adding an attached order and pediment to the front fortunately never materialized, the Hiorns may have been employed as obvious local men or because the old firm was remembered with confidence and re-employed.[9] This may have happened at Lee Place, Charlbury, the Ditchley dower-house, whose conversion from a rambling farmhouse into an elegant villa began in 1725 but shows clear signs of having been started again and finished in the mid-century; it has features characteristically favoured by the Hiorns.[10]

All the Hiorns' work with the Smiths was within the context of the well-mannered but externally unadventurous Palladianism (with occasional Gibbsian touches) which emerged in Francis Smith's later years and from which his son hardly ever departed. But the first documented independent work of the Hiorn building firm was in a Gothic style. According to Messrs Wood and Hawkes, 'in 1744 Hitchcox (Sanderson Miller's own mason) and Hiorn were altering the house' at Radway: if this Hiorn is William or David they were early practitioners of Rococo Gothic[11] and in truth they had not to wait long. In 1748 Sir Roger Newdigate was inspired by his friend Miller to conceive the Gothicizing of his Elizabethan house at Arbury. The process was no hasty one: by 1750 there was a two-storey bay-window at the left-hand end of the south front — an exact replica with slight additional moulding of the bay design for Radway. Behind it, on the upper storey, Lady Newdigate's dressing-room has a pinnacled and ogee-topped bookcase and paper-thin mouldings on the ceiling and in an arched recess. The design, one must say, was Miller's, and both Hitchcox and William Hiorn were employed as masons.[12] Thereafter the gradual Gothicizing of the house through half a century was, it is now clear, to the designs of Newdigate himself, watched over by a series of professional advisers.[13] His detail shows a real eye for a sense of architectural occasion; yet he works it into formally symmetrical compositions. This is most obviously true of the south front which, except for its dazzling centrepiece, all dates from the period up to 1756 when the last payment to the Hiorns is recorded. Their first major experience of building in Gothic was in short to add pointed details to a classic body — a conception which, as with so many eighteenth-century Gothicists, circumscribed their imagination and practice: it would not be difficult for them to absorb a little later Batty Langley's doctrine of Gothic orders.

Most of the Hiorns' rather few authenticated designs are, however, Palladian or in a simple, almost styleless, Georgian which they managed to invest with some elegance. The best-documented of this latter type is Delbury House, near Ludlow, Shropshire built for Captain Frederick Cornwall between 1752 and 1756. In the early nineteenth century wings were added and the roof lowered, and a sad Neo-Georgian doorcase now takes the place of a robust Doric aedicule; but the main house is little changed outside or in. Its façade is just three storeys of seven-bay brickwork with a slight projection for the middle three bays and a light dentil cornice: seemly but unambitious. (The wider middle windows are rather unhappily proportioned, but this may be partly due to later alteration of the glazing.[14]) As often in provincial eighteenth-century houses the richer effects are reserved for the interior, which seems once to have been more highly decorated than it is now; for it is not now possible to find much of Benjamin King's carving described in detail in his invoice. But it can never have been very lavish: as with most Hiorn houses there was little decorative plasterwork. The best room is the combined entrance- and staircase-hall. The staircase, framed by the carpenter William Earl who seems to have been clerk of works, is, as always with the Hiorns, of a type beginning to look old-fashioned by

35. Delbury House, near Ludlow, Shropshire, 1751–6.

the mid-century — open-string with slender balusters (in this case twisted, in pairs) standing on the treads. It climbs slowly through two flights only with an unusual pause for a half-pace in the middle of the second, directly opposite the entrance, and continues into an upper gallery whose supporting rail is carved with a Chinese fret similar to several illustrated in Chippendale's *Director* (the secondary staircase has a cockpen rail throughout). The gallery facing the entrance opens on to the hall with almost Roman grandeur through three widely spaced arches — an adaptation of such gallery schemes as those of Ombersley and Kelmarsh (and ultimately Grimsthorpe).

Delbury was an inexpensive house, costing altogether £1,757; this excluded the stables but did include all the finishing inside, a small amount for furniture and the Hiorns' 5% 'poundage' for design, measurement and supervision. The work of framing and building the carcase of the house represents perhaps two fifths of this. The house was built 'by the great', the Hiorns estimating for the entire scheme and sub-contracting all but the masonry and joinery. Such was their regular practice (they would sometimes additionally do the carpentry themselves), the skilled work always being entrusted to craftsmen from Warwick and the surrounding area whose names occur repeatedly in accounts and letters. Benjamin King, the highly talented Rococo carver in both wood and stone, worked (among buildings where the Hiorns were in charge) at Arbury, Delbury, Farnborough, Kyre, Packington, Stivichall, Stoneleigh, Warwick Shire Hall and Warwick Castle; George Roberts, plasterer (Delbury and Kyre) who did not do anything elaborate, gives way to Robert Moore (Arbury, Charlecote, Compton Verney, Packington, Stivichall, Stoneleigh, Warwick); Richard Newman, mason and stone-carver, who had been at

48

36. Delbury House, the staircase.

Edgcote, was at Farnborough, Stivichall and the Shire Hall; James Bogville, painter, at Delbury, Kyre and Stivichall, and Thomas Blockley regularly provided the locks (Delbury, Compton Verney, Kyre, Stivichall, Wolverley). As with the Smiths and a previous generation of craftsmen, these men would be, and would expect to be, called on regularly by the Hiorns who as master-masons would always be the principal contractors. They appear to have inherited and maintained the Smiths' reputation for economical and reliable building, and the craftsmanship is consistently of an exemplary standard. (The highly experienced builder who recently converted Wolverley House told me that in no other house that he had worked on had he seen such excellent carpentry and joinery, and the brickwork is of wonderful fitness and accuracy.) This, in the exteriors of their houses, went with a characteristic provincial conservatism — the Hiorns were not great inventors and did not, on the whole, design for those who wanted to cut a dash — and almost always one finds old-fashioned elements side by side with others drawn from up-to-date pattern-books. Rococo as interpreted by Benjamin King, for whose work they made ample space within conventionally planned rooms, was obviously much to their taste, representating a lightening of Palladian severity, though sometimes combined with strong volutes or Kentian pediments sustaining a link with the ways in which the Hiorns had been brought up.

It seems likely therefore, on stylistic and geographical grounds, that the Hiorns and their team were responsible for the Rococo Palladianism of Four Oaks Hall, Sutton Coldfield, West Midlands, which evidently was reconstructed in the 1750s

37. Rode Hall, near Alsager, Cheshire, 1752.

and given an Ionic frontispiece, which looked nearly as cramped as that intended for Stanford, and curiously lumpish corner towers. The same kind of elegantly restrained decoration as was once in the hall at Four Oaks, together with plasterwork probably by Robert Moore is still mouldering away at Guy's Cliffe House, Warwick, whose 1751 façade, incipiently Neo-classical with pediments at each end, could, with its skirted architraves and balustraded windows, equally well be by the Hiorns or by Henry Keene, already at this time active in the Midlands.[15] Yet a few years later interiors for Gopsall show the Hiorns in the full flight of the most exuberant Rococo, obviously much under the spell of Chippendale, though not, it seems, copying his designs exactly. Indeed one chimneypiece goes beyond Chippendale in eliminating the horizontal line of the shelf and fusing chimneypiece and overmantel into a single flowing design; a reading-desk for the chapel, however, combines florid Rococo cresting with a formal classicism which looks forward to the Regency.[16]

The entrance front of the new house built on to the old at Rode Hall, near Alsager, Cheshire in 1752 is even plainer than Delbury — five bays wide, three storeys high, with nothing but its fine spacious proportions and excellent brickwork to commend it (though its windows once had architraves).[17] But it originally had polygonal extensions and probably a Venetian entrance. (A Venetian window lights the formula staircase and some robust Rococo plasterwork). Full-height polygonal bays are a striking feature of Kyre Park, near Tenbury, Hereford and Worcester (1751–6 for Edmund Pytts), which was the partial reconstruction of a medieval-cum-Elizabethan house, whose masonry still shows here and there among the Georgian brick and provided very thick walls between which to work in eighteenth-century elegance. For their main (west) front the Hiorns used the well-tried villa formula —

38. Kyre Park, Hereford and Worcester, 1753–6.

five bays, the middle three projecting under a pediment, with an attic storey above the main cornice. On the return façades, beyond the canted bays, are two layers of Venetian windows and in the attic a thermal one — features which the Hiorns obviously delighted in, so that throughout the 1750s there is hardly a building of theirs, house or church, which does not incorporate one or both. But for the date one might have guessed that they picked them up from working to Flitcroft's designs at Stivichall, near Coventry, where they formed a main feature; but that house was not begun until 1755, though thereafter the Hiorns appear to have been in sole charge with their familiar band of craftsmen.[18] Kyre's costing compares closely with Delbury's — £1,944 in all, but this included the stables and an octagonal summer-house. Most of the interiors, which included Rococo chimney-pieces in King's best style, were apparently removed during alterations in the 1960s for the Birmingham Hospital Board, but the characteristic staircase remains, with a variant

39. Wolverley House, Hereford and Worcester, c. 1749–52, the entrance front.

form of the Delbury fret.[19]

Wolverley House, near Kidderminster, also belongs in this group, though the attribution is essentially stylistic: the house was probably built by Edward Knight (who was certainly settled there by the 1750s), ironmaster, uncle of Richard Payne Knight and connoisseur in his own right: he was the most important early patron of Flaxman. A date of 1752 was recently found on a tile in the stable roof. Knight kept diaries, in one of which he notes houses he has visited, sometimes with the architects' names attached. Kirtlington he describes as 'by Smith and Hiorns'; since the Hiorns worked at Kirtlington in a decidedly subordinate role, it seems plausible that Knight's noting of their name implies that he already had an interest in it: he mentions them nowhere else.[20] It is by no means certain that the two main façades of Wolverley belong to one building operation. The entrance front to the west is very plain but extraordinarily stately — just seven bays of three-storey brickwork, with quoins, Doric cornice, plain parapet and Doric doorcase (the latter now rather crudely restored), plain window openings with flat arches and keystones. Nothing could be simpler, and nothing more calmly satisfying in its self-confident dignity. The east front, though it is as long, has only five bays, the very wide central one breaking forward under a pediment with Venetian doorcase and first-floor (stair-case) window and thermal window in the attic: a more spacious paraphrase of the front of Stivichall. All the windows have stepped architraves, keystones and little brackets under the sills — comfortable old-fashioned Hiornish details. The interior, now divided into flats, reveals little apart from some panelling which looks suspi-ciously early eighteenth-century and the staircase crowded into the narrow entrance hall. One enters from the east underneath it, as one does at Edgbaston Hall, whose interiors were done up by the Hiorns in 1751–2; hence the somewhat cramped

52

40. Wolverley House, the east front.

doorcase, whose fantastic glazing is presumably due to a more recent whim.

In the mid-1750s the Hiorns' most important building work was the Warwick Shire Hall. They certainly drew out the working plans, but all the evidence points to their having been in this case simply the executants, though an inscription on a plate fixed to the roof timbers calls them 'surveyors' and Miller was evidently glad of Mr Hiorns' vigorous support (against Thomas Prowse 'and other good judges') for his columnar octagonal court-rooms.[21] Several of the craftsmen they frequently used were on the job too: Richard Newman, Robert Moore, David Sanders the carpenter, and Benjamin King working solely in stone. All the external stonework has been renewed and recarved, but King's capitals and 'festoons' of his favourite fruit and flowers, continuing a late seventeenth-century tradition perhaps passed on to the Warwick men by Edward Poynton, remain inside the hall. His design for the Corinthian capitals drew criticism from Prowse, and in the end it was left to the London sculptor James Lovell to adjudicate. The design chosen, whether or not King's original, is a familiar Vitruvian one, taken ultimately from Fréart's *Parallel* which in Evelyn's translation was still in common currency: the episode indicates how much of the detailed work was settled by craftsmen, and though Miller's festive and imaginative design for the Hall is highly literate, doubtless the Hiorns had to determine the classical detail from their own knowledge:[22] working under Miller would hardly have provided the example they might draw even from a camp-follower like Flitcroft, and since William Smith himself nothing better in that line ever came their way.

But there were buildings to copy and pattern-books to work from. The Hiorns' most substantial church, Holy Cross, Daventry (1752–8), leans very heavily on Gibbs, whose *Book of Architecture* they must have known. Marcus Whiffen has

41. Holy Cross, Daventry, Northamptonshire, 1752–8, the exterior.

pointed out the indebtedness:[23] the nave is that of St Martin's-in-the-Fields converted to the Doric of All Saints', Derby; the tower takes the lower stages of Flitcroft's St Giles'-in-the-Fields (itself an imitation of St Martin's, for which they would have needed a visit to London) and adds, too abruptly, an alternative spire design again from St Martin's. The result, says Mr Whiffen, is hardly elegant: to him the spire is a 'gouty finger'. It is nonetheless robust and dignified, and the departures from the Hiorns' models are themselves interesting. In the first place Daventry has a real chancel (unusual in an eighteenth-century church) two bays deep with a tunnel vault reminiscent perhaps of those in All Saints', Northampton, but semi-cylindrical as at Ingestre in Staffordshire: this makes the east end quite different, both inside and out, from the two Gibbs churches; for there are two distinct volumes of chancel and nave meeting at re-entrant angles, while the east pediment is necessarily much narrower, a feature within, rather than dominating, the elevation. The use of Doric simplifies everything, but a quietly Baroque touch is introduced (perhaps simply to reduce the height) by lifting the upper windows almost to the cornice so that a full entablature can be carried only over the pilasters.[24] In the absence of a portico the tower stands in visibly comprehensible relationship to the body of the church and to the west front which looks, perhaps like the façade of a small town hall. (There is the inevitable thermal window, but the pedimented Doric porch is a felicitous addition of 1951.) Inside, the plaster groin vaults, quite different from the two Gibbs ceilings, give a bare Italian air to an otherwise very English interior rendered somewhat bizarre by the enormously wide slabs of cornice above the dosserets of the columns. [25]

VII William and David Hiorn; Packington Hall, Warwickshire, the stables, 1753–58.

VIII William and David Hiorn?; Harlestone House, Northamptonshire, the stables.

IX William and David Hiorn?; Harlestone House, the stables , portico.

x William and David Hiorn?; Broome Hall, West Midlands, the Gothick front.

XI John Vardy; the New Stone Building, Westminster, 1755 onwards, demolished in 1883.

St Bartholomew's, Birmingham (1749–51, destroyed in the last war) was another Gibbsian paraphrase, this time of the simpler St Peter's, Vere Street; but the Hiorns' third authenticated church — Great Houghton, near Northampton (1754) — is more original. It was miserably mutilated in 1878, when the windows were given 'Norman' tracery and the thermal window disappeared behind an utterly alien porch. But the main lines of the little pedimented box, with another pediment in the middle of the side and tiny lean-to Venetian chancel, can still be seen, as well as the distinctive steeple whose spire is linked to its tower by appearing to rest on a free-standing octagonal colonnade carrying up-turned volutes (and once also urns) above the entablature; a fresh piece of architectural thinking along Hawksmoorian lines.[26]

David Hiorn died in 1758, and it is uncertain whether he had anything directly to do with the design of what is unquestionably the Hiorns' most distinguished house — Foremarke Hall, near Repton, Derbyshire, built for Sir Robert Burdett in 1759–61. It has been repeatedly said that the design is based on, or even that it is 'a smaller and simplified version of', Isaac Ware's Wrotham Park, Middlesex. Doubtless the Hiorns had seen Ware's design in his *Complete Body of Architecture;* yet their design is in no sense a copy. It is at most a free variation on elements taken from Ware. The centrepiece at Foremarke — Ionic tetrastyle portico over a double curved

PLATE VI

42. Holy Cross, Daventry, the interior.

perron – follows that of Wrotham exactly; so (allowing for a change of order) does John Carr's Tabley: it is a standard Palladian formula. Also Wrotham and Foremarke both have domes over polygonal bays. But at Wrotham (on one front only) they are far out at the ends of the wings, forming units entirely distinct from the main block. Though his plan appears continuous, Ware's silhouette is sectional and staccato.[27] Foremarke's domes and canted bays, on the contrary, are integrated into the main body of the house, the round, octagonal and triangular forms thus more tensely and intricately contrasted. Moreover the plan of Foremarke is entirely different from that of Wrotham, which is a double pile on either side of a longitudinal spine wall — the common form of so many eighteenth-century houses. Foremarke by contrast is essentially a very deep single pile: all the main structural walls are transverse, and contain all the stacks, allowing, within the five 'super-bays' of the plan, very flexible arrangements of accommodation on each floor and consequently rooms of varied size and shape.[28] In detail the façades show the familiar

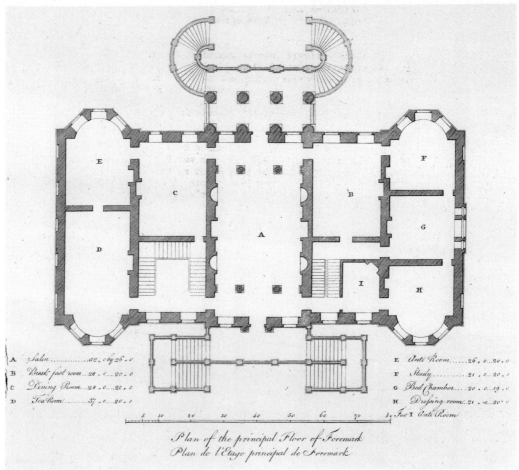

A Salon..............52..by 26..0
B Break fast room..28..0..20..0
C Dining Room..28..0..20..0
D Tea Room..37..0..20..0

E Anti Room..26..0..20..0
F Study..........21..0..20..0
G Bed Chamber..20..0..19..0
H Dressing room..21..0..20..0
I Anti Room

5 10   20   30   40   50   60   70 Feet

Plan of the principal Floor of Foremark
Plan de l'Etage principal de Foremark

43. Foremarke Hall, plan from *Vitruvius Britannicus*.

engaging mixture of the well-tried and the novel — for example windows with lugged architraves on the flat sections, windows without surrounds of any kind in the polygons: the aim seems to be to stress the clear form of the end bays by avoiding any detail which might draw attention away from their plain angular shape. They get fractional but visible further emphasis in the way that the polygons start from a vertical plane a few inches forward of the main wall — touches which reveal an architect who can appreciate and estimate the effects of small variations. Inside, the hall takes one straight across the house through two Ionic screens: it is quite a severe room, but its chimney-pieces combine bold diagonal volutes with tablets carved with fabulous scenes deliberately cultivating the picturesque. Another in the former ante-room, now part of the library, has a high relief of a milkmaid and her cow: all the chimneypieces here are in marked contrast to the swirling Rococo designs made for Gopsall at about the same date. The tall, quite narrow staircase hall, a much tighter version of Delbury, again with a triple-arched Roman gallery, shows an august enjoyment of fresh kinds of volumes, which appears again in the dome rooms in the attic and in vaulted rooms in the basement centred on free-standing columns. The house, with its mixture of something old and something new could be called transitional; but it has achieved remarkable poise and serenity at

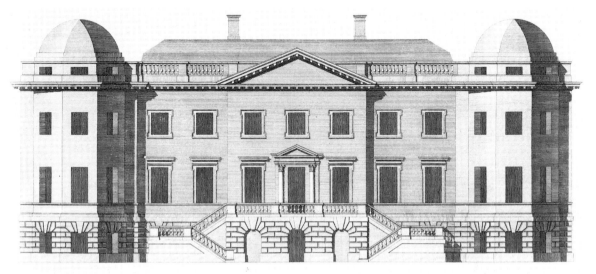

44. Foremarke Hall, garden front from *Vitruvius Britannicus*.

its moment of stasis — a thoroughly intelligent piece of house-planning, full of crisp detail but genial and never overbearing: if indeed it was David Hiorn's swansong, he might, had he lived (he was only in his mid–40s at most) have developed into an architect who would have responded individually to the new movements of the 1760s and 1770s.

All these houses have or had office ranges — of a fairly routine kind until the imposing stable courtyard which the Hiorns are known to have built at Packington and the even more impressive ones they may have built at Harlestone House and Courteenhall.[29] There are frequent payments to them from Lord Guernsey's bank account and from his steward's between 1756 and 1765.[30] Their work must have been partly within the house where King was carving, painting and gilding in 1759 — well before the major remodelling which began under Matthew Brettingham in 1766 with Henry Couchman as contractor. An elevation at Packington, showing a simpler version of the façade design finally adopted, is probably in David Hiorn's hand. It seems likely that the inspiration came from Lord Guernsey himself, and that first Hiorn and then Brettingham were essentially his executants.[31] William Hiorn's 'designs for blacksmiths and coopers houses and shops ... March 1764' survive[32] though the buildings do not. Before them, however, had come the stables which were 'intended' as early as 1750 but described as newly-built in September 1758.[33] The ultimate source for the design, a square courtyard with pedimented centre on

PLATE VII
PLATE VIII
PLATE IX

45. Hiorn drawing for Gopsall Hall, Leicestershire,
c. 1749–60, showing a design for the chimneypiece
in the dining room.

each side and pyramid-capped tower at each corner, is Kentian;[34] but closer in place
and style are Roger Morris's stables for Althorp (1732–3), whose two porticos,
which take off that of Inigo Jones's St Paul's, Covent Garden, are so close to the
main centrepiece at Packington that the Hiorns must have studied them attentively:
indeed the Packington square can be described as a planed-down version of
Althorp.[35] The Courteenhall block (of c.1750) is resplendent for sheer size (though
not a full quadrangle, its façade extends beyond, or as it were through, the corner
towers) but has a simpler Palladian entrance. Harlestone outbraves them all with
heroic entrance temples which, anticipating a favourite device of Scottish Neo-
classicism by more than half a century, sit astride the main ranges: coupled Roman
Doric columns flank arches worthy of Blenheim Palace and with their appropriately
massive entablature and pediment, they give extraordinary solemnity to a now
familiar formula. Other details are supportively strong — double blank arches along
the outer walls, the thermal windows in the towers set within full-height arches.
Were the Hiorns up to all this? Or was the ghost of Morris walking? The stables
fortunately survived the destruction of Harlestone House in 1939–40 but are now in
a sad condition and need full restoration.

There are other ancillary buildings by the Hiorns. At Foremarke miniature

Palladian sentry-boxes peg down the ends of the curved stone screens that hide the kitchen court and gardens from approaching guests — purely decorative finials which have no insides.[36] There was to be, and perhaps was, much more at Gopsall: the Hiorn drawings at the RIBA include a triple-arched loggia deriving, as Dr Friedman points out, from a Palladian formula incorporating lean-to half-pediments but carrying a Baroque dome; three versions of a domed rotunda without and with structural arches between the columns, in the last of which half the floor area is used for a bath-house; a summer-house with chamfered corners and concave walls; a Palladian orangery flanked by two stoves (i.e. forcing-houses); two designs for a Burlingtonian prospect tower; a boathouse; and a Chinese bridge.[37]

Among the Gopsall drawings is one for a Gothick summer-house: apart from Arbury and the repair or rebuilding of two church steeples (St Martin's, Birming-

46. Gopsall Hall, design for a garden temple or summer house.

ham and Holy Trinity, Stratford-upon-Avon — the latter perhaps not to their design) this is the only Gothic work hitherto attributed to the Hiorns.[38] Their engagement with Gothic is a subject about which too little has yet been established for anything more to be said with confidence. A possible addition, however, is the design of Ecton Hall, Northamptonshire. This has been attributed to Miller largely on the grounds of what may have been only a distant acquaintanceship with Ambrose Isted who reconstructed the house apparently in 1755–6. Much of an earlier building was incorporated and this may account for some undigested features on the façade; but the undisputed eighteenth-century work: castellated canted bays,

Tudor dripmoulds over square windows, even the ogee-headed polygonal porch, is not obviously in Miller's style; and it would surely have been uncharacteristic of Miller to put classical interiors in a Gothic house: the hall chimneypiece with diagonal volutes recalls those at Foremarke. It seems, on the other hand, in its rather mechanical way, the sort of tentative exploration of Gothic which one might expect

47. A design for Ecton House, Northamptonshire, now in the Northamptonshire County Records Office.

to follow from a professional acquaintance with Arbury — once again the Gothicizing of a symmetrical classical plan. At Northampton county record office, there are elevations and plans — evidently contract drawings — almost certainly in William Hiorn's hand, annotated in his version of the spidery copperplate which he shared with his brother, the measurements shown in a manner which they had learnt from the Smiths.[39]

This does not prove that William Hiorn designed Ecton any more than their having made working plans unseats Miller's authorship from the Shire Hall. But if he did, and if he also made the Gopsall drawing, he evidently came into contact with Batty Langley in between, and this opens a whole range of possible activity among some tantalizingly elusive Midlands houses done by one who for the moment must remain the master of the ogee gable.[40] (It would also give him without much challenge the vaulted entrance lobby and Gothick doorcase at Abington Hall, Northampton.[41]) I merely make the occasion for a brief shot in the dark. Broome

PLATE X House, near Stourbridge, is remarkable in having two adjacent facades, one Palladian and one Gothick. The Palladian is full of 'Hiorn' features: thermal and Venetian windows with sill brackets, open pediment with small returns of the cornice (cf. Daventry), a little Gothick glazing; the Gothick has classical round-headed windows on the ground floor and then goes into Langleyesque triple lights and an ogee gable sandwiched between castellated towers reminiscent of Arbury: The two façades seem definitely to be part of the same building operation which in fact encased an older, possibly Elizabethan, house. It is a nice fantasy to think of the two brothers doing a façade each and coming to terms at the corner: what other candidates are

48. Abington Hall, Northamptonshire, the lobby.

there for this very individual project?[42]

After David Hiorn's death there are very few documented designs, though William's name continues to appear in major building works. The only classical one was the rebuilding of the east end of St Mary's Nottingham, (1762, re-Gothicized in 1843), and it may be that the classical architectural talent of the firm died with David. Mr Colvin[43] attributes Over Whitacre church, near Coleshill, to 'William or David', but it was not built until 1766. The body of the church is like a simpler Great Houghton, but the tower, though packed with the usual Hiorn items, is so odd an ensemble that one hesitates: was it perhaps the best William could do on his own? Whether or not he went on as an architect, his skill as a mason was in demand. Like the Smiths, he kept a marble yard, which in 1764 provided chimneypieces and other work for Stoneleigh.[44] He must have made more monuments than the two now recorded to his credit, one a noble piece to Edward Acton at Acton Scott, south Shropshire designed by William Baker in 1751 and perfectly executed in grey and white marble by Mr Hiorn, continuing or remaking an old association from their time with the Smiths. Very likely some of the numerous wall tablets in St Mary's,

Warwick come from the Hiorn yard — including perhaps William's own, a characteristic Hiorn melange in which a well-wrought Grecian urn stands on a plinth decorated with Rococo scrolls; the tablet itself, with fluted frieze and guilloche dado, is flanked by sensuous Baroque whorls — an ingenious microcosm of the firm's vocabulary touched now by the young Francis Hiorn's Neo-classical refinement. Doubtless it was he or his brother who phrased the tribute to their father;

> Whose public Character was distinguished by Zeal and Integrity,
> Whose private Life by Humanity and Friendship.

Zeal, integrity, humanity, friendship ... David perhaps, if one is right to see him as the more active designer, had some imagination and flair as well. But the Hiorns would never have led style or fashion: one cannot think of them as ever likely to produce a book for others to follow, at least not an essentially architectural one, not only because they did not see themselves as teachers and did not think theoretically at all, but because they did keep their aprons on, acted primarily as working craftsmen whose job required that they keep abreast of things, but depended above all on the soundness of building methods tested through the practice of generations. This was no recipe for artistic innovation, but a Hiorn house was an economical proposition and likely to stay up. They were favourable examples of the band of architectural middlemen who converted the invention of their artistic masters into a working vernacular which jobbing builders all over the country could use without serious danger of botches or cranks or making utter fools of themselves. There is a kind of *necessary* dullness.[45]

4

JOHN VARDY, 1718–65
Palladian into Rococo

Roger White

JOHN VARDY is one of the faceless men of English architectural history. To most students of the subject he is no more than the name behind a single building, Spencer House, and to some not even that. Insofar as he has been considered at all, he has consistently been lumped together with his colleagues Isaac Ware and Henry Flitcroft and written off as competent but uninspired, worthy but dull, the sort of person Alexander Pope might have had in mind when he prophesied that Lord Burlington's 'just and noble rules' would 'fill half the land with imitating fools.'

Yet for all his obscurity Vardy in many ways hardly qualifies as an outsider; in common with Ware and Flitcroft, indeed, he was very much an insider. The reason for this paradox is that all three were essentially architectural civil servants. Their long careers were spent as members of the Office of Works, working their way up through a succession of posts to positions of eminence in that bureaucracy — Vardy to be Surveyor to the Royal Mint, Ware to be Secretary to the Board, and Flitcroft to the dizzying heights of Comptroller of the Works. This meant job security and a continuous income as well as the occasional official commission, all things which the sensible architect craved then and craves still. But it also meant that much of their time was taken up with purely humdrum work of administration or running repairs: it was, perhaps, rather like working for the Property Services Agency in the 1980s. Their imaginative scope was restricted, their flights of fancy circumscribed, and the effect can sometimes be seen even in the work such men did outside the Office.

The fact remains however that these are the men, or the kind of men, of whom the architectural mainstream in mid-eighteenth-century England was composed, for the Office of Works was by far the largest and most prestigious concentration of architectural expertise in the country.[1] Since the time of Inigo Jones it had been the heart of the English architectural establishment, and in 1726, following the death of the Comptroller Sir John Vanbrugh and of the Surveyor Sir Thomas Hewitt, it was effectively 'captured' by the forces of Palladianism. With the strong backing of Lord Burlington, William Kent was installed as Master Carpenter. Henry Flitcroft ('Burlington Harry') was given the key post of Clerk of the Works at Whitehall, Westminster and St James's. Ware's Office of Works career began in 1728 when he was appointed Clerk Itinerant, while Vardy, a rather younger man, enters the scene in 1736 as Clerk of the Works at the Queen's House, Greenwich.

Little enough is known of Ware and Flitcroft as men, but considerably less is known of Vardy, of whom no personal papers nor even a portrait survive. In the Palladianised Office of Works the dominant personality was that of the genial and bibulous polymath Kent, in the shadow of whose fecundity the lesser talents had perforce to live and work. This is true of Ware, Flitcroft and others besides, but it is the fate of Vardy above all to have come down through history as Kent's particular protégé. In his lifetime the closeness of the identification served him well; thereafter it has made it impossible to see his achievement as in any way individual, or indeed to see it at all. The purpose of this essay is to suggest that he was not simply a Kent clone; that while capable of the restrained urbanity which characterises the designs of Ware and Flitcroft and the Office of Works 'house style' in general, Vardy was also able to develop some of the more idiosyncratic hallmarks of his master to ends which, if not necessarily better than those of his colleagues, are often at any rate more fun.

John Vardy hailed from the city of Durham, where he was baptised on 20th February 1718 (1717 in the Old Style Calendar) in the church of St Mary-le-Bow, hard by the east end of the cathedral.[2] He was the second son of Ralph and Mary Vardy (the name appears variously as Vardy, Verdy, Verdye and Verdey), who had married in August 1715 in the neighbouring church of St Mary the Less. His origins were unequivocally humble, since Ralph is described in the parish registers as a labourer. A total of seven children seem to have appeared at roughly two year intervals, of whom the eldest, William, died shortly after John's christening and the fifth, Thomas (born 1724), was later to join John in seeking his fortune down south. More than this one cannot say, except that by 1722 Ralph Vardy appears to have settled into a permanent career as gardener; and that between at least 1723 and 1744 he owned an as yet unidentified house on the east side of South Bailey. This, presumably, is where John and Thomas Vardy were brought up.

John Vardy's next appearance is at Greenwich in May 1736, where he was appointed Clerk of the Works at the Queen's House, at the age of only eighteen. There is no indication of how he made the transition, though one might speculate that it had something to do with the intercession of the Reverend Dr Bland, Dean of Durham, who in 1738 subscribed (like Vardy himself) to Ware's new edition of Palladio.[3] Most of Vardy's Office of Works colleagues began their professional lives apprenticed to some appropriate London guild such as the Masons, Carpenters or Joiners, but his own name is absent from their records, as from those of the Durham guilds.

In a bureaucracy where patronage and personal favour were all, it is perhaps remarkable that there was so much upward mobility, professional if not social. At the head of the Office of Works was the Surveyor-General, a well paid political placeman; and it says a good deal for the open-mindedness of successive Surveyors and the talent-spotting abilities of their professional subordinates that young men could be plucked from total obscurity and given so thorough a training as to become not only highly competent draughtsmen but also interesting architects in their own right. Vardy arrived in London, inexperienced and presumably speaking a largely incomprehensible Durham dialect, during the Surveyorship of the Hon. Richard Arundell. Arundell, who was half-brother of the 'architect Earl' of Pembroke and an intimate of the Burlington-Kent circle, was regarded by many as a frivolous aesthete (Horace Walpole recalled him drawing pubic hair onto the marble statues at Wilton with black charcoal).[4] There is no mistaking his considerable knowledge of architectural matters, however, nor his willingness to use his position to boost Burlington's campaign for the Palladianising of public works, and it is significant that it was for Arundell himself that Vardy made his first dateable independent designs, ten years after his appointment to Greenwich.

We know nothing of Vardy's activities at Greenwich or at Hampton Court, where he spent two years as Clerk in 1744-6, but during these first ten years he seems to have established himself as some kind of unofficial personal assistant to Kent. In 1737, on the evidence of a drawing for the Board Room chimneypiece which is half in Kent's hand and half in Vardy's,[5] he was assisting in the fitting-up of the Treasury building overlooking Horse Guards Parade, begun to Kent's design in 1733. At about the same time the finished drawings for Kent's successive Houses of Parliament schemes begin to be in Vardy's hand.[6] In 1741 he drew and engraved Kent's delicious Gothick pulpit for York Minister, and three years later he made his sole venture into publishing with a volume of 50 plates entitled *Some Designs of Mr Inigo Jones and Mr William Kent*. As 33 of the plates were devoted to buildings, furniture, vases and other artefacts by the latter architect it is clear where Vardy's prime allegiance lay. Others of Kent's classical designs had been and were to be published elsewhere (notably by Ware), but Vardy performed a particular service both to contemporaries and to posterity by including the Gothick Court of King's Bench and Gloucester Cathedral choir screen, as well as engraving separately both elevations of the Gothicised Esher Place. Apart from Batty Langley's *Gothic Architecture Improved,* published initially in 1741-2, these were the earliest appearances in print of the new Gothick. As such they constituted the principal means of disseminating Kentian Gothick, and they clearly determined Vardy's approach in his subsequent essays in the style.

While Kent lived, Vardy could learn and assist in the usual manner of a talented amanuensis but there was perhaps little prospect of breaking away as an independent designer. It is really only after his master's death in 1748 that Vardy can be seen to emerge from his ample shadow. Kent never lacked commissions, and there remained a ready market both inside the Office of Works and out for one who could adopt his idiom. Vardy was in fact peculiarly well placed in this respect, for at the time of Kent's death and until 1754 he was Clerk of the Works at the palaces of Whitehall, Westminster and St James's. This was always a key post in the Office of Works hierarchy since it provided more than average scope for the holder to carry into execution building projects that would be immediately in the public eye. The first such was the erection of a plain two-storeyed house at the north-east corner of St James's Palace,[7] but a far more prominent and prestigious project concerned the new headquarters for the Horse Guards in Whitehall.

The ubiquitous Kent had evidently prepared designs for the Horse Guards at some point between 1745 and 1748, and Vardy's engravings of the completed building accord him full credit as architect. On the other hand the sole drawing in Kent's hand which can be connected with the scheme[8] is not at all close to the executed design, and it is apparent from the Works records that such plans as were inherited were subjected to extended tinkering both before the foundations of the central block were laid in 1750 and after.[9] To some extent, this arose because unlike most Georgian public building projects, the Horse Guards expanded rather than shrank. Successive dreams for grandiose new royal or Parliamentary buildings foundered for lack of funds, but the Horse Guards grew in scope to become in effect a new War Office. This, plus its prominent site along Whitehall, and the fact that it was to form part of the ceremonial royal route to Parliament, combined to ensure that the Horse

Guards was the one great public project of the Palladian Office of Works not to be severely truncated or abandoned altogether. The Board took such a close interest in the evolution of the design and the progress of work that the finished product might accurately be described as having been designed by a committee. The outcome, though thoroughly Kentian in inspiration and detailing (the four-towered central block is obviously derived from Holkham Hall, Norfolk, for instance), is not a work of undiluted genius, and the fact that Vardy's name became so closely associated with it may have had mixed results for his reputation. He and William Robinson were appointed joint Clerks of the Works in 1750 and Vardy became overall Surveyor of the building in 1753, in which year he unsuccessfully volunteered a swagger design for a great gateway leading from Whitehall into the main court.[10] Had it been accepted, the familiar breast-plated guards and their mounts would now stand sentry duty beneath Vardy's exuberant scrolls, cornucopia, lion and unicorn, instead of ensconced in the present austere pill-boxes.

PLATE XI   A public project for which Vardy can more justifiably be given credit is the so-called New Stone Building which stood opposite the east end of Westminster Abbey and, surviving the great fire of 1834, was finally pulled down in 1883.[11] This too was in some sense a Kentian hangover, since it represented the ultimate boiling down of the magnificent schemes for a Parliament building. Kent had envisaged the wholesale replacement of the jumbled medieval and Tudor Palace of Westminster with Neo-classical, almost Beaux Arts, complexes on an epic Roman scale. What finally went up was in no way compensation for this lost grandeur, but it did make a dignified contribution to the Office of Works' recurrently frustrated efforts to improve the architectural setting of government and Parliament. In 1762 Vardy exhibited at the Society of Artists 'A Design for the Court of King's Bench Records etc. in St Margaret's Lane, Westminster, (made) in 1753, when Clerk of the Works at Westminster'. Typically, work did not start until 1755, and then only the central five bays were built of what was intended as a seventeen-bay composition. The six bays to the south, where a characteristic Palladian tower turned the corner into Old Palace Yard, followed after Vardy's death in 1766–70, and it was left to Soane to complete the composition to the north in 1821. The vocabulary was absolutely mainstream Palladian with no frills or thrills: rusticated basement, piano nobile with pedimented or Venetian windows (set within relieving arches à la Chiswick), and a contribution to the skyline in the form of pedimented attic and pyramidally-capped towers. Opposite the New Stone Building on the south side of Old Palace Yard was a more modest Palladian building in the same astylar vein. This was built in 1754–6 as accommodation for the Parliament Office and is still in place, having escaped the 1834 fire and twentieth-century attempts at bombing and demolition. It has in recent years been ascribed on dubious grounds to Isaac Ware (in stylistic terms almost anyone in the Office of Works could have designed it), but there seems no particular reason to doubt the traditional attribution to Vardy.[12]

It is natural for architects to long for great public commissions which will serve as their own monument to posterity, and in the seventeenth and eighteenth centuries the most consistent and unrealistic longing of the English architect was to be allowed to build a royal palace. Vardy was no exception to this rule, and in 1761 he exhibited at the Society of Artists a 'Design for a royal palace at Whitehall, fronting the park, just before the new building of the Horse-guards was begun, when Clerk of the Works to Whitehall, 1748'. No drawings from this inevitably unrealised scheme survive, and in any case, as his own description of it implies, the commencement of the Horse Guards put paid for ever to dreams of a palace on the Whitehall site.[13]

Vardy's other great unrealised public project was the British Museum.[14] In February 1754 he was summoned by the Trustees of the Museum (founded by Act

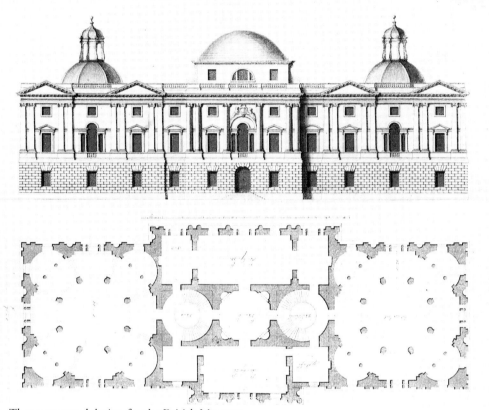

49. The unexecuted design for the British Museum.

of Parliament the previous year) and cross-examined as to the likely cost of a new building on a site in Old Palace Yard, adjoining that earmarked for the new Parliament buildings. The Trustees had explicitly in mind something which would be 'conformable' to Kent's Commons and Lords in the increasingly unlikely event that they were ever erected. Vardy duly produced a plan and elevation which took their cue from the schemes that he as draughtsman knew only too well. At the centre is a low dome with stepped base, by Kent out of Chiswick, flanked slightly awkwardly by octagonal domes with cupolas. The piano nobile on the other hand, with its lively rhythm of varying windows tied together across the facade by a continuous string course and framed by pedimented and pilastered projections, recalls the better known country house designs of the 1750s and 1760s by James Paine, which are often cited as examples of the Rococo in English architecture. Internally two thirds of the plan were to be taken up by vast octagonal galleries with screened exedras at the angles, intended no doubt to evoke antique grandeur in the same way as the Parliament designs. Had the project got beyond this stage Vardy's name might now be almost a household word. Instead, despite a further consultation in 1756 and Vardy's offer to give his services as architect free of charge, the Trustees opted, for reasons of cost, to buy and convert Montagu House in Bloomsbury. There were more disappointed hopes over the design made in 1751 for a new building on the north side of Cavendish Square to house the Society of Dilettanti. This design does not survive and was certainly not executed in Vardy's lifetime, although the striking pair of pedimented ashlar frontages finally erected in 1769–72, after the Society had sold the site and a quantity of ready-cut stone to George Tufnell, bears sufficient similarities to the facades of Spencer House to make it a possibility that the 1751 design may have been kept and used after all.[15]

In 1754 Vardy was moved from his job at Whitehall, Westminster and St James's, where he had been very much at the centre of official building campaigns, to become Clerk at Kensington Palace. This posting lasted until 1761 and overlapped with the Clerkship of Chelsea Hospital, which ran from 1756 until his death in 1765. There was very little work in prospect at either place that would have been professionally or financially rewarding, and it was as well for him that private commissions began to proliferate; their incidence after 1754, indeed, may be a corollary of his less oncrous official commitments. The certain or attributable works of his last decade, in their variety and architectural interest, indicate rather better than his Office of Works products what he might have been capable of had he lived beyond the age of 47.

Vardy's earliest known private commissions were for a church and a sizeable mansion for Richard Arundell's Allerton Mauleverer estate in Yorkshire. The

50. Allerton Mauleverer Church, North Yorkshire c. 1745.

church, said to have been built in 1745, is one of the oddest hybrids of a period that was far from archaeologically scrupulous about its stylistic mixes. There can be little

68

doubt that the central tower (an entirely new feature, since the preceding church had a Gothic west tower) is a conscious emulation of the Romanesque. The west front on the other hand hovers equivocally between the Neo-Norman and the Neo-classical, the round-arched windows and door of the steeply gabled central section being sandwiched between open-pedimented aisles. The aisle walls themselves have simple pointed windows and the transepts Gothic plate tracery. Inside, re-used medieval Gothic nave arcades consort with simple classical transverse arches to the aisles. The elaborate hammerbeam roof, assumed by Pevsner to be seventeenth-century, is proved by detailed drawings (almost certainly in Vardy's hand) to be part of the mid-eighteenth-century rebuild.[16]

The open pediments and porthole west window of this intriguing church carry over into Vardy's unexecuted design of 1746 for the neighbouring mansion, which

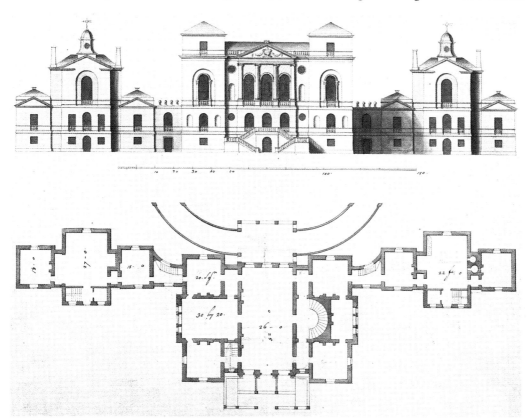

51. Allerton Mauleverer house, design of 1746.

proclaims his interest in the idea of the towered Palladian house.[17] Vardy had an evident pre-occupation with towers, actual or implied, which derives in the first instance from Kent but is also characteristic of the coming generation's desire for greater articulation of both skyline and elevation. His unexecuted design for a house for Sir Thomas Hayles at Howletts in Kent (1755)[18] presents the Holkham theme in its most literal form, condensed and unadorned, whereas Allerton accentuates the verticality and isolation of elements inherent in Holkham. Allerton is an extraordinarily high-waisted design, and a very restless one. The central elements of the tripartite pavilions are elongated upwards until, with their cupolas and weathervanes, they rival the towers of the main block. Wall planes are broken relentlessly backwards and forward, and in the peppering of facades with assorted windows, recesses, bull's-eyes and niches there is that *horror vacui* which was the amateur Burlington's legacy to subsequent architects.

Towers on a much smaller scale recur in the town house he designed for Lord Montfort in 1755 (unexecuted),[19] this time of the pedimented Wilton variety, and again on his house for Colonel Wade in Whitehall of 1753.[20] Wade's house enjoyed particular prominence because it stood in the very middle of Whitehall, facing north

52. Colonel Wade's house in Whitehall, 1753, pulled down 1875.

towards the Horse Guards and occupying one end of the block between Parliament Street and King Street. On both designs the towers are vestigial, being in reality the short ends of raised attics. The stylistic idiosyncracy of these projects leads one to suggest that Vardy may also be the most plausible architect for the facade of Woodcote Park near Epsom, Surrey. This was previously attributed to Ware on the strength of an unsigned elevation in an American collection of drawings that was mistakenly assigned to him in its entirety. The drawings are now accepted as an Office of Works mixed bag, and on stylistic grounds alone the Woodcote façade relates far more closely in its oddity to these designs of Vardy than to anything by the urbane Ware.[21]

The early 1750s saw the beginning of Vardy's professional relationship with Joseph Damer, Baron Milton and first Earl of Dorchester. For this notoriously mean and crusty peer Vardy began two major works, a large ashlar-faced town mansion on what is now Park Lane and the rebuilding of his country seat of Milton Abbey in Dorset. Dorchester (originally Milton) House occupied an awkward triangular site that had hitherto been waste ground along Tyburn Lane. Like most such London mansions it presented an undemonstrative exterior to the world, its gardens concealed behind a high encircling wall but its principal rooms on the first floor

XII John Vardy; Hackwood Park, Hampshire, 1761–3. A distant view by Paul Sandby, now in the collection of the Yale Center for British Art.

XIII John Vardy's tinted drawing for the Alcove Room at Spencer House, now in Sir John Soane's Museum, London.

XIV John Vardy; Spencer House, London, 1756–65, the front to Green Park.

xv Henry Keene's design for an octagonal garden
pavilion, in the Victoria and Albert Museum.

xvi Henry Keene's design for a large classical house, No E 857 in the Victoria and Albert Museum.

commanding views over this directly into Hyde Park. A drawing in the Milton Collection at the RIBA[22] very probably represents Vardy's alternative suggestions for a decorative scheme for the bow-fronted reception room on the park front. If so, it is typical of the compensating richness of the London town house interior and also of the decorative vocabulary of this post-Kent generation, with the rigid Palladian geometry of door frames, dado and eared wall panels counteracted by lavish stucco drops and floral festoons. The house seems, on the evidence of rate books, to have been begun (and probably completed in carcase) in 1751–2, but work on the interior

53. Woodcote Park, Surrey.

evidently proceeded in fits and starts, with the rateable value rising from £150 to £160 in 1755 and then to £180 in 1760.[23] It was completed, and entrance gates added,

54. A drawing of 1828 showing Dorchester House, Park Lane. Begun 1751, demolished 1849.

by Sir William Chambers in 1769–71, only to give way successively to a new Dorchester House by Vulliamy (1850–63) and then to the Dorchester Hotel (1930).

Damer acquired the Milton Abbey estate in 1752, and when Bishop Pococke passed the house two years later he noted that 'Lord Milton is casing it all round in a

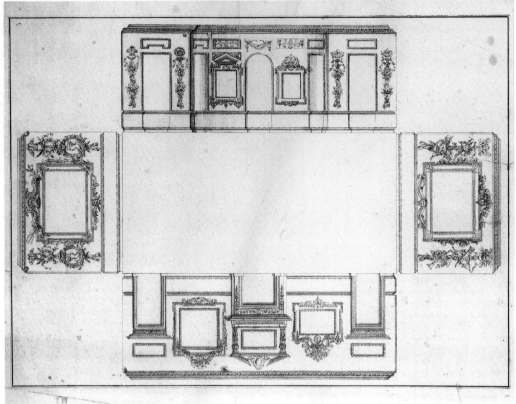

55. A room scheme for Dorchester House, now in the Milton Collection of the RIBA.

beautiful modern taste'.[24] A drawing in the Milton Collection indicates that Vardy had offered his client the choice of a classical or Gothick rebuild of the rambling medieval lodgings adjoining the Abbey church.[25] From Pococke's observation it is clear that work had already begun — but on which option? The idiom of Vardy's Gothick elevation was closely derived from Kent's Esher, which he had engraved, and like that of Wren and Hawksmoor before him was only skin deep, being adopted to harmonise approximately with a medieval neighbour. However, the one certain drawing for the interior shows that, as at Dorchester House, this was to have been in his rather full-bodied and voluptuous version of English Rococo.[26] His section of the Great Room on the first floor, dated 1755, exhibits a deep plain cove lit by a tripartite lunette, and a pair of straight-forward chimneypieces, but the wall surface around and between was to be divided into panels surrounded by a froth of stuccowork. The halting of work in mid-stream, perhaps before the Great Room was even attempted, and the subsequent demolition of what had been completed, may indicate that after an initial choice of a classical exterior the client capriciously and characteristically changed his mind. When Chambers was taken on to direct the resumption of operations in 1770 the unfinished fragment was pulled down and work began again from scratch, with the economical Lord Milton dictating that Vardy's original Gothick plans be adopted and adapted.[27] Chambers found the style almost as uncongenial as he did the client. He did his best to make the elevations as regular and un-Gothick as possible, but if the building as finally executed is compared with the engraving published by Hutchins in 1774, which must surely repre-

56. Vardy's alternative schemes for Milton Abbey, Dorset, c. 1755, offering a classical or Gothick style.

The North West View of Milton Abby   *the Seat of the R.^t Honble Joseph Lord Milton*

57. Milton Abbey: engraving of 1774, probably showing Vardy's Gothick scheme before alteration by Chambers.

sent Vardy's own revised scheme, the extent of Chambers' indebtedness is at once apparent. Vardy's Milton would have been one of the major works of the early Gothic Revival.

Vardy's handling of the Milton façades, and his intimate knowledge of Kent's Gothick oeuvre, suggest that he may have been the architect behind Shobdon Church, Hereford and Worcester, that most intractable of English Rococo Gothick puzzles. The tantalising documentation for Shobdon supplies most of the basic information about its rebuilding except the name of the author.[28] The work was carried out in 1750–52 and the architect, who was taken on and supervised by Horace Walpole's bosom friend Dickie Bateman, was a London man. This rules out Kent, who was dead, and Thomas Farnolls Pritchard, the Shrewsbury Goth, who in any case had been dismissed in 1747 for faulty workmanship on the neighbouring mansion. Stylistic analysis of the sugar-candy interior reveals indebtedness in roughly equal parts to Kent (tripartite arches from the Gloucester Cathedral screen, wall panels from the York Minister pulpit, window tracery from Esher and Honingham) and Batty Langley (columns, window surrounds and chimneypiece all from *Gothic Architecture Improved*).[29] Of all the London architects who would have known Kent's work sufficiently well, perhaps only Vardy could have produced such a convincing

58. Shobdon Church, Hereford and Worcester, c. 1750–52.

fusion of sources, at once frivolous and robust, for Ware's few Gothick essays are on the dour side, while Flitcroft, employed briefly on Shobdon Court in 1746, was too proper an architect ever to have risked this church.

Vardy's ability to combine the frivolous and the robust is best seen in his designs for landscape architecture and for furniture. If propriety or economics constrained his fancy in the external appearance of his public and private commissions, these by contrast were the areas in which he was at greater liberty to indulge the freedoms of the Rococo. In his designs for a boathouse for William Augustus, Duke of Cumberland, in Windsor Great Park (1754, not executed),[30] for a bath house for an unknown location (1754, and probably executed),[31] and for lodges for Hackwood Park

59. A design of 1754 for a boat house in Windsor Great Park. Reproduced by Gracious permission of Her Majesty The Queen.

in Hampshire (1761, executed but since destroyed), he evinces a characteristically Rococo fondness for enlivening the surface texture by means of varying kinds of rustication, from knobbly flints to dripping frostwork. The close stylistic affinities between these designs and the jolly Doric temple in the grounds of Isaac Ware's vanished mansion of Amisfield, Scotland, make an attribution of that building to Vardy, rather than Ware, highly tempting. Another tempting stylistic attribution, on the basis of comparisons with these buildings and with Vardy's designs for pedimented gates at the Horse Guards (already discussed) and for an unknown location,[32] would be the tremendous pedimented gate lodge to Fonthill Splendens in Wiltshire. For Hackwood, where he remodelled the south front of the house in an austere astylar manner known only from a distant Sandby view, he also produced   PLATE XII
alternative versions of a delightful rusticated Gothick lodge, one with the scalloped eaves and trefoil finial of Kent's Esher Place porch and the other (achieved by the lowering of a flap on the drawing) a tea-cosy roof of thatch. Neither version is known to have been built, unlike his other design for a pair of cubic lodges at the

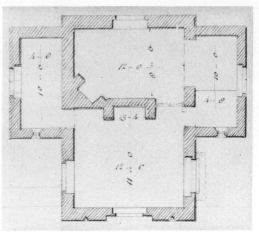

60. Design for a lodge to Hackwood Park, Hampshire, dated 1761.

Basingstoke entrance to the park, whose chunky chequerboard rustication of flint and stone seems almost to prefigure Lutyens.[33]

The fifth Duke of Bolton, at Hackwood and his town house in Grosvenor Square, was one of Vardy's most important patrons. With the subsequent recasting of Hackwood by Samuel and Lewis Wyatt and the demolition of the town house, all that remains of his assorted commissions is a quantity of exceptionally fine furniture. Vardy's furniture designs, for which a number of drawings survive, range from the straightforwardly Kentian through to the Rococo and on to the incipiently Neo-classical. In many cases they relate to architectural commissions where it is clear that Vardy, like Kent before him and Adam and Athenian Stuart after, was employed to design not only the building itself but the integrated decoration and furnishing of its interiors as well. Several drawings of room schemes, indeed, are very early examples of an architect indicating the colour to be adopted for the walls.

PLATE XIII That for the Alcove Room at Spencer House, for instance, has the walls pale green, with the niches flanking the palm tree alcove occupied by negroid youths in fetching pink shifts;[34] and one of the room schemes from the Milton Collection has not only pink walls but festoon curtains drawn in at the heads of the windows.[35]

This versatility, for which no doubt Kent was the exemplar, was presumably facilitated by the arrival in London of Vardy's younger brother Thomas, who in 1740 was apprenticed to the King's Master Carver James Richards.[36] He was admitted freeman of the Joiners Company of London ten years later and we may safely assume that much, if not all, of the outstanding furniture made to John's designs, which depends invariably for effect on virtuosic carved ornament, is the fruit of collaboration between the brothers.

John's drawings for pier tables, mirrors, beds, plinths, and even candle brackets show his draughtsmanship at its most attractive and individual. This is nowhere more so than in those designs where he throws off the corset of Palladianism and embraces the swirling, writhing curves of the Rococo. The finest of a number of surviving executed pieces in this vein are the pair of pier tables and mirrors still at Hackwood, the quintessence of English Rococo in their incorporation of palm branch, shell and feather motifs into a strong and simple overall framework.[37] The exhilarating brio of Vardy's drawings for such pieces is suggestive of the confidence

76

 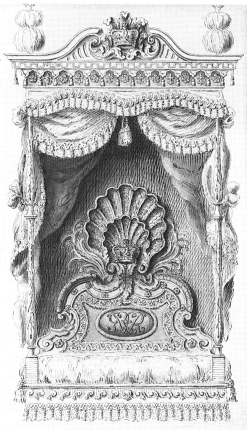

61. Vardy's design for furniture at Hackwood Park. 62. The design for a State bed for St James's Palace.

he placed in his brother to turn them into gilded reality. Yet more extravagant is his design for a state bed for St James's Palace:[38] a love nest of the most regal variety, almost Second Empire in its voluptuousness. Kent's Green Velvet Bed at Houghton, with its great scallop shell head board, is the obvious point of departure, but its bold architectural character is gleefully jettisoned by Vardy in favour of fringes, furbelows, tassles and plumes. A slightly less abandoned version of this design survives in the form of the Cut Velvet Bed now at Hardwick Hall, thought to have come from St James's via Chatsworth.

One might perhaps be forgiven for seeing this furniture as a form of escapism for one who, though he had come a long way since his humble beginnings in Durham, was all too rarely let off the lead as architect or designer. Even at Spencer House, his most celebrated single commission and London's finest surviving eighteenth-century town house, he was not given his head. Spencer House in fact epitomises the frustrations and disappointed hopes of Vardy's career. His design for a house on the site for Lord Montfort was made redundant by the suicide of the client in 1755, and although he managed to secure a prompt replacement commission from the young John Spencer later that year, every part of the external and internal finishing had to be submitted to the scrutiny of Colonel George Gray.

Gray, who was Secretary of the Society of Dilettanti for 32 years, acted as Spencer's mentor in matters of Taste, and the late Lord Spencer was inclined to award him the lion's share of credit for the evolution of the design.[39] Certainly there are Vardy drawings for the interior which bear Gray's imprimatur,[40] and certainly he is likely to have been instrumental in the decision to import James 'Athenian' Stuart over Vardy's head to decorate the first floor rooms after 1758. In general however (and no family papers survive to determine the correct apportionment of credit), there seems no reason to doubt that Vardy was, as he subscribed himself on his engravings and drawings for both exterior and interior, architect as well as draughtsman. For the stately front to Green Park and the incomplete façade to St James's Place (intended to be symmetrical about the entrance door which now occurs at its eastern end) he deployed the full Palladian ordonnance, with an

PLATE XIV

63. Spencer House, London 1756–65, Vardy's design for the St James's Place facade.

expensive Doric order in Portland ashlar instead of the astylar stock brick reticence favoured by most contemporary town house exteriors. The park front is given considerable individuality, indeed idiosyncrasy, by a pediment which spans five of its seven bays, combining with the stumpinesss of the Doric, the absence of an attic, and the long horizontal lines of rusticated ground floor and terrace to emphasize the width rather than the height of the composition. Though Chambers praised it in 1759 for the antique correctitude of certain of its features, there is nothing about the design as a whole which suggests major interference by Gray.

Mrs Delany noted the shell of the ground floor as complete in September 1756. Vardy's scheme for the large dining room on the park front had already been approved in 1755,[41] and this survives as a sober Jonesian apartment with Ionic screens at each end. In a similar vein are the two drawing rooms which turn the corner into St James's Place, one (the former small dining parlour) with a splendid coffered apse recalling Chiswick and Holkham. At the opposite end of the dining room Vardy produced a far more exotic interior in the shape of the Alcove Room,

64. The Alcove Room, Spencer House, as built.

whose south wall is dominated by a palm-tree alcove sanctioned by Gray in December 1757. Though the source was a John Webb design for Charles II's bedchamber at Greenwich (which Vardy thought was by Jones), and the frieze was copied from the Temple of Antoninus and Faustina in Rome (as rendered by Desgodetz and subsequently utilised in the Drawing Room at Holkham), the total effect was without parallel amongst English Palladian interiors of the eighteenth century.

Vardy's ground floor suite was completed in 1760, together with its complement of specially designed furniture.[42] For the Alcove Room there was a mirror and seat furniture which picked up the palm-frond motif; for the Great Dining Room, *en suite* side tables and mirrors (dated 1758), the former supported on winged lions and the latter given luscious oval frames incorporating candle sconces and winged female busts. For the apse of the small dining parlour Vardy designed a related oval mirror, this time incorporating lions' heads (the same mirror design appears on the window wall of his Great Dining Room scheme of 1755). Below it was to be a strikingly Neo-classical side table with the slab supported on a double-bodied sphinx. The source for this appears to have been a Hollar etching after Giulio Romano,[43] and it is possible that in utilising it Vardy may have been vainly attempting to match the developing tastes of his client. In 1757 he produced a design for the closet on the first

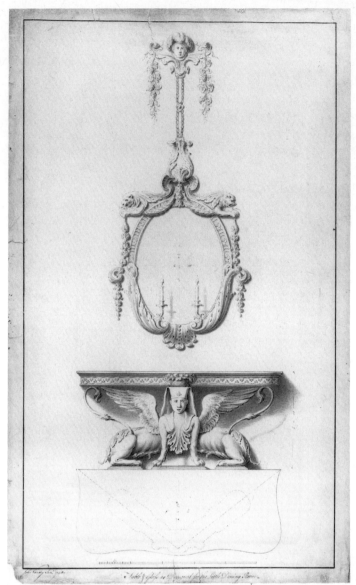

65. Vardy's design for *en suite* table and mirror for the small dining parlour, Spencer House.

floor above the Alcove Room, whose coved ceiling was to have elaborate stucco combining an assortment of Rococo and Neo-classical motifs. But this bid to achieve a toe-hold on the principal floor was doomed to failure, for Spencer and Gray had earmarked it as the proving ground of their new protégé James Stuart, who in 1759 was to create his exquisite Painted Room directly above Vardy's Alcove Room.

Despite this golden opportunity and the enthusiastic promotion of the Dilettanti, Stuart's career was to prove something of a nine day wonder, and indeed his interiors at Spencer House were to be the object of stinging censure from his rival Adam. Nevertheless, the sequence of events there was an ominous pointer to Vardy's fading prospects of employment in aesthetically progressive circles. His supersession at Spencer House did not immediately deprive him of commissions and it may be that, had he lived, he would have been able to modify and up-date his style, tacking to the Neo-classical wind sufficient to please more conservative patrons such as the Duke of Bolton or the Earl of Dorchester. The likelihood however is that, as with the comparable cases of James Paine and Henry Keene, the resultant style would have carried less than complete conviction and that he would have found himself losing out increasingly to the triumphant Adam-Wyatt school.

John Vardy died on 17th May 1765 at the age of 47. His will shows him to have been comfortably off, with property in Derby Street, Westminster and Egham, Surrey,[44] and there were at least three important commissions on his books. His demise prompted no eulogies, however, and the architectural world went on much as before. Vardy had not puffed up his own reputation by self-advertisement, nor built himself into a fashionable pundit. In all probability his contemporaries saw him as posterity has seen him, essentially 'Mr Kent's man', a dependable but ultimately dispensable practitioner of a style created by other minds. To suggest, as far as the evidence allows, that this is not the entire story has been the modest intention of this essay.

5

HENRY KEENE, 1726–1776
A Goth in Spite of Himself

Tim Mowl

IN ROBERT BROWNING's poem 'Andrea Del Sarto' the eponymous painter, musing gloomily upon his life's work, declares: 'Ah, but a man's reach should exceed his grasp, or what's a heaven for?'

Among the architectural drawings in the print room of the Victoria and Albert Museum is a collection of some thirty designs for temples, houses and a palace, all but a handful of them unrealised. These represent the reach, the ideal forms, the careful bait for the potential patron set by the mid-eighteenth century architect, Henry Keene.[1]

Scattered about central and southern England are those few surviving buildings which represent his grasp, structures which the luck of life either allowed him to build or, often more happily, obliged him to build. The interface between Keene's reach and his grasp is an unusually profitable study because he designed through those decades from 1750 to 1775 when Palladian, Rococo, Gothick and Neo-classical modes were interacting uncertainly and died at the age of fifty with his practice apparently on the verge of failure. This was despite the fact that several of the V & A designs and at least four of his realised works suggest that he could have been riding the crest of a new stylistic fashion.

Taken as a whole, these designs go some way to explain the dilemma of direction which must have faced not only Keene but also his more successful contemporaries. They are a casebook to an understanding of how a certain sensibility could fit an architect for mastery in one style, the Gothick, and for meretricious inadequacy in another, the classical.

A mere four of the designs are Gothick, three of them for garden pavilions. All the other designs are classical. None of them are signed by Keene, but at least twelve of the temples and garden buildings are in his hand, then there is the one bizarre, restless design for a palace and thirteen projects for medium-sized houses and villas.

The Gothick designs are relevant to the understanding of his realized work and the attribution to him of undocumented buildings; as architectural drawings only one, a pavilion in an ornamental wall, has been carefully coloured to suggest the effects of light and shade. Significantly, a version of this pavilion was actually built about 1760 as Robin Hood's Temple for Sir Charles Kemys Tynte at Halswell House near Bridgwater in Somerset.

Every one of the classical designs has been accorded this full treatment of colour-wash with a delicate concern for contrasts of light and shadow, particularly where colonnades are drawn across recessed sections of an elevation to create a loggia. Front and rear elevations are provided for almost every house and several of the more ambitious projects have side elevations as well. The impression given by the

66. A scheme for a pavilion in an ornamental wall, one of many designs by Keene in the Victoria and Albert Museum.

whole collection of V & A drawings may be the result of the taste of the original collector. It certainly suggests, however, that Keene saw himself as pre-eminently a classical architect and devoted much time and considerable ingenuity to the preparation of schemes which, if realised, would have made him a serious rival to Sir Robert Taylor and James Paine.

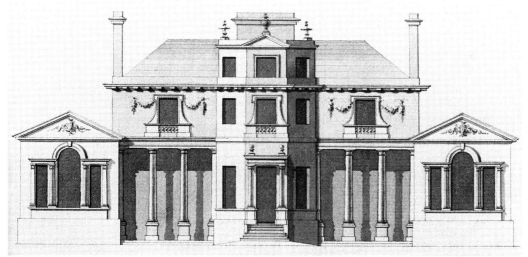

67. An elevation of a small classical house in the V & A collection.

Since none of these classical designs appears in his known *oeuvre* of lost or surviving buildings, it is worth considering what stylistic elements led to their rejection, and so perhaps to the general pattern of rejection that runs through Keene's career as a classical designer. These specimen elevations display outstanding originality in their manipulation of elements and in their spatial subtlety, yet these were probably the very qualities which caused them to lie unexecuted. No single design can be precisely classified as Baroque, Palladian, Rococo or Neo-classical. Keene experimented, like a sophisticated Edwardian architect, with variations on all four styles. He adopted no grand tradition, and this in itself suggests a fatal deficiency in will. In practice it must have meant that he was never taken up by any particular group of patrons.

Keene's misfortune may have been the accidental one of having been born too late, in 1726, twelve years after Robert Taylor. At any given point in English architectural practice there is only room for a limited number of successful designers in one field, and Sir Robert Taylor occupied the niche which Keene must, on the evidence of these designs, have hoped to fill. Both men were 'bred to the profession of architecture'[2] but, apart from his advantage in being twelve years older, Taylor's father was Master of the London Masons' Company. He sent his son on a frugal Italian tour just before he himself died bankrupt. Keene's father by contrast was a mere carpenter. Curiously, both Keene and Taylor achieved their first significant advances at Westminster Abbey, but whereas Taylor's was the prestigious commission by parliament to design in 1744 a monument for Captain Cornewall, a national hero, Keene was simply appointed Surveyor to the Dean and Chapter in 1746.

Even this position was, for a young man of twenty, a remarkable step. He must have owed it to James Horne, a much older man, who had risen from artisan joiner to architectural practice as a surveyor and designer of modest Palladian churches in the London area. Horne had employed Keene's father in the building of a church, St Mary at Ealing, and Horne became Surveyor to the Fabric of Westminster in the same year that the young Keene became Surveyor to the Dean. Keene succeeded Horne as Surveyor to the Fabric in 1752.

Before that year Keene had already achieved his first major commission to design the Flesh Market at Westminster. This project should not be underrated. A row of six three-storey town houses fronted the scheme onto Broad Sanctuary. Behind these was a Doric columned cloister about a central court and no less than twenty-four shops and eighteen family houses. It was a piece of major urban redevelopment in the most prosaic contemporary classicism. Nothing could have been further removed from the restless decorative elaboration of his later ideal drawings than the Broad Sanctuary terrace, with its central feature of a plain pediment with an oculus and a single skirted and balustraded window below.

The paradox of Keene's talent is already apparent. He was of London suburban artisan origin and Ealing background. Intimately involved with the day to day repairs of a great Gothic abbey, his first venture was surprisingly to front a typically capitalist enterprise: the clearance of an area of slum tenements in order to create a new property of high residential density and commercial utility. The mind and the advice of James Horne, that pedestrian Palladian, can be sensed here as it can in Keene's commission to build in 1755, a year before Horne's death, a very dull Palladian house for a Mr Gulston at Ealing. But all this time the mind of the plain suburban classicist was being suborned by the example of the prodigious Gothic structure for the repair of which he was responsible, and whose most ornate features he was absorbing to use as a later vocabulary. 1750 is the date on his stolid Flesh Market designs, yet in the same year he was at work on two of his finest schemes in the wholly divergent Gothick: Hartlebury Chapel for Bishop Maddox of Worcester and the enchantingly original Enville Museum for Lord Stamford.

68. Hartlebury Castle Chapel, Hereford and Worcester, c. 1749–50. Vaulted and fitted out by Keene.

The influence of the Gothic presence of Westminster Abbey was impressed upon another Londoner of Keene's social class in the mid-century. Batty Langley, son of a Twickenham gardener, moved to Parliament Steps, Westminster in 1735 when he was thirty-nine years old and on to Soho in 1740. The Gothick designs of his *Ancient Architecture Restored and Improved,* published in 1741–2, are essentially composite impressions of the slender clustered columns of Westminster's Early English nave, the foliated trefoils and frothy crockets of its Decorated tombs and niches and the Perpendicular fenestration of Henry VII's Chapel.

Keene must have been through a preliminary period of familiarisation with applied Gothick design before his creation of Hartlebury Chapel and the Enville Museum. Regrettably, details of this period in his life are obscure.

In these circumstances, Keene's contact with contemporary architects such as Sanderson Miller is particularly important. A founder patriarch of the Gothic revival, Miller was a gentleman architect whose forte was for rough, indeed

69. The Enville Museum, Staffordshire, c. 1750–2, exterior.

amateurish, pencil sketches. These conveyed a semblance of a particular building or piece of furniture, and were then fleshed out into working drawings by professional architects or master builders. Miller is credited with the Gothick castles at Hagley, Hereford and Worcester (1747–8) and Wimpole, Cambridgeshire (designed 1749–51). It may be a coincidence that one of the undated Keene designs at the V & A is of 'Library Steps, at Ld Hardwickes at Wimple'[3], but he was certainly working for Lord Lyttelton on furniture for the castle folly at Hagley a year after its completion. A letter from Lyttelton to Miller dated 18 July 1749 reads: 'Since I wrote this I have spoke with Mr Keene, who will send you by this post the design for my dining room chimney piece. The other he need not trouble you with. He desires a model from you for the chairs in the castle if they are to be made here'.[4]

This is the first reference to Keene's Midlands practice and a fair indication that in 1749 he already had a working relationship with the gentleman amateur, sending some completed designs for Miller's approval, finishing others without his assistance and requiring, or pretending to require, roughouts of Gothick furniture from Miller. It is clear from the record of Miller's relations with Sir Roger Newdigate at Arbury that Miller needed to have his self-esteem boosted regularly. He actually

XVII Henry Keene; Arbury Hall, Warwickshire, 1762–76, the dining room.

XVIII Henry Keene; the monument to the third Earl of Litchfield in Spelsbury Church, Oxfordshire, c. 1772, and detail.

collapsed into a nervous breakdown when his vanity was not carefully humoured. He was a projector of the Gothick spirit but not the perfector of its finished forms.[5]

What is puzzling is that before any of these hints of minor Gothick activity on his part, Keene must already have been engaged on a major new work in the style: the chapel to the Bishop of Worcester's palace at Hartlebury Castle. Miller's diary for 26 October 1749 describes this as 'very near finished and very handsome'.[6] The entry suggests, allowing for the scale of the work, that it was begun in the previous year, 1748, when Keene was only twenty-two and had no prior designing experience in

70. The Enville Museum, the ruinous interior.

the style. It has to be supposed that the pro-Gothic Bishop of Worcester, by some process of enthusiastic expectation, had persuaded an inexperienced young surveyor to put together several disparate stylistic features of Westminster Abbey, fuse them in a Langley manner, and so produce an interior of rare delicacy and distinction. If Miller had any hand in its design he would most certainly have claimed it. All he ever claimed was that on 15 June 1750 he had begun 'Drawing plan of seat' for the building which he had admired so generously eight months before.[7]

The Enville Museum, a garden temple of an equal lyrical invention, is essentially Hartlebury Chapel turned inside out; an extrovert architectural experience where the chapel is an introverted one. The chapel is a fan vaulted rectangular space containing, and visually dominated by, a screen of three ogee arches carried upon slender clustered pillars. The temple, on the other hand, is a screen of three ogee arches set upon similar pillar clusters giving entrance to a rectangular space under an almost identical fan vaulting. What was a united interior experience at Hartlebury is at Enville made separate. At Hartlebury the screen is two-dimensional, at Enville the screen arches become a three-dimensional pillared portico. Hartlebury rejects the outside world; the Enville Museum works outwards into its garden. It was in the

71. Hartwell Church, Buckinghamshire, 1753–5, the vaulting.

chapel that Keene first revealed his inclination to make a vaulted roof the dominating feature of an interior. This was to be a constant of his career until he died with his superb series of ceilings for Arbury Hall still unfinished. In these at least he had no rival in the mid-century.

72. Hartwell Church, the exterior.

Hartlebury Chapel was complete in 1750, the year when Keene is likely to have become occupied with his vast project for the Westminster Flesh Market. The date of the Enville Museum is less certain but it was probably complete by 1752.[8] The vaults of Henry VII's Chapel were probably the models for the Enville and Hartlebury ceilings, but Keene modified and simplified them extensively. He was perhaps influenced by Christopher Wren's solution in St Mary, Aldermary, to the problem of setting fans across a narrow rectangle. Wren gave his fans a small radius and filled the intervening spaces with cusped roundels and saucer domes. Keene's fans have a similar projection and the gap between their leading edges is filled by rosettes and simple pendants.

As in so much early Gothick work, (these two buildings predate most of Strawberry Hill), the Enville Museum has faults of design. When an architect with a classical background works in the Gothick he is inclined to fumble in his placing of the string courses. That at Enville has no *raison d'être*, structurally or visually. The small side rose windows sit uneasily high in relation to the large central rose and the two simple side windows have no stylistic relationship to the complex triple ogees of the doorway. But all these flaws are excused by the engaging restlessness of the whole. It is in the nature of the Gothick to provoke and disturb, not to calm and satisfy. Even in ruin, the Museum remains the first lyrical and successful Gothick façade of the century.

If we suppose that Keene found time to design and supervise the Museum before 1753, he was then in the midpoint of his first Gothick period and had moved from ecclesiastical to lay patrons. The church at Hartwell, Buckinghamshire, for Sir William Lee, Bart., marked, literally, a high point in his handling of fan vaulting and its collapse in 1951 was a disastrous loss.

A series of designs in the Bodleian Library record his early ideas for this extraordinary building.[9] These prove that initially he projected a cruciform church with a wide nave and narrower chancel and transepts with a ludicrously small east tower. But he found, when he sketched out the vaults for this ground plan, that he was creating a series of illogically related vaulting units over the chancel and transepts with one large rose motif over the nave. He then abandoned the cruciform ground

PLATE XV

plan and devised the existing octagon. One of the V & A designs for an octagonal Gothick garden pavilion is so close to Hartwell Church as Keene finally devised it that he may simply have taken the design and projected it on a larger scale.[10] This would explain the unusual height and proportions of the building.

Hartwell Church marks Keene's absolute capitulation to the vault as a controlling feature. The church is conceived in terms of its ceiling and designed as an octagon but not for the Palladian associations of that form. An octagon is a mathematically ideal setting for a virtuoso display of eight true fans centred at its corners and touching at their leading edges a vast open central rose. Each fan is allowed its complete spread without cutting into its neighbour; the eight interstices are filled with elegant tri-lobed mouchettes. As such the design was a *tour de force* of spatial exploration, but it is functionally questionable whether the eyes of the worshippers should always be drawn upwards to a Rococo-Gothick heaven and distracted away from both altar and preacher.

From the outside the church is a charming curiosity. Because a tower on one side of an octagon would have looked unbalanced, Keene gave it both east and west towers. It might have made more sense, since the church was only an enlarged version of the octagonal Gothick garden pavilion, if Keene had topped it with an ogee dome like that on the pavilion. Placed at the end of a straight vista from the house the church doubles, in fact, as a rather ungainly garden ornament.

Hartwell Church was completed in 1755 and Keene's classical work on Hartwell House was not begun until 1759. If the early Flesh Market is ignored, his architectural career divides into two Gothick periods neatly alternating with two classical periods. He was now moving into his first classical episode (1755–60). Since the design for the Gothick garden pavilion in the V & A seems to predate the building of Hartwell Church, it is not unreasonable to suppose that the main group of classical house designs were also early work, prepared by an ambitious young architect hoping to achieve, in the near future, the patronage of the wealthy.

The designs are the work of an impatient Palladian with a strong preference for schemes where the central block is full of activity with much interpenetration of its spaces through loggias, balconies and deep colonnades. Side pavilions are the rule, but the connecting wings are usually so complex as to detract from the three main units of the facade. There is a grudging anticipation of Neo-classicism in the scale of some of his colonnades, but decorative detail in the form of swags, cartouches, urns, ball finials, oculi, recessed arches, tapered pilasters and skirted and balustraded windows is applied so lavishly as to suggest that Keene was more of a Rococo

73. Design for a classical house in the V & A collection, by Henry Keene.

architect by inclination. The exuberance of his Gothick work would support this view. But in his Gothick and in his classical designs there is such a strong spatial feeling that the mass of superficial detail tends to be justified. Every one of his classical designs in the V & A is actively three-dimensional with his favourite canted bays pressing out aggressively. Domes, pyramids and pediments rise upwards and deeply recessed loggias cut into the body of the houses. Attenuated colonnades emphasise the recession of the loggias with a play of shadows. The designs are, in fact, far too eclectic to be called truly Rococo.

These designs make a fascinating series, but all that can be said of them historically is that Keene's patrons were not fascinated. Perhaps if he had pressed his work upon new men, city merchants and bankers, as Sir Robert Taylor with his Masonic connections was able to do, he might have got further. Several of Taylor's surviving villas, like Asgill House, Richmond and Harleyford Manor, Buckinghamshire, resemble Keene's projects in their ingenious deviation from the norm. But Taylor's best work has an astylar grace that Keene's designs consciously avoid. Keene's patrons seem to have had too strong a sense of what was architecturally fitting in a classical elevation to allow him to express himself and his actual classical work between 1755 and 1760 is disappointing.[11]

He designed for four patrons in this period. The first, Mr Gulston of Ealing, was clearly a home town connection. Only the spindly proportions of the portico reveal Keene's hand in the design of this now demolished house.

The second patron, the first Earl of Shelburne, presented Keene with the chance for which the V & A drawings suggest he was waiting. Impressed, presumably, by Hartwell Church, Lord Shelburne asked Keene to put a new Gothick parapet on High Wycombe parish church and to design a bizarre pew in composite style, Gothick, Jacobean and Rococo, to be placed above the chancel screen. This now serves more appropriately as a minstrels' gallery to the assembly hall of a nearby girls' school. It reveals a weakness in Keene's sense of the integration of modes, but must have pleased Shelburne, since he gave Keene the task of designing and supervising the erection of a Guildhall as his gift to the town. This still functions admirably, and its light arcading allows outside space complete access to internal volume. It is appropriately civic in its first floor suite of rooms and its vigorous Baroque tempietto supplies that upward thrust upon a relatively narrow base which is characteristic of Keene's liveliest elevations.[12] The Guildhall was completed in 1757. Meanwhile, in the Earl's country seat, Bowood House in Wiltshire, matters were proceeding less happily.

The building history of Bowood is tangled. After the first Earl died in 1761, his heir brought in Robert Adam and sent Keene packing. This was Keene's first real setback — a sign that at thirty-five he had already missed the tide of fashion.

Keene's west front of the house, destroyed in 1955, was a tame affair. Only the delicacy of the Rococo cartouche in the plain pediment suggested his taste. The south front was a stylistic confusion but it is fair to suggest that Keene was preparing a more ambitious elevation typical of his three-dimensional designs. The canted

74. The Guildhall, High Wycombe, Buckinghamshire, 1755–7.

bays, projecting cornice, balustrade and decorative urns were his and he seems already to have assembled on the site, before he was dismissed, the stones for a giant portico.[13] Saddled with these expensive materials, Adam was obliged to continue the project, which had, indeed, a Neo-classical grandeur. He merely re-cut the capitals in an elegant reeded design of his own contrivance.

This must have damaged Keene's reputation and it is significant that Sir Paul Methuen at neighbouring Corsham Court rejected, at about that time, all three schemes which Keene had devised for enlarging his house. The designs were, for their time, astoundingly sympathetic to an existing Elizabethan front. Keene had proposed to double the original bays and gables, and in one of the three elevations for the south front, he had set double height Doric and Ionic colonnades between the Elizabethan gables to achieve his favourite effect of depth and shadow.

There remained, in his first classical phase, his rebuilding of the east and garden fronts of Hartwell House, a project on which he worked from 1759–63. It is by this, by the west front of Bowood and by the later Provost's Lodgings at Worcester College, Oxford that Keene's ability to devise a successful elevation for a large classical house must be judged.

75. Bowood House, Wiltshire, 1755–65. Destroyed 1955–6.

It is instructive to compare the garden front of Hartwell with design no. E857 in PLATE XVI
the V & A — the real and the ideal, the grasp and the reach. William Lee was of the
party of Frederick, Prince of Wales whose equestrian statue still stands at Hartwell.
Frederick favoured the Rococo if only because his father was officially Palladian. So
at Hartwell Sir William seems to have asked for an essay in his political style: astylar
and facetted on the exterior with interiors dramatised by Rococo decoration on
ceilings and around chimney pieces. What is most interesting at Hartwell is to see
how the realities of an existing Elizabethan house and the taste of an English baronet
have modified Keene's ideal scheme for such a house.

Design E857 is of eleven bays, Hartwell extends to fifteen. In all this space
Hartwell retains the canted bays and the recession of the three central windows of
E857, but gone are the pediment, the columns, the rusticated basement and the side
pavilions with their battery of swags, garlands, pilasters and Viennese domes. To
compensate, Hartwell can only muster a balustraded cornice with urns and a
stronger emphasis upon the first floor windows with flat and triangular pediments.
An architect's achievement depends upon what he can persuade a client to let him
build. Keene's surviving interiors at Hartwell are vigorously, though not riotously,

76. Hartwell House, Buckinghamshire, 1759–63.

Rococo; his two elevations for the exterior are only modest compromises in that direction. The house reveals none of his favoured upward thrust of elements and no trace of his three-dimensional devices of columns set across recessed sections. In short, he had failed for a second time to point towards a new and individual direction in the development of English classical architecture — an insular Rococo.

Long before Hartwell was complete, Keene was back in his second Gothick phase and moving towards the design of his masterpiece, the Dining Room of Arbury Hall in Warwickshire.

Robin Hood's Temple at Halswell House in Somerset and the Tynte Pew in nearby Goathurst Church, both of 1760, were minor commissions. So too was his chancel roof of 1768 for Harefield Church, Middlesex, but this last with its uninspired barrel vaulting of linked trefoil-headed panelling was commissioned by the strong-willed and opinionated Goth, Sir Roger Newdigate, himself a capable draughtsman. Harefield is, therefore, part of the story of Keene and Arbury which began in 1762 and which represents one of Keene's rare triumphs of will in a struggle between designer and client over the forms of an evolving house.

Newdigate began the Gothick evolution of Arbury in 1748, taking advice from Sanderson Miller but using William Hiorn as his executant architect. The earlier rooms of this transformation are fine but markedly inferior in spatial exploration to the room for which Keene was responsible. 'H. Keene, Architect', is first mentioned in the Arbury account books in 1762.[14] He seems to have taken a leading role at the house when the Library was complete and the Parlour, now the drawing room, was under construction. Both the Library and the drawing room are rectangles with shallow barrel vaults. The walls of both rooms and the vault of the drawing room are surfaced with repetitive ranks of cusped panelling. The effect is rich, late

94

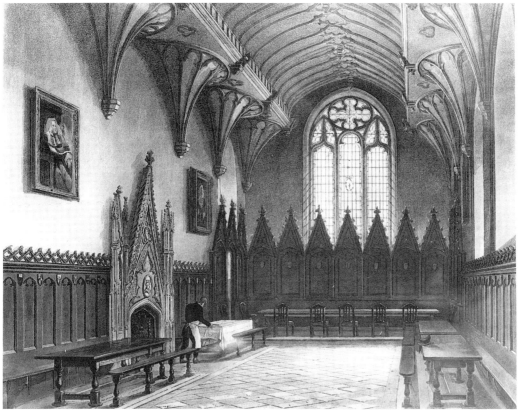

77. The Hall of University College, Oxford, remodelled in 1766. The ceiling and woodwork were destroyed in 1904.

Perpendicular, and uninventive. One notable relief in the drawing room is the chimney piece, carved by Richard Hayward in 1764, a year after the room was fitted up. A similar chimney piece was set up by Keene in the Hall of University College, Oxford in 1766.[15] Both were based on Aymer de Valence's tomb in Westminster Abbey, so it is fair to assume that in 1764 Keene was beginning to vary and enrich the Newdigate house-style of panelled Perpendicular, though he still deployed it dutifully at Harefield in 1768.

Keene's remodelled Hall for University College was a compromise between his favourite fan vaulting and a Newdigate barrel. Newdigate was paying for the scheme, so both men were presumably satisfied. In his next and probably final room at Arbury Keene had sufficiently gained Newdigate's confidence to be allowed his own way. The resultant Dining Room is Keene's finest achievement, a room which PLATE XVII appears 'less like a place to dine in than a piece of space enclosed simply for the sake of beautiful outline', a room that impresses 'with its architectural beauty like a cathedral'. So wrote George Eliot about the dining room of Arbury's fictional equivalent, Cheverel Manor.[16] The great fans of the vault are simple in detail but generously calculated in proportion to sweep across and just touch at their fullest extent. Niches of complex late Decorated ornament are placed symmetrically in the vault wall spaces. The room is given an added depth and richness by a piece of planning which also enabled Keene to achieve his favoured effect of projection and recession on the outside of the house. This was a broad aisle on the south side of the room internally enriched by the Newdigate panelling and compressed fan vaults. Externally it was expressed in a projecting frontispiece of three crocketted and traceried windows which verge upon the archaeologically correct and suggest that Keene, just before his death, was travelling fast towards authentic mediaeval revival.

78. Worcester College, Oxford, the Provost's Lodgings, 1773–6.

Keene was working on Arbury when he died, but his last seven years, from 1769 to 1776, constitute his second classical and Oxford phase. This includes his fitting up of the Library at Christ Church, the designing and initial stages of building of the Radcliffe Observatory and his work on the Provost's Lodgings at Worcester. It can hardly have been a happy conclusion to his career. The continuing work at Arbury must have been clouded by the financial troubles revealed after his death.[17] At the Radcliffe Observatory he had begun some work on the first floor with fidgety Palladian detail. Then, just when he had the perfect opportunity to design with his favourite upward emphasis, public criticism of his design led to James Wyatt being called in with his dashing Grecian scheme. Keene had then the ignominious task of supervising the construction of Wyatt's work on the ground floor of his own rejected scheme. The Provost's Lodgings at Worcester can hardly have satisfied the man who drew the V & A designs. The recessed arch of the main façade provides a little relief and there is a fashionable touch of Adam detail in the swags and paterae about the central windows of the first floor, but it is a heavy house, a fitting finial to the oppressive north range.

There was to be one last dazzling flash of Keene's skill in a small masterpiece which combines his intemperate eclecticism with his feeling for spaces penetrating within further spaces. Appropriately, this was a design for a funerary monument, PLATE XVIII · not his own, but that to the third Earl of Litchfield in Spelsbury Church, Oxfordshire. Behind and rising above it is a grey marble pyramid on which a cherub climbs an improbable tree. The monument itself is a tight spatial sophistication of Rococo

96

design in contrasted marbles. This contrives to centre all attention through a convex oval opening upon two mysterious urns, consciously scaled as if caught in perspective, receding from view like some metaphysical insight into the calm finality of death. In three years Keene was to explore this finality himself, his schemes for the Arbury interiors only half completed. Apart from this one intensely conceived monument at Spelsbury, all the feeling for an evolving classicism which his designs had promised was achieved only in the market hall of a small Chiltern town.

Keene was an architect open to influences, consciously in search of solutions. It was his error of judgement that he did not analyse his own early practice to anticipate the direction in which English taste was moving: not towards a native Rococo, but towards a revived Gothick. Had he produced a tempting range of houses in the Gothick style, their exterior elevations diversified by his highly individual spatial invention, he might have saved English architecture from the later crudities of Milton Abbey and Tong Castle.

Caught up by circumstances rather than seeking to control them, he produced Gothick designs only to order and expressed his genius in a series of limited and largely interior schemes. In these he acted rather as the secondary agent of a patron's vision than as an initiator of that new style which he was uniquely qualified to develop.

6

JAMES ESSEX, 1722–1784

Archaeological Integrity

Thomas Cocke

JAMES ESSEX is one of the most interesting provincial architects of the eighteenth century. He is important in a local context, being associated with most of the major commissions of the period in and around Cambridge. Essex also has a broader appeal. His life shows how it was possible to rise, professionally, from joiner and general builder to architect and socially, from artisan to gentleman and antiquary. Furthermore, in Essex's circle of acquaintance, different intellectual and artistic worlds met. Through his father, also James Essex, and through his patron, Sir James Burrough, he was linked with James Gibbs with whom both older men had worked on the Senate House. Essex's own interest in ancient building brought him into contact with the Cambridge antiquaries, notably William Cole, Michael Tyson, Thomas Gray, James Bentham and Richard Gough, and, thanks to Cole, with the more fashionable world of Horace Walpole at Strawberry Hill. But in the final count Essex is of most significance to posterity for his precocious practice and studies of Gothic. His restorations of such great medieval buildings as the cathedrals of Ely and Lincoln, and King's College Chapel, Cambridge were exceptional in their period for their efficacy and for their concern for authenticity. In his unpublished treatise on Gothic as well as in his articles on such topics as the Round Church at Cambridge, he tried to investigate the structural logic of medieval building rather than to amass attractive decorative details or curious historical fact.

His buildings in the classical taste of the period are soundly constructed and sensibly planned but reveal no great imagination in their design. His college buildings in Cambridge whether new-built, as at Sidney Sussex, or refacings of earlier structures, as at St John's, have façades composed of conventional pedimented doorways, dentil courses and raised window architraves, with the orders used only for frontispieces. His stylistic vocabulary changed little over the years. The elevations of his 1773 design for the new Court at Corpus Christi are like those he made for a similar commission twenty-five years earlier. The influence of the emerging Neo-classical style can be perceived, for instance in the Trinity College Combination Room, in an increased refinement and economy of detailing rather than in new motifs. Even his more ambitious façades at Clare College Chapel, for all the refined elaboration of their mouldings, are derived from Christopher Wren's Chapel for Pembroke College erected a whole century before.

His lack of adventure can partly be explained by the limited means available to Essex's patrons. Colleges were not the wealthy institutions then that some became in the nineteenth century, and the dons and clerics who commissioned him privately were comfortably off rather than rich. Corpus was twice forced to abandon well-considered plans for a new court:[1] The heightening and refronting of the Tudor

79. James Essex, from a contemporary miniature.

buildings at St John's was given up after one side of one court had cost £2,700.[2] Even where a scheme was completed, money could run very tight. The erection of a new chapel and library range at Sidney Sussex was only achieved by a forceful Master who kept four fellowships vacant in order to divert their endowments to building.[3] Essex, when asked by the University in 1766 to front the unfinished west façade of the Senate House, cannily produced first a cheap design without orders, which could then be rejected in favour of one with pilasters, at an additional cost of £310.[4]

The restraint of Essex's style must also be due to the influence of his mentor and patron in architecture, Sir James Burrough. It was the influence of Burrough which helped to lift Essex from artisan-builder to gentleman-architect and Essex remained ever grateful to him. In or about 1775 he piously had printed the engraved design for the new University Library which Burrough had prepared in 1752 but which had been rejected in favour of the present building by Stephen Wright, the protégé of the Chancellor, the Duke of Newcastle.

Burrough's architecture can perhaps be described as Hanoverian Tory, conservative but not reactionary. The connection between Burrough and James Gibbs over the building of the Senate House, so close that Burrough was credited with the design, meant that Burrough was never an orthodox Palladian. It was possibly thanks to Gibbs that Burrough held and passed on to Essex a respect for Wren unusual for the period. Their borrowings at Clare from Wren's Pembroke Chapel have already been mentioned. In his designs for a new court at Corpus, Essex planned a chapel flanked by porticoes, incorporating a library imitating Wren's

80. St John's College, Cambridge; Tudor college architecture remodelled by Essex 1773–75.

arrangement at Emmanuel College. Burrough used Palladian motifs but not Palladian principles and proportions. In his Peterhouse building of 1736–8 he crowded finely executed rustication and Venetian windows on to a tall, narrow block.[6] Essex

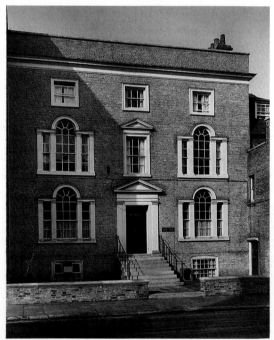

81. Kenmare House, Cambridge, 1768.

continued this tendency in a frankly provincial way at Randall House (now Kenmare) of 1768 where four Venetian windows jostle each other in a three-bay facade. Burrough retained throughout his career a taste for internal richness typical of the 1720s. His woodwork is robust and architectural as in the fireplaces in the halls of

Queens' and Trinity Hall; the plaster rose in the ceiling of Sidney Sussex hall is almost Baroque. Essex, far from reacting against Burrough's conservative style, seems to have regarded it as definitive, to a degree that makes it difficult and to an extent profitless to disentangle their respective hands in the commissions they undertook jointly. The two men were not only like-minded but in such close contact that even on the day Burrough died Essex had been with him discussing business.[7] A comparison between the hall lantern erected for Gonville and Caius in 1728 and the antechapel lantern at Clare of the mid 1760s does however suggest some development in style.[8] The earlier lantern has an octagonal dome, articulated at the angles by engaged composite columns, an attic lit by wreathed oeil-de-boeuf windows, and a shallow ogee cupola. The Clare lantern is a simpler and stronger composition with the attic omitted, Ionic pilasters substituted for the columns, and the ogee cupola heightened.

The antechapel and chapel of Clare, begun to Burrough's design in 1764, the year he died, and carried to completion by Essex, are undoubtedly their masterpiece. Cole who, as a firm friend of Burrough and Essex, could judge between them, gave the credit to Essex: 'His knowledge and abilities in modern architecture is (sic) sufficiently evident by his performance at Clare Hall Chapel.'[9] The design exploited the awkward site at the north east angle of the seventeenth-century court by creating a progression from the dark access passage to the domed and top-lit antechapel and, beyond, to the barrel-vaulted and cross-lit chapel. Although the external elevations were based on Wren, the plan and internal detailing were untraditional. Antechapels were usually either simple lobbies or when on a large scale, as at King's and Trinity, continuations of the space of the chapel proper. At Clare the antechapel and chapel are distinct, contrasting spaces. The mouldings of the woodwork of the stalls and altarpiece are as subtle and delicate as anything by 'Athenian' Stuart or Robert Adam in the same decade.

In contemporary architecture however, Essex's concern was usually practical utility rather than aesthetic effect. He was an improver not only of buildings, but of roads and bridges. His 'great services, care and attention to improve the Navigation' between Littleport and Clayhithe won him the offer of the Freedom of Cambridge in 1779.[10] He shared the enthusiasm of his age for new techniques of bridge building. Presumably in his construction of the 'Mathematical' bridge at Queen's he learnt much from William Etheridge, its designer, who had worked on Westminster Bridge and went on to build the bridge over the Thames at Walton.[11] Essex's Garrett Hostel Bridge, built in 1769 but replaced in the nineteenth century, was another 'Mathematical' bridge with brick piers and timber superstructure.[12] His Great Bridge at Magdalene of 1754 was demolished in 1823, unrecorded save for a note about its foundations,[13] but his beautiful Cycloidal bridge at Trinity, erected in 1764-5, survives as testimony to his skill. Drawings in the British Library show how carefully Essex worked out the geometry of the arches, perhaps under the influence of the revolutionary Pontypridd bridge by William Edwards of which Essex made a drawing, now in the RIBA.[14]

PLATE XIX

In Essex's domestic work, whether for individuals or for institutions, the overriding requirements were not for greater or grander accommodation but comfort and convenience. Without nineteenth or twentieth-century techniques of heating or lighting late medieval or even seventeenth-century rooms could be dark, damp, low and cold. Essex's task in both restorations and new buildings was to make wide, stout, well-lit staircases and decently proportioned and panelled rooms with efficient chimneys and generous windows. Gabled garrets were heightened into full storeys, again with comfortable if lower rooms, and clunch or red brick façades faced with good ashlar or stock brick. Essex's last such job for a college, First Court in St John's, is an instructive example, especially as only the southern range was completed so that the eastern and western ranges survive as comparisons in their original state. The College order of 1772 was that the block should be 'covered with

82. Gonville and Caius College, Cambridge, the hall lantern, 1728.

83. Clare College, Cambridge, the antechapel lantern, 1763–69.

stone, sashed and otherwise improved'.[15] The early sixteenth-century red brick building was heightened by a full storey built of grey stocks, the contrast being left visible at the rear but concealed towards the court by an ashlar facade. The two-light mullioned windows were replaced by sashes. Yet the Georgian decoration was no more elaborate than the Tudor, with, externally, simple pediments to the doorways and raised architraves to the windows, and, internally, turned balusters to the stairs and plain panelling to the rooms. At First Court, Christ's College, where Essex's work amounted to refacing rather than internal remodelling, his technique was to enlarge windows and doorways and to make the court regular by breaking the ranges up into acceptable classical compositions. In rooms of greater pretension the same priorities applied. The Combination Room at Jesus, fitted up in 1762, has attractive but old-fashioned fielded panelling with a lugged overmantel: that at Trinity ten years later is larger and slightly more Neo-classical, but such grandiose PLATE XX elements as the chimneypiece have been introduced in recent times. Halls and chapels were also in need of greater comfort. The introduction of plaster ceilings, xix James Essex; Trinity College, Cambridge, the Cycloidal Bridge.

xx James Essex; the hall of Emmanuel College, Cambridge, repaired and refitted 1760–4.

xxi Rowlandson's view of the West Room and Dome Room in the old University Library. The Dome Room was fitted out by James Essex, 1750–1.

84. Clare College, the interior of the antechapel lantern.

new and more complete panelling and larger windows made these large rooms less cold and dark. Cole disapproved of Essex's refashioning of Queens' chapel in 1772–5 as altering an old building which 'seemed to want it very little' but the new ceiling, new paving, altered panelling and the painting of the plain parts of ceiling and walls 'Naples Yellow' must have created a more cheerful room for college worship.[16]

85. Christ's College, Cambridge; First Court, refaced by Essex 1758–75.

Essex's career was a success story. He was born in 1722, the son of an artisan who, in spite of the reputation he acquired for his joinery and the expansion of his business to cover general builder's work, seems to have had little to bequeath his son besides the family firm.[17] The house James Essex senior leased from Corpus Christi College in the last decade of his life, the Hartshorn tenement in Trumpington Street, was modest in size and value.[18] The elder Mrs Essex, Bridget (née Prigg) is unlikely to have brought much money of her own, since her son had to pay her an annuity of £30.[19] Yet when Essex died in 1784 he was worth over £20,000, mostly in cash and Bank Stock, which he seems to have accumulated patiently over the years, rather than gained in one windfall or lucky speculation.[20] He had risen to the rank of gentleman, addressed as 'Mr Essex, Architect' not 'joiner' or 'carpenter'. In 1772 he had been elected a fellow of the Society of Antiquaries, and was almost certainly also a Freemason, at that time a mainly upper class interest.[21] His professional income in the 1750s and 1760s must have been based on his building business. As an architect he was of course paid only a few guineas for designs, unless he was responsible for the erection of the building, in which case he charged the standard five per cent commission. Thus the refacing of First Court, St John's, which cost £2,700 brought Essex £135;[22] the rebuilding of the Combination Room at Trinity, which cost about £4,500 brought £223.[23] Surveying was less profitable. For 'surveying repairs and new buildings' at Trinity, which include the rebuilding of Nevile's Court, for the four years 1754–8, Essex received only £120.[24] By the 1770s, Essex had withdrawn from the joinery and building business but was in demand from Lincoln to Winchester as consulting architect. This brought him honour, rather than financial reward. For his last works at Lincoln, which included the repaving of the cathedral, he was given an inscribed silver salver.[25] At Strawberry Hill Essex refused any fee for his initial designs and only took £31–10s for the later Beauclerk tower and office range.[26]

His artisan background in some ways aided his later career. Essex was acknow-
ledged to be a man of common sense and practical judgment. He was invoked as
arbitrator in professional disputes, for instance when the lawyer James Ind quarrelled with the builder Charles Cole and his brother over a house they had built at
Fenstanton.[27] Thanks to his intimate knowledge of the various branches of the
building trade, especially carpentry and joinery, Essex could ensure that in a complex restoration, such as the rebuilding of Nevile's Court, each element was properly coordinated within the general programme. His practical skills also helped earn
him his place as an expert on Gothic since it confirmed his unique understanding of
its technical aspects. But such a reputation also kept him tied to the tedious minutiae
of building, consulted over faulty tiling or passage doors.[28]

Essex's activities in both his professional and his social life were not confined
either to Town or to Gown. His advice·and his company were sought by both
parties. His position in Cambridge's small but closely-knit middle class was streng-
thened by his marriage in 1753 to Elizabeth Thurlbourn, daughter of a leading
bookseller of the town and sister-in-law of an eminent local doctor, Richard
Hayles.[29] There was much intermarriage between such families and University
dons. The Essexs' daughter Meliscent married John Hammond, fellow of Queens'
and Elizabeth's niece, Sophia, married Thomas Kerrich, fellow of Magdalene and PLATE XXI
University Librarian. Essex was thus not far removed socially from the dons and
clergy who made up his local antiquarian circle and who were themselves often the
sons of provincial merchants, professional men, clerics or minor gentry. Burrough's
father was a doctor of Bury St Edmunds, Cole's a middling Cambridgeshire
landowner, Tyson's Archdeacon of Stamford. Personal, professional and academic
ties were all interconnected. Essex knew James Bentham as patron, fellow antiquary, partner in building, family friend and trustee. Cole's papers or Tyson's letters
show how constantly they visited each other to dine or take tea.[30] The almost
claustrophobic closeness of the circle is demonstrated by the way that Essex who, in
his youth, had publicly accused Dr Masters of Corpus Christi of plagiarism, had to
associate with the man constantly for the rest of his life.[31]

The antiquaries amongst whom Essex moved were far more than an assortment
of provincial clerics. Cambridge in the mid-eighteenth century was the centre for a
group of medievalists who, in accord with their academic background, were interested in the history and theory of medieval architecture rather than in being
dilettante patrons of buildings and decoration in a neo-Gothic style.

The weightiest figure in every sense was William Cole, an insatiable and meticulous recorder of the past, whether expressed in documents, buildings or anecdote.
Cole already knew of Essex as a young antiquarian in 1742-3 but their acquaintance
only became close when Cole decided in the 1760s to retire to the Cambridge area,
eventually renting a house in Milton for which Essex designed alterations and
additions. (Essex refused payment so Cole eventually gave him a book, hitherto
unidentified, of prints of castles in France and Spain).[32] Antiquarian tastes were
complementary, with Cole educating Essex by lending him manuscripts and books
and Essex in return explaining how Cole's beloved Gothic worked. Cole had a
genuine affection for Essex. Although he could be patronizing and sometimes
exploited Essex by making him run errands in London, Cole spared the acid asides
with which he damned friend as well as foe. He claimed that Essex's restoration of

Ely had made the cathedral 'one of the noblest, grandest, and finest things of the sort in England'[33] and asserted that Essex's reredos in King's Chapel showed him to 'know more of Gothic architecture than anyone I have heard talk of it.'[34]

Cole advanced Essex's career by recommending him to Horace Walpole as an architect for Strawberry Hill, which led to the commission for the Ampthill Cross

86. Essex's reredos for King's College Chapel, Cambridge, removed 1897.

from Lord Ossory. Cole's own architectural patronage was limited but, besides his house, he asked Essex to design his monument. This eventually consisted of a design, now lost, for a tower for St Clement's Church in Cambridge, as requested in Cole's will.[35] Cole's final tribute was to make 'my old friend Mr James Essex, Architect'[36] one of his two executors, and thus responsible for the precious folio volumes, containing all his research and thought, his 'wife and children', which were bequeathed to the British Museum.[37]

The Cambridge antiquary best known to the world, though not in that role, was the poet Thomas Gray. In his later years Gray devoted much of his time to the study of medieval architecture but none of this work was published, except the analysis of Romanesque ornament, which formed part of the advice he gave James Bentham on the historical introduction to the latter's *History of Ely*, which was used almost verbatim in the final text. Essex must have known Gray through Cole and Tyson, though Gray kept himself apart from Cambridge society.

The other two important Cambridge antiquaries were James Bentham and Michael Tyson. Bentham of Ely was a curious figure, proudly provincial and of no apparent brilliance, but indefatigable in pursuing contemporary improvement in areas as diverse as turnpike roads, liturgical chanting and cathedral restoration. His

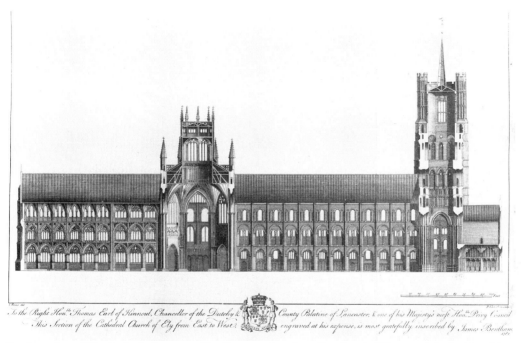

To the Right Hon.ble Thomas Earl of Kinnoul, Chancellor of the Dutchy & County Palatine of Lancaster, & one of his Majesty's most Hon.ble Privy Council. This Section of the Cathedral Church of Ely from East to West, engraved at his expense, is most gratefully inscribed by James Bentham.

87. A section of Ely Cathedral surveyed by Essex: a plate from Bentham's *History and Antiquities of the Conventual and Cathedral Church of Ely*, published in 1771.

History and Antiquities of the Conventual and Cathedral Church of Ely, published in 1771, though despaired of during its slow and stately progress into print, became one of the authoritative books of the Gothic revival. Essex was first associated with Bentham as an assistant, to make surveys and perspective drawings of the cathedral for Bentham's book, but they later collaborated on equal terms in establishing the architectural history of the church and precinct, and in carrying out the restoration of 1757–61 and more especially, the removal of the choir ten years later. Bentham, who acted as Clerk of the Works, and the Chapter did not always follow their architect's advice; Essex complained that they had spoiled the paving of the new choir by preferring a cheap estimate from, as it proved, incompetent London masons rather than a more realistic one by proved Cambridge workmen.[38]

Michael Tyson is also a difficult figure to evaluate. He died suddenly at the age of forty, leaving scores of topographical and portrait drawings and engravings but little published work to confirm the high reputation as an antiquary which had brought him the friendship of both Essex and Richard Gough. It was Tyson who was to join with Essex and Walpole to produce a monumental history of Gothic in all its aspects.[39] It was he who encouraged Essex to join him in an antiquarian tour of Normandy in 1772, which did not take place, and of Flanders the next year, which did.[40]

Closely associated with these two men was the Director of the Society of Antiquaries, Richard Gough, mentioned above. Gough was also a Cambridge man, at Corpus with Tyson. Perhaps through Tyson Gough became one of Essex's firmest friends and strongly encouraged his medieval studies. It was largely due to Gough that Essex was elected Fellow of the Antiquaries in 1772 and that he published his articles on such subjects as Round Churches, Lincoln Cathedral, and the abbey and bridge at Croyland.[41] Gough particularly prized Essex's practical understanding of Gothic, for instance asking him to evaluate the structural feasibility of a proposed reconstruction of the early timber bridge at Rochester.[42]

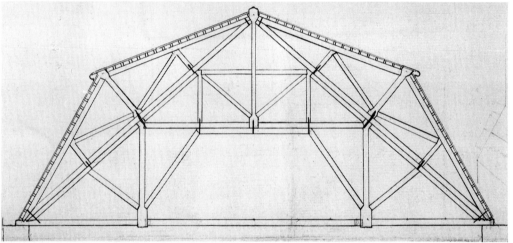

88. Essex's drawings of the low pitched roof he erected over the chapter house of Lincoln Cathedral, 1761–2.

Essex must have had a greater knowledge of the techniques of medieval construction than any other practising architect of the eighteenth century. The first paper he read to the Antiquaries covered the whole subject of the origins and types of brick building in England. The notes and drawings he assembled for his history of Gothic included details from a great variety of buildings, mostly in East Anglia and the East Midlands, but also from as far as Devon and Kent. These were to illustrate sections on such elements of the fabric as vaults, windows, doorways, capitals, bases and mouldings 'with their proportions'.[43] Essex was not trying, like some other eighteenth and early nineteenth-century writers, to assemble eye-catching examples of Gothic ornament for builders to copy, but to establish a dated typology of the successive styles of medieval architecture. He was concerned with the very structure of ancient buildings. 'Time must be spent in measuring their parts, comparing them with each other and ascertaining the proportion they bear amongst themselves'[44].

His lack of interest in ornament, although an advantage in his quest for the essence of Gothic, meant that he could be dismissive of detail. 'There being generally a superfluity of ornament in Gothic architecture it will be often found that where (?) one is defaced another may be taken away to preserve the symmetry without spoiling the appearance of the work.'[45] This stray note amongst some papers on Lincoln referred to the screens in the east transept of the cathedral, but it could equally apply to the sculpted portals of the west front. Elsewhere he remarked that it was 'not necessary to restore every broken ornament, which will waste much time and expense in beautifying the church. If the proportions are good, ornaments will not be missed.'[46] This economical approach to detail helps to explain the rather bald external appearance of the Ely lantern which Essex restored with simple tracery and low pinnacles and which survived until Scott's restoration in the nineteenth century.

Essex was confident he could improve on the techniques of the medieval masons and carpenters. He replaced the pyramid roof of the Lincoln chapter house by one with a low hipped profile on the grounds that it was more economical in timber.[47] He considered the risk taken by the builders of King's Chapel in having such a shallow-pitched roof that it tended to force out the buttresses, could not be condoned even though it had succeeded.[48] His general attitude was the realistic one that 'we are not to imagine everything done in the past was good architecture any more than in the present age.'[49]

Essex was conscious that his approach to designing in Gothic differed from 'the ridiculous imitations frequently made by our modern builders, who, mistaking the principles of pure architecture, think they have produced something in the Gothic style when they have collected together a jumble of discordant parts of old buildings (?) which have no relation to each other and supported a string of pointed arches by a row of broomsticks instead of pillars.'[50] He also blamed incongruities on the frequent 'striking absurdities' of the originals and the 'injudicious additions' often made in later times.[51] He was scornful of the way a transept turret on Norwich cathedral had been rebuilt with Tuscan pilasters in 'no way agreeable to the rest of the building, a fault always to be avoided in repairing old Buildings.'[52]

The great achievement of Essex as a restorer of medieval buildings was his attempt to think himself into the mind of the original builder. In 1774 he wrote that he had made a design for the cresting on the central tower of Lincoln cathedral 'as near as I could agreeable to the ideas of the architect who built the tower.'[53] The next year he again claimed, in his survey of Gibbs's classical screen wall at Lincoln, that 'in order to correct the disagreeable appearance of this wall, I was desirous of tracing the original state of this part of the church and if possible restore it to the state which the builders intended it'.[54] So, when he had to design new work which would be seen in conjunction with the original fabric, he made a deliberate attempt to use detail which suited it. At Lincoln the central arch of Gibbs's screen wall was rebuilt in the Early English of the rest of the nave, complete with Purbeck shafts, while the Tuscan capitals of the side arches were recarved with the leaf forms of the fourteenth-century capitals to be found within the vestibule to the west. Significantly, the vestibules themselves, shut off from any comparison with the rest of the building, Essex left classical, just as he was content at the same time to provide the equally secluded canons' vestry off the south transept with Gothick furnishings of almost churchwarden simplicity.[55]

Essex's attempts at authentic detail at Lincoln were greatly aided by the skilled workmen he employed there, the masons John Hayward, who repaved the cathed-

89. Essex's drawing for his high altar scheme at Lincoln, c. 1768.

ral, and James Pink, who carved the reredos and restored the pulpitum, and the carpenters, Thomas Lumby and his son William. Essex had a high respect for the 'more than common abilities' of Thomas Lumby, whom he chose in 1775 for the dangerous work of erecting the cresting on the central tower even though Lumby was at that time bankrupt.[56] It must have been partly due to Essex that William Lumby, who succeeded him as Surveyor of the cathedral, achieved such a good understanding of Gothic detail. The designs for transept screens which he drew up for Essex in 1779–80 are both authentic and sensitive.[57]

It was the reputation of Essex as a surveyor rather than as a designer of Gothic that led cathedral Chapters to consult him first at Ely and at Lincoln and then as far afield as Salisbury, Canterbury and Winchester. It is significant that at Canterbury and Winchester cathedrals his advice was asked about roofs, and at Winchester College about the structural condition of the chapel tower. He was not invited to make designs for decoration. It was only gradually that he became associated with antiquaries and, at Strawberry Hill and Ampthill Park, with the virtuosi of Taste.

The invitation of 1773 to advise on the 'propriety' of moving the choir in Westminster Abbey eastwards brought Essex into direct contact, indeed competition, with his fellow Goths, Henry Keene, James Wyatt and Horace Walpole.[58] Essex was presumably consulted because of the name he had recently made as the designer of the newly-moved choir at Ely and the new east end at King's College Chapel, Cambridge. The reports of the architects, which had all been submitted by 1773, have not survived, but drawings by Essex in the British Library must relate to the project.[59] The stalls were to be set right against the piers of the apse; the altar screen was to resemble his Lincoln design except that the gabled central tabernacle would have been much taller.

Essex's academic reputation as an expert on medieval architecture was based not

90. Lincoln Cathedral, the canopy of the bishop's throne,
designed by Essex, 1778.

so much on his papers for the Society of Antiquaries but on his projected *History of Gothic*. Plans for the book went through several forms and occupied many years. His first scheme was a book on King's College Chapel for which he published proposals as early as 1756 and still hoped to produce in 1772.[60] It was based on the measurements and observations he had been able to make during his restoration of the chapel during the early 1750s. The book would have resembled that which Francis Price published in 1753 on Salisbury cathedral both in its emphasis on plans, elevations and sections and also in its proposed publication of the medieval sources for the building history. The full-scale history of Gothic was mooted not later than 1769 when Essex, inspired perhaps by a recent visit from Horace Walpole, asked Cole to procure Walpole's help in 'putting all his collections towards a regular treatise on Gothic Architecture together'.[61] The idea blossomed of a collaborative work in which Essex, Walpole and Tyson should all be involved but only Essex proved to be in earnest, continuing studies for it almost until his death: there are

91. Debden Church, Essex, showing the spire added to Essex's design in 1786, removed in 1930.

drawings of column types on the back of auction particulars of February 1781.[62] The title varied from 'Gothic Architecture ... viz. Little Essays towards ye history of it' to the 'An Historical and Architectonical Description of Gothic Buildings, with Observations on the Habits, Customs and Particulars Relating to the Antiquities of those Times'.[63] This latter plan, of December 1776, still envisaged contributions from Tyson and Horace Walpole, so it could promise not only an explanation of 'the origin, progress and theory of Gothic from the best examples, illustrated by plans, elevations and sections' and including chapters on geometry, changes in style, prices of material and workmen, and technical terms — all of which were to be contributed by Essex — but also 'observations on the sculpture, statuary and paintings'.[64]

Essex's own drafts were not unambitious. He sought to trace architecture from its beginnings in biblical and classical antiquity, with illustrated reconstructions of the tabernacle of the Israelites and Solomon's Temple, to its climax in Rome and then through its corruption and changes by the Barbarian invaders to its renewed flowering in the middle ages.[65]

That the book was never published was due partly to the failure of the other contributors to give serious support and partly to the cost of the plates. Essex reckoned that he would need a hundred plates distributed through the different sections.[66] Lack of money cannot however have been the deciding factor since by 1779 Essex himself reckoned his property to be worth over £15,000.[67] A more serious difficulty may have been the diffidence of Essex in literary and academic fields. His lack of confidence was not helped by the sneers of some of his more educated friends. Tyson complained to Gough of Essex's verbosity[68] and Cole patronisingly remarked that Essex should not make 'a parade of learning, with which he is totally unacquainted; so much that I have corrected at least a hundred false spellings in his own language.'[69]

Essex collected an impressive variety of testimonials to his knowledge of Gothic. Cole's tribute has already been mentioned. Walpole wrote of Essex's Beauclerk tower; 'he has built me a tower so exactly of the fourteenth century. It ... puts one in mind of that at Thornbury'.[70] Gough mourned Essex's death for the 'irreparable loss of this great master'.[71] Even forty years after his death E.J. Willson, in his introduction to the *Specimens of Gothic Architecture* by the elder Pugin, praised Essex as the 'the first professional architect whose works displayed a correct taste in imitations of ancient English architecture'.[72] Willis and Clark, whose researches in Cambridge into University and College archives revealed something of the extent of Essex's practice, admitted that 'his name is associated with several works of merit' although they deplored the 'melancholy attempts ... to convert the medieval style of our colleges to Italian by a mere mask of ashlar'.[73] By 1910 Essex's 'architectural sins' were considered 'heinous'.[74] More recently Pevsner reinstated him as an important figure of the early Gothic revival.[75] Perhaps now, two hundred years after his death, it is possible to view his achievements in a wider context and to value not just individual works but the whole range and variety of his practice.

7

THOMAS HOPPER, 1776–1856
The Drama of Eclecticism

Neil Burton

THOMAS HOPPER's obituary in 1856 declared that 'probably no other architect of about the same period, except James Wyatt, was so extensively employed in erecting new and extending old mansions'.[1] This is patently rubbish. Wyatt designed over thirty new houses, Hopper less than ten and it is easy to name a dozen late Georgian architects with more domestic works to their credit. While the obituary suggests that Hopper's name may once have been well known, it is now almost forgotten. Perhaps this is because he left behind him nothing but his buildings. None of his family papers and only a few letters have come to light. He was not a member of the architectural establishment, did not belong to any of the architects' clubs which were beginning to spring up and is not mentioned in the writings of his contemporaries. He himself published nothing except a handful of bitter little pamphlets about the architectural competitions that he failed to win.

Probably the most familiar thing about Hopper is his declaration in one of these pamphlets (Hopper versus Cust on the New Houses of Parliament 1837) that 'It is an architect's business to understand all styles and to be prejudiced in favour of none'. This is the kind of attitude which used to make architectural historians wince: Sir John Summerson voiced a widely held opinion when he wrote 'In this universal, hasty, slick eclecticism we recognise unmistakeably, the end of an epoch. When the time has come that everything can be done quickly and easily, it is time for someone to think again'.[2] But there is no escaping the fact that all late Georgian designers were eclectic, even the intellectuals like William Wilkins and Sir John Soane. This eclecticism has proved a continuing puzzle because it was the product of a period when fashions in architecture seemed to change almost annually. Perhaps one of the most valuable things about Thomas Hopper is that his buildings taken together, reflect most of the architectural fashions of the decades after 1800. Taken singly they are often surprisingly powerful and show their architect to have been someone with an eye for the picturesque, a particular flair for the design of exciting staircases and a considerable ability in planning.

Hopper was born in Rochester in 1776. His father was a measuring surveyor, 'clever and prominent in his business, but of intemperate habits'.[3] The younger man spent his first years in his father's office and this was apparently the only formal training he received. He is first heard of in London in 1802 and appears in the Directories as a building and land surveyor at 42, Upper Berkeley Street. He remained in London all his life, living subsequently in Connaught Terrace on the Edgware Road and later in a large house on the Bayswater Road. He married and had two daughters and one son. Although Hopper himself never drank anything stronger than water, his son became a hopeless alcoholic and the male line of the

92. One of the four relief panels at the base of Nelson's Column, Trafalgar Square, which is alleged to depict Thomas Hopper. He has been identified as the supporter of the expiring mariner, bottom left.

family expired with his death.

Nothing at all is known of Hopper's working life before he reached the age of thirty. His father's only known commission was supervising the building of houses in Southend as a speculative venture (unsuccessful as it turned out) and the younger Hopper may have been engaged in similar activities.[4] Whatever his early career, matters took a sudden turn for the better in 1806. Biographies of architects are full of anecdotes about the recognition of unsuspected talents by discerning patrons, and in Hopper's case the fairy godfather was Walsh Porter — a picture dealer and one of the influential but obscure men of taste in the circle of the Prince Regent. Joseph Farington's diary[5] contains several observations on Porter, none of them flattering. Lord de Dunstanville thought him a very slight man, with nothing in him either of knowledge or understanding; Sir Francis Bourgeois considered him very eccentric and entertaining and said his society was much relished by the Prince of Wales who, in his associations, was sure to fix on a man who, with singularities, had something in him.

Porter used to exhibit the paintings he wished to sell in his own house, Craven

Cottage at Fulham. This modest rustic cottage had been built for the Countess of Craven in the 1780s, but was much enlarged and improved by Porter. With Hopper's assistance the main living room was changed into an Egyptian Hall, 'being an exact copy from one of the plates of Denon's Travels in Egypt ... the interior is richly painted in the Egyptian style and is supported by eight immense columns covered with hieroglyphics, and at each corner of the room is a palm tree. A sphinx and a mummy are painted on each side of the door, the ceiling is painted with hieroglyphics: a lifesize female figure in bronze stands near the door holding up a curtain in imitation of tiger skin; a moveable camel stands near the entrance: the whole of this room is striking and characteristic.'[6]

93. The Egyptian Living Room at Craven Cottage, Fulham, c. 1806, burnt down 1888.

The living room at Craven Cottage was an early manifestation of the Egyptian craze in England, though the style was far from being an absolute novelty. G.B. Piranesi's *Diverse Maniere d'Adornare i Cammini,* published in 1769, had illustrated a whole series of Egyptian decorative motifs which were taken up especially in French interiors of the later eighteenth century, while in Britain both James Playfair and Joseph Michael Gandy used Egyptian elements. But what prompted the Regency interest in things Egyptian was firstly Thomas Hope's mansion in Duchess Street, off Portland Place, completed in 1800 and regularly open to fashionable visitors from 1804. An Egyptian room was one of the attractions, along with an Indian room and the strictly Greek Doric picture gallery. Napoleon's Egyptian campaign and Baron Vivant Denon's *Voyage dans L'Egypte,* published in 1802, along with Thomas Hope's *Household Furniture* of 1807 stimulated a fashion for the Egyptian manner which reached a peak in about 1810.

No doubt Porter was trying to imitate Hope's London house by making his own a compendium of styles. Besides the Egyptian room there was also a Gothic room painted in imitation of Henry VII's Chapel at Westminster and several other apart-

94. The cast iron colonnade at Woolverstone Hall, Suffolk, 1823.

ments fitted up in the style of different countries including a Persian chieftain's tent ornamented with panels of looking glass between the blue striped lining. Porter's efforts were sneered at in some quarters; an article in *Ackerman's Repository* derided his efforts as grotesque and ridiculous. But the Prince Regent evidently admired Porter's taste and in 1805 he commissioned him to redecorate Carlton House, finished by Henry Holland only nine years previously in a refined Neo-classical manner. From 1807 Porter was employing Thomas Hopper as executant architect and Hopper continued working at Carlton House for several years after Porter's death in 1809.

At Carlton House, attention was concentrated on the range of rooms facing south across St James's Park at ground level. At the west end of the range, opening out of the dining room, a large Gothic conservatory was added, to Hopper's design. This PLATE XXII conservatory, which attracted an enormous amount of public attention, was a paraphrase of Henry VII's Chapel, one of the favourite models in the early years of the Gothic Revival. The main members of the building were apparently of cast iron, and the interstices of the tracery of both windows and roof were filled with coloured glass. Contemporary illustrations convey something of the exotic and theatrical interior but the descriptions which accompany them make nothing of the novel method of construction. Although warehouses had been made out of prefabricated

95. Melford Hall, Suffolk, 1813, the staircase.

XXII Thomas Hopper; the interior of the Conservatory, Carlton House, 1807, destroyed 1826.

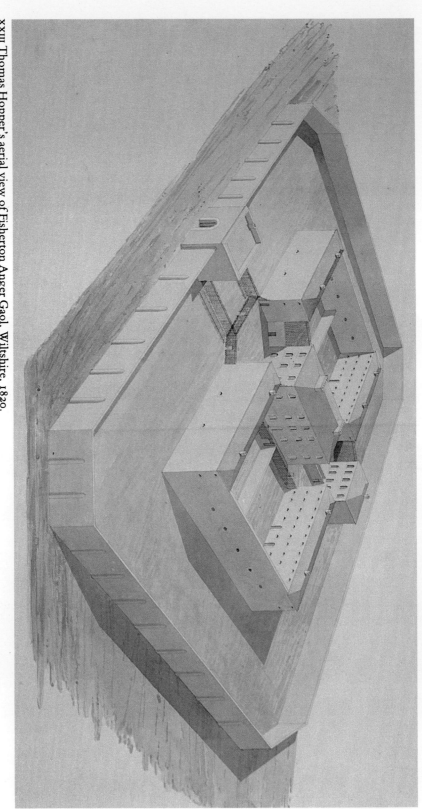

XXIII Thomas Hopper's aerial view of Fisherton Anger Gaol, Wiltshire, 1820.

iron parts since the late eighteenth century, it was still a very unusual material for polite buildings. A few years later Thomas Rickman designed two churches in Liverpool to be built mainly of cast iron, but this was at the instigation of a local ironfounder. There was no such incentive at Carlton House, so perhaps the use of such a novel material was proposed by Hopper himself. In some of his later works he used iron extensively, in preference to more conventional materials. At Woolverstone Hall in Suffolk, where he carried out alterations and improvements to the late eighteenth-century house of the Berners family in the early 1820s, Hopper introduced long Doric colonnades flanking the main house, in which every architectural element, from the column bases to the balustrading, was made of cast iron. In this instance the ironwork has proved very durable: the Carlton House conservatory, unfortunately, was demolished together with the rest of the building in 1826.

Hopper's association with the Prince was amiable and certainly helped him towards a profitable career as a country house architect. It is said that he was offered a knighthood by the Prince when George IV, and was pressed by Czar Alexander I to settle in St Petersburg, but he received no further royal commissions after Carlton House. His next works were small ones: a building for the Royal Society of Musicians in Lisle Street, an entrance lodge at Dromoland Castle in Ireland and the re-casting of part of the interior of Melford Hall in Suffolk for Sir William Parker. All these were in the Greek style, which was becoming particularly popular and fashionable in domestic work.

Melford Hall is a red brick Elizabethan house of conventional form and plan, whose main door opens into a screens passage serving a great hall. In his alterations Hopper made no attempt to imitate the Elizabethan style, but instead provided a new main staircase rising in two straight flights from the service side of the screens passage. On either side of the stair are galleries with Ionic colonnades supporting an elliptical coffered roof. The obvious prototype is the great staircase at the Palais de Luxembourg in Paris, designed by Jean-Francoise-Thérèse Chalgrin and built in 1795. Hopper is not known to have visited France, but he may have seen engravings of the French stair. Elsewhere in the house Ionic columns and the anthemion frieze of the library are taken directly from the engravings of the Erecthion in Le Roy's *Ruines ... de la Grece* of 1758, or a later derivative.

But perhaps the most intriguing features of the work at Melford are to be found in the great hall. The walls are covered with Victorian panelling but there is a handsome and massive marble chimneypiece of early eighteenth-century character, and the screen has been replaced by two Doric columns which could well be of the same period. It has always been assumed that these were introduced by Sir Cordell Firebrace, who made some alterations in the 1740s, but it seems more likely that they are Hopper's work. The columns only make sense as a prelude to the new main staircase and there are some Greek details in the scrolled brackets supporting the overmantel which suggest a later date. If the chimneypiece is indeed by Hopper it is an astonishing example of early Georgian revival.[7]

Immediately after Melford, Hopper embarked on the design of a new house which he considered his masterpiece in the Greek Revival manner. This was Leigh Court at Abbot's Leigh outside Bristol. His client was P.J. Miles, an extremely wealthy West Indian planter. In its present state as a medical institution, the house stands rather baldly amid the decaying remains of a once enormous park. The

96. Leigh Court, Abbot's Leigh, Bristol, 1814.

exterior is of Bath stone and rather heavy in appearance, though the three main elevations are varied in a Wyattish way, recalling nearby Doddington, which had been finished the previous year. The north and south elevations have tetrastyle Ionic porticoes projecting from the plain two storey fronts, while the east elevation has its four massive columns *in antis*. The boldness of this front especially recalls Belsay Hall in Northumberland and since the stair hall at Melford has obvious parallels with the hall at Belsay it is possible that Hopper had visited the north of England and seen this austere exercise in domestic classicism.

Hopper's interior at Abbot's Leigh is a complete contrast, and displays the same dramatic sense as the Carlton House conservatory. A chaste domed and colonnaded vestibule leads into a great central hall with a sinuous double staircase rising to an Ionic gallery which runs round the entire hall. The decoration is extraordinarily rich, from the brass dog-tooth inlay in the mahogany stair rail, to the tiers of richly-moulded anthemion ornament in the cove of the heavily coffered ceiling. Though the hall is now stripped of most of its fittings, the automatic organ installed by Miles survives. Its case is decorated, presumably to Hopper's design, in a manner congruent with the rest of the room and the instrument still plays excerpts from Mozart's *La Clemenza di Tito*.

All the principal rooms at Leigh were on the ground floor and retain much of their former opulence, with very heavily moulded ceilings in gilded plaster and handsome mahogany doors with ornamental surrounds and door-furniture. The original effect when the walls were hung with Miles's outstanding collection of Old Master paintings must have been magnificent and old photographs show the handsome shelving of the library. Unfortunately all the original furniture has now been dispersed, except the couches in the hall.

For the park surrounding the house, with its views over Leigh Woods and the Severn estuary, Miles sought the advice of Humphry Repton. His recommendations of building an eye-catching circular temple to the east of the house and adding a bow

97. Leigh Court, the staircase.

window to the saloon overlooking the Severn seem not to have been followed. Repton was critical of the siting of Leigh Court, but the appearance of the land surrounding it is now so altered that it is difficult to follow his remarks.

Besides the house itself, Hopper was responsible for the original main entrance, a handsome Ionic gateway with commodious lodges. It is tempting to ascribe to him a splendid Gothic conservatory in the village of Abbot's Leigh, effectively the estate village and wholly owned by the Miles's. Although the conservatory has been

98. Margam Abbey, West Glamorgan, the entrance front, 1830–5.

ascribed to the 1830s, both its cement rendered exterior and its cast iron interior are reminiscent of Hopper's work.[8]

The fashion for pure Grecian domestic architecture was fairly short-lived, but in official architecture the Greek style, backed by authorities like Thomas Hope, Lord Aberdeen, William Wilkins and the ruling clique at the Royal Academy, was dominant. Very many public buildings were erected in the twenty years after Waterloo, from large institutions, through County Courts and Shire Halls down to provincial Athenaeums. Architects for such lucrative commissions were usually selected in competition; Hopper competed for the General Post Office, the Carlton Club, the Conservative Club and the Houses of Parliament, but without success. The only public buildings to his name were designed in his capacities as Surveyor to the Atlas Assurance Company and to the County of Essex.

Hopper was appointed to the Essex County Surveyorship in 1816 in succession to Robert Lugar. The reasons for his selection are unclear, though he did have a prior connection with Essex. At the very beginning of his career, in 1804, he had worked as surveyor on the rebuilding of Chelmsford parish church after the collapse of the nave and south aisle in 1800 and the architect for the rebuilding was the then County Surveyor, John Johnson. This official post carried a salary of £250 a year and it was expected that the holder would also have his own business. Hopper's major task in office followed soon after his appointment with the building of a new county gaol at Springfield outside Chelmsford. The first plans were submitted in 1819 and the prison was completed in 1826. All the prison buildings were contained within a high brick wall, with rounded buttresses like miniature bastions, and could be reached only through a massive primitive Doric gateway topped by the gallows. The encircling wall remains, but the prison itself has been much rebuilt. Hopper himself

99. Melbury House, Dorset, the sixteenth-century tower.

was required to alter the buildings in 1834, and again in 1843, to take account of the rapid evolution of penal conventions, and the splendid entrance gate has been obliterated more recently in the interests of greater security. Two other prisons by Hopper were the House of Correction at Little Ilford in Essex and the gaol at Fisherton Anger in Wiltshire. The reason for the selection of Hopper by the PLATE XXIII Wiltshire justices is unclear, and the building he designed was more remarkable for its economical construction and as an exercise in the use of blank wall surfaces than for its awareness of current experiments with radial plans and other features.[9]

Most of Hopper's work for Essex was architecturally unremarkable. It included various highway improvements, bridges, minor official buildings and alterations to existing buildings. He retained the post of Surveyor until his death in 1856. Although it was moved earlier in that year that he should resign, since age and ill-health made him unable to attend to county business, the motion was subsequently withdrawn 'from the desire signified by many influential magistrates to act with the most kind consideration towards an old and faithful servant of the county'.[10]

The Essex connection gave rise to a considerable number of private commissions in that county, both for alterations and for new building. Among the former was Terling Place, a late eighteenth century house by John Johnson where Hopper was employed in 1818 by Colonel Strutt to make improvements. The wings of the house were greatly enlarged and the interior re-cast to provide a grand central saloon, whose chief ornament was a Parthenon frieze by John Henning senior, who had made a long study of the Elgin Marbles and provided similar friezes both for the Athenaeum Club in Pall Mall and for the stair hall of the Royal College of Surgeons.

Perhaps the most successful of Hopper's new Essex houses was Danbury Park, begun in 1830 for James Round and built of red brick in an ebullient Tudor style, apparently derived from an earlier house on the site which Round had pulled down. The Tudor style was among the most popular for country houses in the late Georgian period because of its picturesque appearance and because it facilitated flexible planning. Associations with Elizabethan and Jacobean nobility also appealed to those who wished to show, or imply, ancient lineage. An early and influential example of the style was William Wilkins's Tregothnan in Cornwall, built in 1818, which received much praise in Neale's *Views of Seats*. One of Wilkins's models was East Barsham Manor in his home county of Norfolk, and Hopper also used the East Barsham turrets together with gables, pinnacles and elaborately moulded chimneys to create a bold and varied outline. The apparent irregularity of the exterior is belied by the efficient internal planning, with the family and service quarters linked by a central corridor.

Bold handling of ornament was one of Hopper's distinguishing skills and makes his 'period' work seem less anaemic than the general run of historicist buildings of the time. Perhaps the most striking of all his houses in the Tudor Gothic style was Margam Abbey in West Glamorgan, begun in 1830 for Christopher Mansel Talbot. The old house of the Mansels had been demolished in the 1780s and the family lived mainly on their estate at Penrice. Proud of his ancient lineage and attracted to the romantic landscape of Margam with its ruined mediaeval abbey, young Christopher Talbot determined to build a new house in a suitable style. Both the Talbot family seat at Lacock in Wiltshire, and Melbury House in Dorset, which was the home of Talbot's mother, were ancient houses; Lacock formed out of an abbey cloister with eighteenth-century improvements by Sanderson Miller, Melbury dating principally from the mid-sixteenth century with seventeenth-century enlargements. As early as 1828 Talbot had decided on a similar style for Margam. After one of his visits to Lacock, his aunt there wrote to her son,

> Kit seems to like this place extremely and is determined to build a tower to his new house and a large hall like this and above all *secret staircases*.

His first choice of architect was Robert Lugar, a well-known exponent of picturesque Tudor, whose Cyfartha Castle in Glamorgan had been finished in 1825. But Lugar proved too expensive, charging £250 for a single drawing, and Talbot turned instead to Hopper, Lugar's successor as Essex County Surveyor, but more probably known to Talbot as the architect of Penrhyn Castle in North Wales. Hopper's relationship with his client seems to have been cordial, though distant; he provided the design and remained in contact with Talbot by letter, but the work on site was supervised by the Shrewsbury architect Edward Haycock.[11]

By far the most conspicuous feature of Margam is the staircase tower, copied directly from the mid-sixteenth-century tower of Melbury. Of the three principal elevations of the house, those to the north and south are asymmetrical in themselves

100. Margam Abbey, the staircase.

and extended by the service wing to the east. The west elevation has a symmetrical arrangement of bay windows, with two small towers reminiscent of those on the main front of Lacock. The interior was also Gothic, with some magnificent ogee arched chimneypieces and a splendid theatrical central stair hall with a vaulted lantern, which recalled Smirke's Lowther Castle or even Wyatt's Fonthill. One curious exception to the Gothic rule was the great library on the west side which had a heavy compartmented ceiling with three great roundels, recalling the seventeenth century work of architects like John Webb. The plan of the house was compact and efficient, with the three principal living rooms grouped tightly round the stair. Sadly, Margam has been neglected since the Second World War and the interior was

101. Gosford Castle, Armagh, begun 1819.

burnt out in 1977. The house is a ruin in the centre of a country park, but it seems that the shell, at least, is now safe.

Given Hopper's liking for the bold statement it is not surprising that he proved successful with the Neo-Norman style. Like so many late Georgian styles, it was popularised by James Wyatt, first in his Broadway Tower of 1799 and subsequently in three castellated houses at Shoebury in Essex, Pennsylvania in Hampshire and Norris Castle on the Isle of Wight. Nash and Smirke both toyed with round castellated towers but it was not until the publication of Thomas Rickman's *Attempt to Discriminate the Styles of Architecture in England* in 1817 that approved models were readily available for architects to follow. Hopper's first Neo-Norman work was Gosford Castle in County Armagh for the second Earl of Gosford, begun in 1819,

xxiv Thomas Hopper, Penrhyn Castle, Gwynedd, 1825.

xxv Thomas Hopper; Penrhyn Castle, the Great Hall

XXVI Thomas Hopper; Penrhyn Castle, the Ebony Room.

and he showed at once that he could handle the rather clumping vocabulary of the style with ease. The grouping of the towers and other elements of the house is masterly, though ornament is a little scanty, and the great boundary wall of the estate, with its capping of massive boulders, is impressive.

Gosford was completed in 1821 and the following year Hopper began his connec-

102. Penrhyn Castle, Gwynedd, detail of the staircase.

tion with the Pennants of Penrhyn. George Hay Dawkins-Pennant was a wealthy slate quarry owner with extensive interests in the West Indies. It is not clear why he picked the Neo-Norman style; perhaps because it was fashionable in the early 1820s, or perhaps to outface the genuine medieval castles of Conwy, Beaumaris, Harlech and Caernarfon which dominate the coastline of the Menai Strait. With a virtually unlimited budget and the services of the local stonemasons, Hopper created for Pennant the most impressive Neo-Norman house in Britain. The keep, loosely based on Castle Hedingham in Essex and the keep in Hopper's home town of Rochester, dominates the composition and forms a pivot around which the drive sweeps to arrive at the main front. Here the rest of the house unfolds, lying along the top of a shallow ridge. The main body of the building, though looking defensible

PLATE XXIV

and studded with towers, is not strictly Neo-Norman and some of the ornamental details, for example the projecting oriel over the porch, are obviously invented, not copied.

What makes Penrhyn really extraordinary is that Pennant's wealth, enthusiasm and patience allowed the interior to be treated in the same vein as the exterior. The PLATE XXV great hall is loosely based on the nave of Durham Cathedral, with some curious PLATE XXVI lights contrived in the vault — a distant echo of the Carlton House conservatory. The library is divided by an arched central screen much like that which divides the PLATE XXVII great hall in the keep at Rochester and the staircase is decorated with a disturbing synthesis of Norman grotesques, fan vaulting and oriental arabesques. It might be

103. Birch Hall, Essex, 1843–7, the exterior.

said that where proportion flags, detail is used to distract the judgment, but the total effect is convincing, the more so because Hopper designed much of the furniture, also in a Neo-Norman manner. Penrhyn's unaltered interiors still convey, as few others now do, the thoroughgoing romantic historicism of the late Georgians.

Hopper evidently liked the Neo-Norman style. It chimed well with his own taste for massiveness. At Gosford, at Penrhyn and at Butterton in Staffordshire where he built a Neo-Norman church in the 1840s, he shows a skill in the massing and handling of Norman outline greater than any of his contemporaries. But the critics were not impressed with Penrhyn. The *Gentleman's Magazine* commented, 'It seems to have been built rather as a striking object than as an elegant or commodious residence. The material, (Mona Marble from Anglesey) 'is so dark that it would remind the spectator of the black castle of an enchanted tale: the shrieks of an enthralled damsel and the grim head of a giant crowning the dark keep would be

128

only wanting to complete the illusion'.[12] By the time Penrhyn was finished in 1837 Neo-Norman had been displaced by Italianate as the fashionable alternative to Tudor Gothic. Italianate houses were thought more original and convenient, besides being cheaper and offering just as many opportunities for picturesque towers and other ornaments.

Although he could produce delightful Italianate houses, like Birch Hall in Essex, Hopper seems to have preferred a more formal Italian classicism which at times looks like English Palladianism. This back eddy of Palladianism in the 1830s is a phenomenon which has seldom been remarked. Hopper's Kentian chimneypiece at Melford is perhaps the first indication of his liking for the style. Just over ten years

104. Birch Hall, the staircase.

later he designed Arthur's Club, now the Carlton Club, in St James's Street. Although forced to alter some features of the exterior by the Crown Surveyors, Hopper's design, with its rusticated lower floor and Corinthian colonnade between the windows with their alternating triangular and segmental pediments, is still effective. The interior, with its massive staircase hall, black marble fireplaces and rich plasterwork by Bernasconi, is more Hopperish than Palladian and the library bookshelves are very like those he designed for Leigh Court.

Undoubtedly the most significant Neo-Palladian building executed by Thomas Hopper was Amesbury Abbey in Wiltshire. In 1834 he was called in by Sir Edward Antrobus to reconstruct the old house, built in the 1660s to the designs of Inigo Jones's pupil, John Webb. Hopper produced a new house based on the old, but with

105. Amesbury Abbey, Wiltshire, rebuilt 1834–40.

a wider portico and a secondary front facing across the park to the river. He retained the external form of Webb's central tower as shown in *Vitruvius Britannicus* and used it to contain a massive and imposing staircase hall with two tiers of round-headed arches, strongly reminiscent of the work of Vanbrugh or Hawksmoor. It has been pointed out that the stair has elements of Vanbrugh's work at Kings Weston near Bristol. This house was owned by the Miles family of Abbots Leigh and it is probable that Hopper was familiar with Kings Weston and may even have been responsible for some of the alterations made to the house in the early nineteenth century. In any event, his sympathy for early eighteenth-century English architecture was distinctly unusual in the 1830s.

Another work in this manner was the head office of the Atlas Assurance Company at 94, Cheapside. Hopper was Surveyor to the company and in 1834 he was required to replace two old houses on the north side of Cheapside with a new building. The replacement resembled an Italian palazzo with a rusticated ground floor faced with granite and two floors above articulated with Corinthian pilasters and with handsome pedimented aedicules to the windows. The principal entrance in the narrower Cheapside front was set into a deep niche, a rather French feature, but one which Sir Christopher Wren used in the tower of St Mary-le-Bow only a short distance away. Hopper's building survives, but has been completely altered internally, given a new roof, and has had a pedestrian arcade driven through it, behind the façade.[13]

106. Amesbury Abbey, the staircase.

Hopper continued in practice until his death in 1856, an eclectic to the end. His last houses were Kinmel Park in the classical style, Birch Hall in the Italianate manner, Wivenhoe Park in the Jacobean style and Easton Lodge in Tudor Gothic. There is certainly more of his work, especially his restoration work, still to be discovered, but even on present showing he was an architect whose achievements are bewildering in their diversity.

8

SAMUEL SANDERS TEULON, 1812–1873

A Pragmatic Rogue

Matthew Saunders

THE NAME of Samuel Sanders Teulon has become synonymous with Victorian architecture at its most roguish.[1] In the great age of stylistic licence he tried the patience even of contemporary critics. *The Civil Engineer and Architects Journal* of July 1862 warned its readers that 'the mention of Mr Teulon's name is quite sufficient to prepare one for seeing some curious achievement, in the way of novelty at any rate'. He was, and has remained, an Architectural Outsider, adopting the Victorian rediscovery of polychromy, asymmetry and Romantic drama, but with such a liberality that, at their best, his buildings remain among the most extraordinary of English architectural experiences.

Almost everything in Teulon's character seems to belie his architectural persona. His life was an archetype of Victorian respectability — his wife Harriet, whom he married in 1835, bore him four sons and four daughters before her early death. His churchmanship was Evangelical. His industry was such that the obituary in *The Architect* specifically alludes to overwork as a cause of death. The only full-length photograph we have of the man even shows him complete with mutton chops and top hat.

He was born on 2nd March 1812. His mother, Louisa, hailed from Rotherhithe but his father, Samuel senior, had been born in 1785 in Greenwich. From 1810 he had been resident at the substantial stuccoed house named 'Hillside' in fashionable Crooms Hill, built by the Georgian architect John James for his own occupation. There seems no reason to doubt that Samuel junior was born there. His father was at the time a cabinet maker and upholsterer although later in his long life he advanced into the profession of surveyor. As the surname implies, the family's origins were French.

1812 had also seen the birth of that other famous Goth of French blood, Augustus Welby Pugin, although Teulon's origins were Huguenot rather than émigré. The Teulons had originally fled after the Revocation of the Edict of Nantes in 1685,[2] and the family remained proud of its French descent, several members becoming Directors of the French Hospital in South Hackney. These included Samuel in 1862 and his brother, William Milford[3] who was also an architect, in 1863. There was a second family home on the estate of 'Tenchleys' at Limpsfield Common, Surrey, which remained in Teulon hands from the late eighteenth century until the early twentieth century. Samuel took the name of the estate for the eighteenth century house which he acquired in 1846 at 3, The Green, Hampstead where he was to live for twenty-seven years until his death.

Samuel's marriage in 1835 to Harriet brought incidental financial advantage, in the form of a capital sum of £4,225, which he passed on at his death in unequal

107. Samuel Sanders Teulon, photographed at his desk.

measure to three of his four sons: sons who seem to have been both the joy and bane of his life. Josiah Sanders, the second, born in 1838, went on to become Principal of the Chichester Theological College although there is obviously a history behind a touching legacy in the father's will[4] of £100 'being the amount which I promised. him when I learned that he had paid the sum of £50 out of his pocket money in part satisfaction of his debts at Oxford'. There is an even more enigmatic bequest to another son, George Alexander, to whom he left 'a packet with three seals on it contained in my iron chest'. Maurice Beveridge has all the appearance of a wayward younger son. His father looked to him to succeed in the practice, bequeathing the goodwill of the business 'with my architectural books, casts, busts, drawings and drawing instruments' together with the lease of the office at 9, Craigs Court, off Charing Cross, which Teulon had occupied since the mid-1850s. However in just over a year, in the first of no less than five codicils, this bequest was struck out, as Maurice had 'so misconducted himself whilst in my office that it became impossible for me to retain him there and instruct him in my business'.

The conventionality of his domestic life, so much at odds with much of his style, was paralleled by Low Christianity, thoroughly in accordance with his Huguenot origins. His friends and clients were of similar persuasion. Sampson Kempthorne, (1809–1873) — with whom he prepared his first known design, the unexecuted Market House at Penzance, exhibited at the Royal Academy in 1835 — was described by a mutual friend, Gilbert Scott, as being 'very worthy and religious'.[5] Another lifelong friend, and eventual executor, Ewan Christian (1814–95), who took over the practice during his last illness, ran a Sunday School in Hampstead and gave a sgraffito roundel of Bishop Latimer for the nave of St Stephen's, Hampstead 'in order that his speech to Ridley at the stake might be brought into prominence in these Romanizing times'.

Among his principal clients, the Calthorpe family (Elvetham Hall, Hampshire; St James's, Birmingham; Woodlands Vale, Isle of Wight) was strongly evangelical. Lord Robert Grosvenor (Lord Ebury) who laid the foundation stone of three of his churches, (Agar Town, London; St Stephen's, Hampstead; St Andrew's, Watford) and who commissioned a fine conservatory for his house at Moor Park in Hertfordshire, introduced a Bill to close all public houses and stop all trading on a Sunday. On occasions, Samuel's Christianity could be stern-faced. There is a surprisingly detailed correspondence between Teulon and the Duke of Bedford about the design of a conduit he was asked to provide for the village of Thorney. The Duke wanted it to be open. Teulon pressed with passion the advantages of doors, for the village lay 'on a great thoroughfare, for labourers (many of them Irish) during all hours of the night in summer'. The sincerity of his belief can be tested by the extent that principle impeded his practice. The Teulons were directly related to the Wagner family, through the female line, and yet because that family's religious persuasion was High and Tractarian, Teulon played no part in their great church building campaign in Brighton. He was regularly criticized by the Ecclesiological Society for the introduction of galleries and prayer desks facing west. Beneficiaries in his will included the Church Missionary Society, the Society for the Propagation of the Gospel, as well as other charities like a Reformatory for Women.

His training began with a studentship at the Drawing School of the Royal Academy, a normal avenue for young architects but a heady one, as Turner and Soane were among the instructors. Thence he passed into practical education at the hands of two London builders, George Legg (1799–1882) and George Porter (1796–1856).[6] He entered independent practice in 1838 and was buoyed up two years later, when he won First Premium in a limited competition for Dyers' Company Almshouses in Islington. Meanwhile his visual self-education continued with a long tour of France, Belgium, Italy, Switzerland and Germany between 1841 and 1842 in the company of Ewan Christian, (Sir) Horace Jones, later architect to the Corporation of London, (Professor) Hayter Lewis and Arthur Green, nephew to Sir William Tite. The results are seen in several drawings preserved in the two sketchbooks now in the RIBA Drawings Collection. Subjects illustrated include fittings in Ulm Cathedral, various churches in Caen and the Duomo in Florence. His personal copy of *The Ecclesiologist* volume for 1855, now in the library of the Council for the Care of Churches, indicates by its careful annotation of G.E. Street's account of his tour through Lille, Ypres, Rheims, Cologne and Munster (p. 361), that Teulon was a diligent and attentive traveller. He and Christian returned to Genoa in 1863.

Very few of his early designs were realised as buildings. Those for the new Town Hall and Market Hall at Penzance in 1835, the Baths at Lee, Kent of 1836 and the County Hall and Law Courts at Ipswich of 1837 were all unexecuted, and the first documented work to be carried out was the rebuilding of the long-standing home of the Limpsfield branch of the family, Tensley Villa, where his client was Thomas Teulon (1764–1844). The work was completed in 1838. As well as this useful family commission, Teulon received help from George Porter who employed him in the

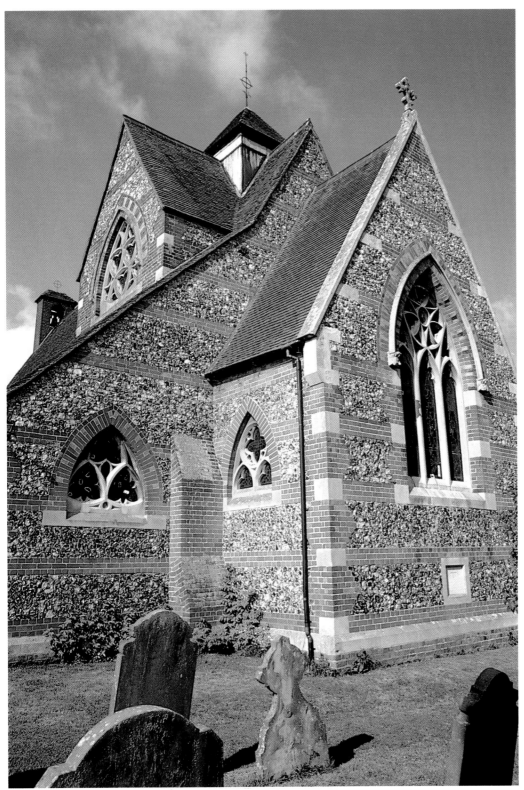

XXVIII Samuel Teulon; Leckhampstead Church, Berkshire, built 1859–60.

xxix Samuel Teulon; Leckhampstead Church, Berkshire, the interior.

completion of his last known and most important work, the Watermen's Company Almshouses at Penge, London of 1840–41.

In his later, productive years Teulon's practice specialized entirely in country houses, urban villas, estate cottages, churches and ancillary parsonages and schools. His failure to win public commissions was primarily due to his reticence in using the

108. Teulon's unexecuted design for Eastbourne Market, dated 1852.

system of architectural competitions, by which the vast majority of municipal commissions were allocated. This seems a pity because in the 'Proposed Market' at Eastbourne, dated 15th January 1852, some ingenuity was shown in the plan. The octagonal Chapter House at the head of the composition was to serve as a Fish Market, isolating the noxious smells from the remainder of the trading areas. He entered at least one church competition, that of 1860 for Holy Trinity, Knightsbridge, although he was not successful.

His success in the 1840 Dyers's Competition was never to be repeated and the only public accolade he was to receive in his career was 'Honourable Mention' for his reredos, carved by Thomas Earp, exhibited at the 1862 International Exhibition. This was intended for, and survives in, his most lavish ecclesiastical composition, St John the Baptist, Huntley in Gloucestershire. He was a regular exhibitor until 1864 at the Royal Academy, where his work received very mixed reviews. Circumstances thus limited his early practice in the first decade mainly to rectories in East Anglia and Lincolnshire, somewhat uncaring church restorations, and cheap and fairly conventional churches. The rectories were almost all in the Old English style advocated by J.C. Loudon. A good example is that provided for the village of Wetheringsett, Suffolk in 1844, for which the design survives.

The first large scale commission for estate cottages came from the Dukes of Bedford and their Steward for the Thorney Estate, Mr Tyro Wing. The Duke was closely involved in the model house movement and the Russell papers contain a detailed memorandum of 1848 in which the Duke and Teulon argued the merits of the external appearance and internal lay-out of cottages being planned on the estate.[7] Teulon suggested sanitation on principles advocated by the Society for Improving

109. Teulon's drawing of Wetheringsett Rectory, Suffolk, 1844.

Labourers' Cottages (of which Lord Calthorpe, another loyal Teulon client, was Vice-Patron). The Duke accepted many of his points, but Tyro Wing was sceptical over the advantages of hollow bricks, which Teulon championed. (These he was given the chance to employ in cottages for the Royal Estate of Windsor in 1856, where the bricks were laid in a rat-trap bond, the heavily vitrified stretchers laid on edge appearing externally as black bands).[8] It was his involvement in that Society, and his clear openness of mind to technical innovation, that probably first brought him to the attention of Prince Albert. In the early 1850s he designed extensions to cottages off Alexandra Road, Windsor which had been built by Henry Roberts (1803–76), the master of Gilbert Scott and one of the most effective advocates of model housing.[9]

Teulon remained in favour beyond the death of Prince Albert and was responsible for new workshop buildings at Windsor of 1858 and the Royal Lodge Chapel of 1863. The Prince of Wales also admired Teulon: there was indirect flattery in the Prince's decision to rebuild the whole of Sandringham House, which he had ac-quired in 1862, with the exception of the porch and conservatory added by Teulon for the previous owner. Teulon benefitted from this Royal association. At least three of his most benevolent clients, the Duke of St Albans (Bestwood), the Earl of Strafford (Bentley Heath) and the fifth Lord Calthorpe (Elvetham) were members of the so-called Marlborough House Set which revolved around the Prince.

In the 1840s Teulon's other main projects were ecclesiastical: both the restoration and fresh construction of churches. These efforts suffered three successive rebuffs in savagely critical reviews of his new church of St Paul, Bermondsey (1847), his restoration of All Saints', Icklesham, East Sussex (1848–49) and Christ Church, Croydon (1851). These appeared in *The Ecclesiologist,* mouthpiece of the

136

extremely influential Ecclesiological Society, published between 1841 and 1868. Its writers were given to terse, vitriolic criticism, occasionally inaccurate and frequently offensive. At Bermondsey Teulon had tried to save his client's money by facing the two principal elevations in stone, leaving the others in brick. The expense spared allowed a full tower and spire, something which the architect had more often than not to excise from his plans for lack of resources. *The Ecclesiologist* first noticed the work at Bermondsey on the basis of a lithograph drawing supplied by Teulon. Despite a homily about 'a master always being known by the harmonious simplicity of his work' the review offered congratulations to the architect and declared its wish that 'he may produce yet worthier designs'. Within a year, however, an actual visit to the site had prompted a violent volte-face. The brick walls were discovered, as

110. Tortworth Court, Avon, 1849–53.

was the 'very coarse' stone carving, 'a vulgar gilt representation of the Holy Spirit' over the altar and all in all 'a pretence about the whole design which makes it far more repulsive to us than a church which is honestly cheap and bad'. At Icklesham the reviewers were no doubt prepared for the worst, and pilloried the architect for removing the original medieval roof and inserting a clerestory. They declared 'we had not much opinion of Mr Teulon's ability but we were not prepared to see him or any other architect in the present day so wantonly destroying a feature of extreme singularity and picturesque effect in an ancient church'. It is hard to gauge whether it was Teulon's outrage or indifference which allowed three years to pass before he presented his defence in a letter of 20th May 1852, in which he claimed to have found archaeological justification for his proposed clerestory.

The third cause for a critical thunderbolt, Christ Church, Croydon, was a commission from no less than Archbishop Sumner of Canterbury. *The Ecclesiologist* review of 1851 was unequivocal — 'we have rarely seen a more mediocre design' although this was a denunciation which the vituperative writers handed down with a frequency that blunted its edge. Teulon was clearly stung, but he did survive. Other conventional church buildings of this period included SS Peter and Paul, Birch, Essex and St Mary's, Benwick, Cambridgeshire where spires were provided, and a series of diminutive churches which dot the hills and fields of Lincolnshire, examples being North Elkington, North Ormsby and Riseholme.

Then came the middle period in Teulon's career in which he produced his best known works. With a fondness for exuberance and abandon that was not prefigured in the early works and which was belied by contemporary commissions such as the large church of All Saints, Benhilton of 1863–65 (where £24,000 went to provide a

111. Bestwood Park, Nottinghamshire, 1862–4.

work of utter conventionality) Teulon suddenly embarked on works of unflinching individuality. The first of his great country houses, Tortworth Court in Avon of 1849–53, had been determinedly asymmetrical and dominated by a huge staircase tower inspired by Wyatt's exemplar at Ashridge in Hertfordshire. However, despite its particular personality, it takes its place in the late Georgian tradition of Romantic design and is in stark contrast to the great houses of Bestwood, Elvetham, Hampshire and Shadwell, Norfolk which now emerged from his office. Tortworth's comparative normality was not due to lack of money — it required some £45,000 — but may well be explained by the client, the second Earl of Ducie who went on to commission from Teulon in 1861 his most tranquil and harmoniously composed church, constructed in warm Cotswold stone, St Mary's, Woodchester, Gloucestershire. Perhaps in both commissions the Earl conveyed to Teulon his own desire for restfulness.

The three great houses by contrast play with colour, interpenetrating forms, riotous skylines and a studiously observed imbalance which amazed contemporaries and present day observers alike. The front porch at Bestwood has been justly celebrated by Mark Girouard as a prime example of architecture and sculpture. The great courtyard tower at Shadwell was known by the joint client, Lady Victoria Buxton, as 'the Tower of Babel', although the language is not that of many nations, but Gothic regarded primarily as geometric form, enlivened by animating detailing. At Elvetham the tracery is entirely *sui generis* in its looped forms and was to be used again by the architect in his schools at Netherfield, Sussex. At the same time Teulon was providing churches like Leckhampstead, Berkshire; Silvertown, London; Huntley, Gloucestershire (which rivals the work of William Burges), and Hunstanworth, Durham. It was fortunate that Teulon's enthusiasm was supported by generous

PLATE XXVIII

112. Shadwell, Norfolk, the courtyard tower,
1856–60.

budgets: at Elvetham the house alone cost £70,000 and the man who commissioned both Huntley and Hunstanworth, the Rev Daniel Capper (died 1886), was a man of prodigious wealth who also paid Teulon to execute works at his own house of Letton (or Lyston) Court, Hereford and Worcester. In the lavish reordering of the private chapel in Blenheim Palace for the Duke of Marlborough, money again was clearly no object.

However Teulon could be equally inventive when designing within financial constraints, especially where brick was the material. Leckhampstead, Berkshire cost just £1,745, and closer inspection shows that the black bricks are all in fact painted, and that the black mastic in which the bricks appear to be coursed is tuck mortaring. The massive timbers which give the roofs such a sturdy medieval quality are simple unvarnished planks, visibly jointed. In his work at Silvertown, the striking use of lightly coloured terracotta drainage bricks within the walls may have been an

PLATE XXIX

economy measure used to aesthetic effect in what was a very poor parish. This capacity for invention within meagre budgets puts paid to the criticism that Teulon's roguishness was the result of having an unusually rich and trusting clientèle. His secular patrons, no less than his ecclesiastical ones, were rarely keen to squander their resources, however vast. Although Peter Allen points out that at Elvetham he

113. Elvetham Hall, Hampshire, 1859–62, the tower.

had the advantage of 'a wealthy, absentee and trusting client',[10] the Duke of Bedford, who commissioned the marvellously Puginesque Post Office and Village Constable's House at Thorney, initially sent back the design as 'much too expensive and elaborate and overdone'.

Almost to a man, the clients of Teulon's most lavish and roguish works were satisfied customers who remained loyal when further work, even of a very different nature, was required. The Duke of St Albans returned to Teulon for the construction of the new church at Bestwood 1868–69. The Calthorpe family, before entrusting Elvetham to Teulon in 1859, had already tried him out on St James's, Birmingham, in 1851–52 and Perry Hall, West Midlands and Lt Col Somerset Calthorpe was to use him again in 1870–71 for the extensive and lavish remodelling of his house at

Woodlands Vale on the Isle of Wight. The Buxtons of Shadwell likewise tried out Teulon on rebuilding the local church at Brettenham and stayed with him for the Buxton Fountain of 1863, now at Millbank. The latter, in its freshly restored state, is a particularly charming proof that the man's genius could manifest itself equally well on a small and a grand scale. Teulon evidently satisfied his clients for reasons both

PLATE XXX

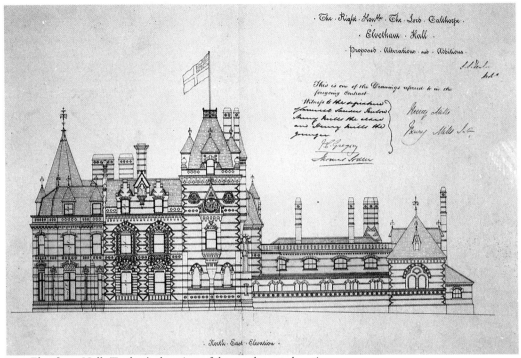

114. Elvetham Hall, Teulon's drawing of the north-east elevation.

aesthetic and practical: he was recommended to the vicar of St Mary's, Ealing, a church he recast from 1863, as a man who kept to his estimates (the recommendation coming from the relieved client at St Mary's, Sunbury). It says a lot for Teulon's business sense that an additional reason for his success in obtaining the Ealing commission was that he was a good correspondent. The vicar initially approached Butterfield, but told the *Ealing Post* that he despaired of ever receiving a reply after a silence of four months.[11] There was perhaps some element of sailing with the wind in Teulon's winning the commission to rebuild St Nicholas's, Guildford. Henry Woodyer, an architect of ample private means, was the first choice but he argued too strongly for the retention of the existing 1836 church. Teulon, less independent financially, did not.

It might be assumed that skill in architectural display need not necessarily be accompanied by structural competence. On at least two occasions disaster did strike. The walls of St Silas's, Pentonville had only risen to five feet when they began to subside. The enraged client promptly sacked Teulon and the contractor. Similarly the great Monument to Tyndale on Nibley Knoll had reached only half of its intended height of 120 feet when it collapsed. As at St Silas's the main blame seems to have resided with the builder's use of faulty materials.

These misfortunes were very much exceptions; Teulon used technical and structu-

115. Elvetham Hall, detail showing Teulon's use of polychromy.

116a and 116b. Elvetham Hall, sculptural details.

ral innovations to make his work both secure and commodious. At Tortworth he introduced gas lighting, heating by warm air and a luggage lift. St Stephen's, Hampstead is maintained by a complicated system of arched foundations and as early as 1847 he was employing deep concrete foundations at Bermondsey. An ancient wall in the parish church at Horsham which he repaired in 1855 was jacked back into an upright position and consolidated rather than taken down and rebuilt. He used iron both decoratively, in the pulpit at Christ Church, Croydon and in several Commandment boards (as at Hunstanworth and at St Andrew's, Lambeth) and constructionally, as in the nave columns at Ealing. Rectangular steel joists were employed at Elvetham.

Teulon's handling of brickwork, even when necessitated by the stringencies of finance, almost always resulted in a striking decorative display. He favoured certain types of design; bricks laid in herringbone patterns, 'tumbled' or arranged to make diaperwork were typical of his style. Their use at St Andrew's, Lambeth occasioned an illustrated article in *The Builder*. *The Ecclesiologist* reviewing the same building in June 1856, declared itself 'glad to see that All Saints', Margaret Street has set an example which is likely to be followed in the proper treatment of brickwork'. Teulon's meticulousness is shown in the few surviving contract schedules. The most complete and most important in this regard is that for Elvetham which runs to no less than fifty pages and is preserved at the house, with a copy in the National Monuments Record. This stipulated that Teulon was to approve the choice of brickyard and in the end he set up kilns in the woods to the east of the house.

Once he had found good craftsmanship he was determined to take advantage of it. He urged the trustees to bear the expense of bringing a Mr Chapman of Hanworth, near Norwich, to London to carve the new seating for St Andrew's, Holborn at a cost of £989, because 'he is a first-rate church carpenter who has done important work under me'. In supervising his projects he was never less than diligent though his personal workload was immense. Even in his most successful years he never entered into a partnership, and although the office was well stocked with assistants

117. Elvetham Hall, fireplace.

118. Silvertown Church, London, 1862, gutted
by fire 1981.

and pupils (a letter survives from him to Scott in 1853 asking the latter to suggest
suitable entrants into the office), he seems to have been a poor delegator. In the early
years, when there was perhaps not much choice, it was always he himself who

144

119. Huntley Church, Gloucestershire, interior looking east.

supervised the work at Thorney. The very greatest ecclesiastical artists worked under him and to his designs including Thomas Earp, the favourite sculptor of G.E. Street, and Forsyth and Skidmore of Coventry, for metalwork. The most famous of Victorian mosaic workers, Salviati of Murano, was described on more than one occasion as a personal friend. J.R. Clayton and Alfred Bell, who together formed the most successful of all Victorian stained glass practices, were both on the building

120. Huntley Church, window tracery.

committee for St Stephen's, Hampstead, Bell providing the east window at no cost. It would be idle to defend Teulon as a restorer of churches. However even here respect for ancient craftsmanship could be explicit. He made a point of keeping the Norman door at Stibbington during his thorough reconstruction and in the contract of works prepared for the restoration of South Carlton church in Lincolnshire he proposed that his new porch be constructed in oak from the old roofs wrought and carefully framed together, a move which might now be seen either as imaginative conservation, or as architectural piracy, but which did stop short of ruthless destruction.

Individuality, or if you will roguishness, in Teulon's churches confined itself mostly to detailing. On some occasions when the spirit of adventurous design was allowed to sweep through the whole building, there were extraordinary and un-archaeological essays in Neo-Norman, as at Hawkley in 1865 where violent chevron toothing and decorative cushion capitals try to endow a rectangular box with central transeptal gables on the long sides with echoes of the twelfth century. The little church at Oare in Wiltshire of 1857–58 is a Romanesque essay in brick, the style dictated by the client Mrs Mary Goodman who intended it to commemorate the life of her husband. At Hawkley and the now demolished St Stephen's, Southwark of 1850, full-blooded Rhenish helm roofs copy the sole surviving Saxon example at Sompting in Sussex. Only Salvin at Flixton in Suffolk in 1856 and the more obscure O.B. Carter at St Peter's, Southampton in 1845–46 did the same.

Teulon was even more on his own in his espousal of the horseshoe arch. This, to present Western thinking, has almost wholly Islamic resonances, although it was

The Story of AGAR TOWN
the Ecclesiastical Parish of
ST. THOMAS', CAMDEN TOWN, N.W.I.

Woodcut by MR. C. R. KEATES, 1886.

By Rev. R. Conyers Morrell, M.A., etc. (Vicar).

(With Historical Maps and Notes on BATTLE BRIDGE, OLD ST. PANCRAS, SOMERS TOWN, CAMDEN TOWN, etc.).
SIXPENCE.

121. St Thomas's Church, Agar Town, 1863, demolished c. 1960.

employed quite frequently in nineteenth-century synagogues and for obvious symbolic reasons in picturesque smithies in the eighteenth and nineteenth centuries. He used such an arch within the school hall at Thorney and much more publicly as the chancel arch within St Mary's, Ealing where the Islamic effect is heightened by the application of striped polychromy. In the extraordinary square-sectioned windows lighting the lower half of the tower at Silvertown, the indebtedness to the Alhambra is direct. His favourite corbel in a chancel arch has two profiles on either side as if the second were a petrified shadow. Another favourite motif was internal buttressing to towers and roofs. These could have structural function but at Rye Harbour, Burringham and St James's, Birmingham they were pure conceit. Exaggerated self-consciousness disguises structural superfluity. Smaller examples of his wayward

122. St Stephen's Church, Rosslyn Hill, Hampstead, London c. 1869, the vault.

148

approach to ornament abound. Surely tongue was firmly in cheek when the foliated capitals in Christ Church, Wimbledon were carved complete with flower pots? At Bentley Heath, Hertfordshire and Hopton, Suffolk the northern and southern nave walls are self-consciously different. A further analysis of Teulon's ecclesiastical repertoire is given elsewhere.[12]

123. Thorney, Cambridgeshire, the post office and village constable's house.

Roguishness is what gives Teulon churches their compelling atmosphere. However, they could be innovatory in plan and detailing. There was a particular plan form which he developed from the 1850s, designed to suit a Low congregation of limited means. In these churches, the maximum need was to house as many people as possible with clear sight lines to the pulpit and display was reserved to the west front and to the roof. This plan form, directly indebted to the Dominican church at Ghent and the Franciscan form of nave, was most remarkable for the complete lack of longitudinal arcading and the division of the east end into the chancel and two side chapels. The best examples of this form are St Paul's, Hampstead completed in 1864 and now demolished; Christ Church, Croydon of 1851–52 which faces demolition, and St James's, Birmingham of exactly the same date, and which has been redundant for almost a decade. Joseph Hansom's magnificent Roman Catholic church of St Walburge in Preston of 1850–54 shows a common source of inspiration, although the completely unecclesiological interior is cloaked by a full-blooded Gothic exterior complete with tower and spire.

Teulon also brought to a fine art, albeit now a highly discredited one, the 'recasting' of Georgian churches. Others such as Blomfield acquired reputations in this field, but Teulon was in regular demand to carry out such work, from the first such commission for St Peter at the Arches, Lincoln of 1854 through to the last, Holy Trinity, Leicester of 1871. The most important example and the most complete is St Mary's, Ealing which received a massive new western tower and complicated roofs consisting of minimal Gothic-shaped apertures in wood suspended on

149

124. Hawkley Church, Hampshire, detail of east wall, 1865.

both the east-west and north-south axes and looking like stencil moulds or lace on an elephantine scale. The round arched Georgian windows and long naves make it easier to introduce an approximate Byzantine quality. Dr Tait, the Bishop of London, on re-opening St Mary's praised its transformation 'from a Georgian monstrosity into a Constantinopolitan basilica'. Even Wren was not spared and although Teulon's efforts at St Andrew's, Holborn were not too radical, the placing of the original wooden pulpit on a new Gothic stone base complete with four angels seems wholly gratuitous.

Teulon died on 2nd May 1873 at the age of 61 after a clear and prolonged breakdown in health. Work at St Andrew's, Holborn, one of the last commissions, was marked not just by tension over the bill but also by the resignation of a highly favoured Clerk of Works, settlement due to the laying of sewers beneath his newly completed Court House in St Andrew's Street, and a strike at the organ builders, Hill and Company (no doubt made the more embarrassing by the presence of Ernest Teulon, Samuel's cousin, as a director of the company). The death certificate, registered on 5th May, gives as a cause of death 'paralysis insanorum' indicating that he had been in such a condition for five months. The phrase is not an exact one, but medical authorities could take it to indicate the coma which constitutes the final stages of tertiary syphilis. Having revoked his previous wish to be buried near his

xxx Samuel Teulon; the Buxton Fountain, Millbank, London 1861–6.

xxxi David Rhind: the Commercial Bank of Scotland, Edinburgh, 1843–7 David Rhind's watercolour of the façade.

125. Hawkley Church, Hampshire.

parents at Greenwich, he was interred, following a service in the freshly completed St Stephen's, Hampstead — 'my mighty church' — beneath a simple monument in Highgate Cemetery. There were three memorial windows, one in St Mary's, Ealing and two in St Stephen's, Hampstead erected by friends and family respectively. These last two have been stolen during the church's long period of redundancy.

Despite the controversial idiomatic nature of his work, Teulon does not seem to have been a polemical animal. He wrote no apologia, no books, not even an article. He was a faithful attender of the Ecclesiological Society meetings but never participated in their public debates. Nevertheless he was not backward in self-

126. Teulon's sketch of the castle at Elz.

advertisement and diligently pursued reviews, particularly in *The Ecclesiologist* and would attend the Committee of the Ecclesiological Society in person to explain his schemes or send drawings or photographs. Moreover, he was clearly known within the profession. In his service on the RIBA Council between 1861 and 1865 he overlapped with Scott, Street, Owen Jones and Sir Matthew Digby Wyatt. Through Ewan Christian he no doubt was acquainted with Pearson, who married the latter's cousin.

Perhaps he was not so much an architectural outsider as an insider anxious for acceptance and respectability, but possessed of an artistic genius unsatisfied by conventions. The man who could sketch the great castle at Elz clearly shared the Victorian love of the Middle Ages but looked upon it primarily as an inspiration for the Romantic imagination and not as the creator of Gothic, the 'Christian style'.

9

DAVID RHIND, 1808–1883
The Master of Mercantile Ornament

Ian Gow

ROM THE scant facts about David Rhind which can be gleaned from his obituary, he appears to qualify very much as an outsider. Unlike most contemporary Edinburgh architects who had been bred up in the Scottish building trades, Rhind received 'the rudiments of his professional education in London'. His training was completed with a spell in Italy, which suggests a certain independence of means and sets him apart from his compatriots in the field.

If he is a neglected architect it is not because his reputation, which rests securely on a handful of sumptuous head offices for prominent Scottish companies, has ever been in doubt but because so little is known of the man who designed them. Neither his personal nor office papers survive and it is impossible to distil his character from the bland phrases written in the boardroom minutes of his corporate clients. There is not even a surviving portrait.[1]

Without such documentation it is impossible to reconcile the apparent contradictions in his career. On the one hand he appears to be an architect with a view of his calling as high art: the man who gave his Glasgow bank a belvedere as though it were the Quirinal, who monitored the efforts of his sculptors and modellers in Rome and London through the new medium of photography, and who was brave enough to let David Ramsay Hay, the founder of Scottish art decoration, loose on his masterpiece, the Head Office of the Commercial Bank. On the other hand, he hardly ever exhibited his designs; he took a deep interest in the more technical and professional aspects of his calling, and was content to spend much of his life as 'official' architect to the Established Church of Scotland and the Prison Board, both of whom were fonder of economy than aesthetics. Despite the successes, there is a list of competitions entered and unwon. On his death he was able to leave his widow only a few hundred pounds to support their large family, which suggests that profitable commissions may have proved few and far between.

There is no mystery about who he was, since the Rhinds were firmly established in the ranks of Edinburgh's professional families. Despite the widening of his contacts in London and Rome, it was the commercial class of his native city and his father's world, which provided his clients. John Rhind was Cashier to the Edinburgh Friendly Insurance Company but the inventory of his heritable estate, drawn up after his death in 1826, reveals interests in the city's legal world. At some stage he acted as clerk to Lord Balgray,[2] and his sons capitalised on these connections. The eldest son, John, succeeded his father as cashier, while no less than three were bred to the law. McDuff and Williamson became advocates, while Robert was a solicitor in Cupar, Fife. Of David Rhind's mother, Marion Anderson, nothing is known except that her brother Robert had retired to Edinburgh after a career as a merchant in Antigua, which may have been unsuccessful, since he is included in the list of his late brother-in-law's debtors.

John Rhind senior's profits were invested in property. The very family home, a pretty villa called Marine Cottage, Pinniefield was probably a speculation. With its neighbours, Marine Cottage comprised the little villa village of Seafield which was being promoted as a potential fashionable sea-side resort for Edinburgh. It is possible that David Rhind's interest in architecture was awakened when his father feud the western boundary of their miniature park to build a terrace of houses. The scheme, like Seafield itself, was a failure, but two plots were taken for houses which were sufficiently elegant to stand alongside John Paterson's stylish hotel and baths of 1812.

With this family background it is unlikely that David Rhind's desire to be an architect would have been received with enthusiasm. After his father's death and with his brothers on the path to more sensible careers, he was more likely to be indulged.

The only document at present available to describe his architectural training takes the form of a reference written in 1836 which William Burn provided for — or rather against — him. In fairness to Rhind, Burn's information is little more than idle gossip and was designed to persuade Burn's patron and protector, the Duke of Buccleugh, to appoint Burn's own man and former clerk, McGregor, instead of Rhind. Since any impression of Rhind is rare, it is worth quoting in full:

> Mr Rhind is the son of the late Cashier to the Friendly insurance Office — he was a pupil for two years with a clerk of mine who was with me only for three years and left me in 1826 or 7 — because I found him ignorant and useless and none of my officials would take instructions from him, they being in truth better informed — he must therefore have been with my old clerk (Smith) in 1827, 28 or 29 — since which I understand he was a short time in some office in London — on his return to Edinr. & thro' the influence of some of his relations in the Commercial Bank he got some of their small branch offices to build, and I rather think he has built a small house in Roxburghshire, having been employed thro' his brother an advocate who married a Miss Oliver from that part of the Country — he is a very young man — about 28 or may be 30 and has not had one half the experience and practice of McGregor, altho' from his more favourable station in life he possessed better means, and greater opportunities of advancement. Of his talents I cannot speak from personal knowledge, altho' I understand it is respectable he has however had very little experience, and his practical knowledge is yet to be acquired. [3]

There are few enough facts to corroborate Burn's account, but his dates must be accurate enough. George Smith seems an odd choice, when the Rhinds had money enough to buy a more prestigious pupilage. [4] Perhaps he was seen as an inexpensive dummy run to test the strength of the youngster's interest. The move to London was a much more serious and costly form of preparation. The biographical note on Rhind in the catalogue to The Edinburgh Architectural Association's Exhibition of 1907 identifies the London office as Pugin's. This is less improbable than it may at first appear; in 1830 this office would have been that of A.C. Pugin[5] rather than of his brilliant son. Of much more importance for Rhind's development as an architect, was the friendship he struck up at this time with Charles Barry who was twelve years his senior. It is again fanciful, but not improbable, that Barry would have impressed on Rhind the vital importance of foreign travel. It was in Rome that Barry, as the protégé of an older student, J.L. Wolfe, had buckled down to the serious study that provided the foundation for his later dazzling success. Rhind's visit to Italy must have been in about 1831. All that is known of his studies there is his claim to a future client in 1848, that:

> I spent some time in Rome and the neighbourhood
> making myself familiar with its monuments.[6]

'David Rhind, Architect' makes his first appearance in the Edinburgh Street Directory for 1834–5. The address given is his mother's house at 6, Forres Street. Since his advocate brothers, McDuff and Williamson, practised from the same address which was also the home of his brother John, the house must have been a hive of industry. Rhind's first commissions were for the Commercial Bank; the family's connections with it are uncertain, but there is evidence to confirm that Rhind designed branches of the Bank in the 1830s. It surely cannot be a pure coincidence that the Bank's official architect was James Gillespie Graham, who was so closely connected with the younger Pugin; Gillespie Graham would be a convincing link between the Rhinds and the Pugins.[7]

127. Sunlaws, Borders, c. 1835.

As for the 'small house in Roxburghshire', it is certainly true that Rhind's brother McDuff married Jane Oliver, who died shortly after the birth of their only child. The two brothers were sufficiently close to share a house at 11, Abercromby Place after this tragedy so McDuff is quite likely to have used his and his in-laws' influence to help a favourite brother. A likely candidate for the house is Sunlaws, at Heiton near Kelso. Rhind certainly made additions to it in 1853 and since he had neither sought nor achieved a reputation as a country house architect, he would have been a singularly odd choice at that date, had he not been there before. By the ducal yardstick, and before the additions, it was a 'small house'. Sunlaws is a plain essay in the Tudor style, possibly incorporating an existing building. It is distinguished by a fret-toppped, pencil-like tower joining the main body of the house to its subordinate office wing.

While occupied with these jobs, Rhind dreamed of greater things and worked at his competition entry for rebuilding the Houses of Parliament. It is interesting to speculate whether any of the entrants discussed their ideas with each other. Rhind's friend Barry, of course, won, while A.W.N. Pugin was busy ghosting Gillespie Graham's entry. Rhind's design was not placed among the prizewinners. Sadly it has not survived, since it would surely be of value as an architectural curiosity, in case its author, as a member of both the Barry and Pugin circles, had anticipated their collaboration on the actual Palace of Westminster.

The late 1830s brought some small church commissions, including St John's, Leith which the Rhinds may have attended when they were in residence at nearby Seafield. Rhind's task was to upgrade and Gothicise a small chapel of ease, making it into a more imposing church. His scheme is creditable, with a centrally placed tower of unusual elaboration, rising in stages to a clock which may have been intended to carry a spire. On either side of the tower pavilion-like schoolrooms enclose a little forecourt. The congregation was sufficiently well pleased to make him a present of thirty guineas in August 1839. Rhind's identification as a bank architect was continued by his competition entry for the North of Scotland Bank, Aberdeen. He was again unsuccessful and the building was erected to the design of the local man,

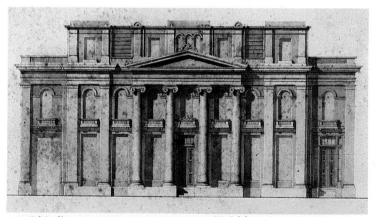

128. Rhind's competition entry for the North of Scotland Bank, Aberdeen 1839.

Archibald Simpson, but Rhind's surviving drawings show his mature manner and contain many of the seeds of his design for the Head Office of the Commercial Bank.

Of much greater importance in the development of Rhind's style was his design of 1838 for the column which supports the statue of Sir Walter Scott at the centre of George Square, Glasgow. This brought Rhind into direct contact with the nascent school of Scottish sculptors whose works were to play so prominent a part in his later buildings. The commission for the statue had been given in 1834 to the local sculptor John Greenshields. Scott had met this 'rustic genius' and admired his talent. Greenshields' death before its completion led to the employment of Handyside Ritchie to execute Greenshields's design. Ritchie was another talented native sculptor from Musselburgh, near Edinburgh. After this first meeting, Ritchie became the principal executant of Rhind's ornamental enrichments. Rhind's design for the Scott column is the first intimation of this interest, and is a rich play on traditional monumental themes. The base combines the pylon and sarcophagus in a most imaginative way and carries no less than eight boldly modelled lion masks, which

129. Rhind's design of 1838 for the Scott Monument, George Square, Glasgow.

became Rhind's trademark. The focus of interest for the development of Scottish sculpture was to have been the Scottish National Monument on Edinburgh's Calton Hill. Intended as an exact facsimile of the Parthenon, it was to be equipped with the Scottish equivalent of the Elgin marbles. Few public buildings had a sufficient budget to permit sculpture on any scale, as Playfair was to discover when he was prevented from employing Steele on figurative sculpture in the pediments of the Royal Institution. Unfortunately for both the sculptors and the Edinburgh skyline, the National Monument remained unfinished, and so opportunities for sculptors passed to commercial premises, a building type that was to become Rhind's speciality.

The Bank, Rhind's first employer provided him with his finest opportunity when it asked him to design its Head Office in 1843. The Commercial Bank, founded in

1810, was one of the most successful joint-stock companies ever created in Scotland. It continued to swallow its rivals until it nobly gave up its name in 1969 on merging with the longer established Royal Bank of Scotland. As its name implied, its purpose was to facilitate trade and look after small investors and businessmen who had not been well served by the older public banks and private bankers. By the 1840s, its success was assured and its directors hankered after architecturally more ambitious premises that would appropriately reflect its role in Scottish life.

They were also anxious to replace their old Head Office in the High Street with one in the New Town, an area gaining in commercial importance at the expense of the Old Town. In 1828 the Royal Bank had acquired Sir Laurence Dundas's splendid

130. Calotype taken by D.O. Hill during the construction of the Commercial Bank showing the sculpture of the pediment.

townhouse, designed by William Chambers, in St Andrew's Square, for its enviable headquarters. The Commercial Bank bettered this in 1843 when they snapped up one of the very few free-standing public buildings in the first New Town, the Physicians' Hall. While the Royal Bank was content to adapt Chambers's building, the Commercial swiftly demolished their £20,000 purchase. It was Rhind's good fortune to be asked to design a replacement with an instruction to eclipse its rivals.

PLATE XXXI   Rhind's design owes something to Playfair's first scheme for Surgeons' Hall in Nicholson Street.[8] The Bank's setting in George Street, a wide gap-site between unbroken lines of terrace houses, was similar to that which had confronted Playfair. Unlike Playfair however, Rhind was not subject to the financial constraints which had reduced Playfair's scheme. Rhind's design in its massiveness and in the strong horizontal band that runs between the columns at floor level, owes something to the strong-box aesthetics which were usual for bank buildings. Its huge areas of plate glass windows and its great portico breaking forward to the street, make it a much more welcoming building than Playfair's original. Rhind's confidence in proportioning the parts and his skill in handling profiles shows that his time in Italy had not been misspent. The most novel feature was the degree of sculptural enrichment which culminates in the deeply undercut and largely free-standing figures in the pediment. For this important sculptural work, which set a new standard for Scotland, a competition was organised by Rhind. The competition was won — possibly with Rhind's connivance — by James Wyatt.

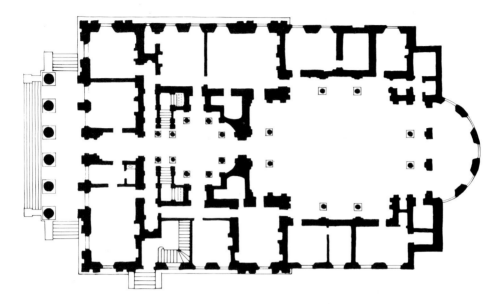

131. The Commercial Bank, Edinburgh, ground plan.

The iconography of the sculpture is elaborate: 'Scotland' is shown surrounded by personifications of the benefits which accrue from successful commercial enterprise. This design, which for many years graced Scottish banknotes, was executed by Handyside Ritchie. In the interior, Rhind had to provide for the requirements of one of Scotland's largest banking enterprises. These included the necessary vaults and safes as well as a house for the general manager. Rhind arranged these necessities around an unfettered central axis, with such a magnificent processional sequence of grand interiors as to leave no doubt that the Bank's house is a palace. Because Rhind's building also covers the garden behind the old Physicians' Hall, the Bank itself is unexpectedly deep in plan. A passage leads to a theatrical top-lit Saloon with a double tier of columns which is a cross between the courtyard of an Italian palace and the cella of a Greek temple. Behind its ranks of columns, symmetrically placed Roman staircases ascend to the boardroom where windows look down into the PLATE XXXII portico and where a coved ceiling breaks up into the roofspace. Beyond the Saloon lies the cruciform Banking Hall, top-lit from an oculus in its dome and approached through screens of columns. The most notable feature of the interior is the deeply projecting plasterwork. At the direction of architects like Rhind, Scottish plasterwork took on a boldness which was not matched in the rest of Britain.

The opulence of the original interior was the result of the contributions of two allied trades whose work has now disappeared. The first of these losses is that of the original furniture by Taylor of George Street, whose design, as surviving photo-

159

132. The Commercial Bank, Edinburgh, interior.

graphs show, had a swagger which suggests the hand of Rhind himself. The second
and more serious loss is that of the original painted decoration carried out by David
Ramsay Hay, the most innovative decorator of his day. The Bank was one of his
most important commissions and the relatively free hand that he was given confirms
that the directors were aiming at a quite exceptionally magnificent effect. To achieve
the requisite tone of purple on the columns of the Saloon and Banking Hall, Hay
imitated a rare marble which he had found in a chimneypiece at Floors Castle. Hay's
painted marbles were pretentiously replaced with real marble of a more mundane
variety by Sidney Mitchell in 1883. Despite their loss, the splendour of the original
interior is not beyond the imagination, and is hinted at in the recently painted ceiling
of another Rhind bank, the former Head Office of the Central Bank of Scotland,
PLATE XXXIII   Perth. On the opening of the Commercial Bank Head Office in 1847, the richness of
the decoration was immediately recognised as a triumph.

Unfortunately for Rhind the felicitous circumstances of this unique commission were not likely to be repeated in his lifetime. In the short term, however, there was an understandable desire that the opulence of the Head Office, which had become identified as the Bank's house-style, should be reflected in its country branches.

These branches made the post of architect of the Commercial Bank one of the prizes of the day. As Rhind's obituary in *The Scotsman* claimed without exaggeration:

> In almost every provincial town of importance in
> Scotland, the building in which the Bank's business is
> carried on is generally a structure of considerable
> architectural pretension from the pencil of Mr Rhind.

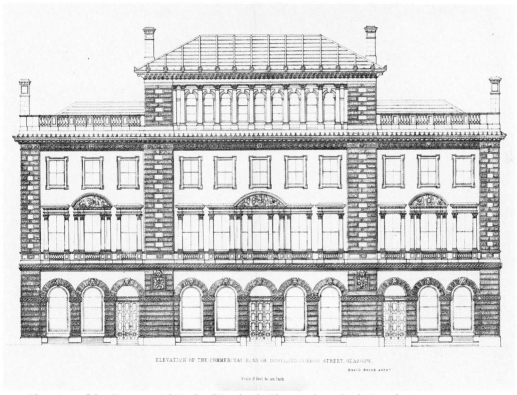

133. Elevation of the Commercial Bank of Scotland, Glasgow branch, designed 1854.

The most ambitious branch was naturally that in Glasgow which he designed in 1854. For branch offices Rhind favoured a Roman palazzo type which his friend Barry had popularized in the South. The Glasgow branch had the further advantage of a fine site. The bank owned a number of terraced houses, centrally placed on one side of Gordon Street which were demolished to create an unusually wide street frontage. Massiveness and strength appropriate to the building's purpose are suggested by the great rusticated piers which divide the façade into three, and which are united horizontally by heavily enriched ornamental bands. The building is unusual on account of these unbroken horizontal lines. Rhind's fastidiousness is shown in his choice of enrichments of which the most telling is the vermiculated rustication, which was often imitated though rarely with that degree of visual success here achieved by Rhind. In place of a pediment he crowned the centre section with an adaptation of a Roman belvedere. Today the Bank is dwarfed by tall buildings but originally it towered above its modest neighbours. Its impact was further increased by Rhind's care, as in the Edinburgh Head Office, to carry its oversailing cornices round onto the flanks, visible, in raking perspective, along the street. As always, Rhind gave meticulous care to the design and iconography of the figurative sculpture. The modeller employed here was John Thomas who had been discovered by Barry. On either side of the entrance he placed tablets representing 'the gold and paper currency of Scotland'. According to the *Building Chronicle,* each of these 'tells its part of the story simply and effectively, and in combination they appear very happily to represent Scottish banking'. These ambitious premises were far larger than the needs of the bank warranted, so that a large part of the building was sublet as chambers on either side of the splendid telling room with its caryatid attic.

The extraordinary feature of the Commercial Bank branches was that while Glasgow obviously deserved such splendour, the Bank and its architect chose not to deviate from the same pitch of magnificence in less important towns. If the effect of the Farnese cornice rampant is merely impressive in a polite town like Perth, the planting of a palazzo, which would not have looked out of place on the Corso, at one end of Hawick's main street must have been astonishing. Few building campaigns so effectively altered the character of Scottish towns until the Free Church, swollen with legacies, and architecturally ambitious, attacked their silhouettes during the 1870s. There were occasional concessions as at Linlithgow, whose old world charm merited a proto-preservationist baronial mode in 1859. In 1865, *The Builder* questioned the wisdom that led the Bank to introduce Morayshire sandstone into Peterhead, a town which up to this point had been wholly granite. In fact the sandstone was necessary to permit the desired quota of enrichment. Nothing underlines the quality of Rhind's work more than the inferior imitations by less fastidious and less scholarly architects which jostle Rhind's branches in the high streets of Scotland.

Rhind's success at the Bank brought him further commissions. The newly completed Head Office of the Commercial Bank is specifically mentioned in the minutes of the Trustees of Daniel Stewart as their reason for appointing Rhind as their architect without recourse to a competition. Since the Trustees' task was to build a charity school and orphanage, the designer of the most sumptuous Scottish Bank 'which had elicited so much approbation' may seem a curious choice. In Scotland the model for such institutions had been set by Heriot's Hospital in Edinburgh of 1628, one of the most ornamental buildings ever erected. Rhind's path was smoothed by two circumstances during this commission. Firstly the Trustees had had a frustrating and infinitely prolonged wait until one of the beneficiaries of the original will had died, and they wanted to build immediately. Secondly the Trustees had their eye on the muddle which the Donaldson Trustees had made of their remit to build a similar charity school, caused by their decision to run a competition. The Stewart Trustees possessed a fine site, crowning a ridge in the countryside to the west of town, and Rhind was instructed to prepare sketch designs in different styles for a building of £20,000 to house eighty to a hundred boys. Having examined his proposals in the Gothic, Elizabethan and Italian styles, the Trustees concurred with Rhind's opinion that the Elizabethan was the happiest. It was subsequently alleged that Rhind's design was a *rechauffé* of his Houses of Parliament entry which is not improbable, but this being Edinburgh, it was inevitably tempered by the omnipresent spirit of Heriot's Hospital. When the provisional contract drawings were put out for estimates, the Trustees took fright when the cheapest tenders exceeded £23,000. Since so little is known of Rhind's professional manners, it is interesting that the Stewart's minutes record that when he was asked to reduce the design, Rhind 'stated very decidedly that he could not without curtailing the accommodation of the Hospital and injuring the effect of the design'. The Trustees deferred to his judgement. To critics outside Scotland unfamiliar with the peculiar twist which Heriot's had given to the Scottish school, the result seemed both old fashioned and cluttered. 'It bears aloft a multitude of little turrets and cupolas, which are presided over by two towers of larger dimensions, reminding one of a box of toys arranged by the hand of a child at play'. Rhind must have been well aware that the School's elevated site allowed its fantastic silhouette to be appreciated from great distances. It was also, in comparison to Playfair's Donaldson's Hospital and Bryce's Fettes College, a very much cheaper structure despite its staccato display of seemingly expensive ornament.

PLATE XXXIV

Rhind's elaboration of some of the details led to litigation with the contractor Hutchison. Although this proved trivial when compared to the problems at Donaldson's Hospital, the Trustees expressed their irritation by withholding what they chose to call Rhind's 'cab fares', until he proved that Playfair was allowed similar extraordinary expenses in addition to his percentage.

At Stewart's Hospital there are hints of Rhind's arrogance and inability to work within budgets. The spoiled darling of the Commercial Bank, happiest playing Severus to their Nero, was unlikely to find such congenial conditions elsewhere. Rhind's appointment as architect to the Life Association of Scotland was again probably the result of family connections. That the relatively straightforward task of providing the Association with a Head Office became a matter of public controversy was largely Rhind's fault. The affair offers a further insight into his artistic and professional personality. It had modest beginnings. In 1851 Rhind was asked to convert 37, George Street, a typical New Town house, into their office but since the eighteenth-century house survives, the work must have been relatively minor. By 1885 the Association felt the need for more ambitious premises and therefore acquired a pair of adjacent houses at 81 and 82, Princes Street for £11,000. By New Town standards it was an exceptionally fine site, fronting Playfair's 'beloved Mound' on which not inconsiderable town planning expertise had been exercised for the preceding thirty years. In spite of the splendid setting, the Association's instruction was merely that 'he should convert part of the buildings into offices', leaving the rest, especially the ground floor shops, intact so that they could be let to earn revenue.

Rhind's solution inevitably involved uniting the two houses with a palazzo front, along similar lines to William Burn's adjacent New Club. On this occasion Rhind's proportions were to be dictated by the existing buildings. By February 1856 the architect and the Directors' delegates on the Building Committee had reached an impasse. It is not clear exactly how the dispute arose but there is no doubt as to its bitterness. As a solution to the problem of the shops Rhind had hit on the idea of incorporating a mezzanine. Whether his choice of the style, Venetian High Renaissance, was in response to the particular site and problem, or whether his interest in

134. Office of the Life Association of Scotland, Princes Street, Edinburgh 1855–8.

figurative sculpture had led him to it, is not recorded. What is certain is that he was designing a much more elaborate building than was required and one which would involve much more destruction, particularly of the shops. In Rhind's own statement later, 'economy was found somewhat to interfere with, and hamper the design'. In spite of ignoring his client's instruction, Rhind regarded himself as professionally piqued when challenged. Whereas a lesser architect, with fewer relations in Edinburgh's commercial world, might have been dismissed, Rhind persuaded the Association to refer the matter to a professional authority. Sir Charles Barry, then the leading architect of the day, was the highest authority in the land but he ought to have been disqualified as a personal friend of Rhind. If the Association were aware of this they may have chosen to overlook the fact because, as far as Edinburgh was concerned, he was a leading authority on the 'Mound'. Barry had not only acted as a judge for the New College Competition at its head, but had also acted as a professional advisor to the Treasury over the design of the National Gallery.

Both sides committed their opinion to writing and were permitted to read each other's version before they were sent, with a photograph of the New Club — a Rhind touch — to the great man. In Rhind's presence, the Secretary consulted Barry in his London chambers. The result was that Rhind was instructed to build the ground floor to Barry's design and the latter was paid twenty five guineas 'for his trouble'. Unfortunately for Rhind the Association was now star struck with 'Sir Charles'. The committee questioned the propriety of a building where the upper half was by one architect and the lower floor by another. Conveniently Barry showed no sign of losing interest. The Association was now perfectly content to have two architects spurring each other on to yet further refinements of design in a style which itself was highly novel. Economy was forgotten. It was equally ominous that one of the Building Committee, Professor Kelland, whose knowledge of mathematics presumably made him a useful adviser on assurance, was also a member of the Aesthetic Society, founded by D. R. Hay. The arcane mysteries of architectural proportion were an abiding interest of the Society. The neighbouring proprietors, particularly the articulate New Club, were less amused by this turn of events especially when the joint architect wanted to increase the intended building's height. The Club, probably well aware of Rhind's predilection for Farnese cornice effects, complained to the Dean of Guild with the result that the Association's wings were clipped. Among the compromises, the most uncharacteristic instruction, for Rhind, was issued that 'the building shall be arranged that the minor cornices & string courses shall profile in their returns within the site of the building.' For the rest of the decoration of the exterior the usual Rhind team of Thomas and Handyside Ritchie created its architectural ornaments, including a heavenly host of putti.

Handsome or not, according to taste, the result was certainly a scandal. In a piece that was probably intended as sarcasm, the *Building Chronicle* saw it as the defeat of the Greek orders in Edinburgh. Playfair, whose final statement at the National Gallery had rejected all sculptural enrichments and who had devoted a lifetime to perfecting the Mound, did not live long enough to see it but would surely have been less than enthusiastic. For Rhind it is difficult to see that it can have been anything other than professionally damaging, despite its undeniable visual opulence. His failure to cater to his client's initial request was not helped by the building's own structural failures when it became apparent that the old backwalls would not support the rearing colossus. The affair was the subject of considerable gossip in the building trade, which not unnaturally wished to know the identity of the architect. Rhind's statement in *The Builder* that he was responsible, can only have contributed to further discussion. The final irony perhaps was that the building, in common with some of its Venetian originals, was merely a façade. Life assurance made fewer planning demands than banking, so much of the property was sublet to an hotel.

In the mature Rhind, Scotland possessed an architect of great ability, but one for which she had little use. It is therefore not surprising that Rhind continued to try his hand at competitions, including those for the Government Offices in Whitehall and the Edinburgh Memorial to the Prince Consort. In 1863 he drew up a plan for incorporating the latter in a grandiose town planning scheme. Centering on the monument was to have been a Town Hall on a terrace adjacent to the Bank of Scotland, looking down on to Prince's Street Gardens. The scheme topically suggested rebuilding Trinity College Church to balance the Bank. It proceeded as far as a lithographed plan, and *The Builder* at least made out that Rhind's lobbying on its behalf was meeting with success. On a marginally more substantial scale than this paper architecture, Rhind's talents were exploited in the fantastically elaborate illuminations in which Edinburgh indulged to celebrate the wedding of the Prince and Princess of Wales in 1863. For a night the very contours of the hills and every fashionable window were picked out in lights in an extravaganza worthy of the Italian Renaissance, a land and a period which could have more fully stretched Rhind's abilities. The effect was so wonderful that the citizens could not resist repeating the spectacle the following night.

Like every other Edinburgh family the Rhinds must have joined the throng who promenaded in Princes Street that night and would presumably have headed for the

135. The elaborate illuminations in Edinburgh to celebrate the wedding of the Prince and Princess of Wales in 1863.

Life Association Building, which was dressed with Chinese lanterns. Rhind had a large family which seems to have been affectionate and happy, if touched by tragedy. His first wife, Emily Shoubridge, died in 1840 when she was only twenty eight. His second wife, Mary Jane Sackville-Pearson, was eighteen years his junior when they married in 1845 and began a second family. Mary Jane seems to have added the 'Sackville' to her new surname. There were eight surviving children when Rhind himself died in 1883 and five more may have died in infancy. By 1883 Lucy was married, while Agnes, Emily, Marion Alicia and Edith were still at home. Two sons, Ernest Sackville and Williamson, were probably also at home while the family's black sheep, David Edward, whose education at boarding schools in Jedburgh and Switzerland has a certain eccentricity, was exiled to New Zealand, but came home on a visit in September 1878. The fact that his father put him up in an hotel for his stay suggests that he may have been unusually difficult. Perhaps because of the second young family Rhind did not retire until 1882. The family seems to have leased their Edinburgh town houses and it was only in 1878 that Rhind left the New Town for a villa, 'Lindenlee' in fashionable suburban Trinity, easily accessible by train from his business.

Meanwhile, Rhind's professional advancement proceeded along conventional lines. On his return to Edinburgh, he was elected to the Royal Society of Edinburgh in 1836, when he was seconded by Dr Russel MD. He also contributed to the Society for the Promotion of the Fine Arts in Scotland. He took an active part in Masonic affairs and was the architect to his Lodge, St Luke's No 44,[9] although his attendance seems to have been irregular. The Society which came closest to his heart was the Scottish Society of Arts, whose interests were technical rather than aesthe-

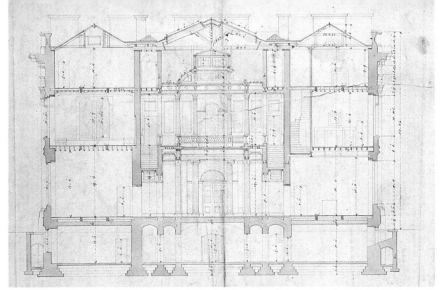

xxxii David Rhind; the Commercial Bank of Scotland, cross-section.

xxxiii David Rhind; Central Bank of Scotland, detail of ceiling.
(Now St John Street branch of Bank of Scotland, Perth.)

xxxiv David Rhind; Daniel Stewart's Hospital, Edinburgh, 1848–53.

tic. In 1855 he became its President, the first architect to be so honoured and the Society resolved that his presidential address should be published.[10] Its main theme was a call for improvements in the technical side of the building trades. Rhind was also a founder member and Treasurer of the short-lived Institute of Architects in Scotland[11] in 1840, which reflects honourably on his standing and ability when he was both so young and had built so little. When the Institute was reformed in 1850, on less exclusively professional lines, some of the old guard refused to rejoin, but Rhind showed no such scruples about associating with this somewhat motley band. Rhind was an active member of the Established Church and both he and his brother McDuff, were elders of St Andrew's Church, whose portico nods across George Street to that on his Commercial Bank Head Office.

Rhind's early church commission and his loyal support of the Established Church, when architects like Cousin had deserted to the Free Church, must have recommended his appointment as architect to the General Assembly of the Church of Scotland in the early 1860s. He extended the Assembly's meeting place, Victoria Hall on Castle Hill (now Tolbooth St John's) so skilfully that it was said to his credit that it 'cannot be distinguished from the original work'. Since the original was by Gillespie Graham and Pugin he perhaps felt a sense of piety. A more substantial Church of Scotland commission was the design of its Normal School in the new Chambers Street.

As 'official architect' to the Church, he continued to attract ministers and heritors as anxious for his advice as Dr Farquarson minister at Selkirk who, on his own volition, obtained plans for rebuilding the Parish Church in 1859. Rhind's 'great experience and eminence in the profession' was recommendation enough for Farquarson, whose inability to persuade his heritors that Rhind's estimate was credible led to subsequent litigation.

Rhind's experience in building branches for the Commercial Bank in remote corners of Scotland stood him in good stead for a similar exercise in architectural colonisation when he got the job of architect for Scotland's Sheriff Court Houses. To be strictly accurate he was more probably architect to the Prison Board, although so few papers survive that his role is anything but clear. What is certain is that he got the job, as at the Bank, more on account of family string-pulling than in tribute to his ability. The Court House styles are as varied as their location. They took on local colour as the towns where they stood became both more sequestered and more native the further they were from Edinburgh. This is clearly illustrated by that at Oban, the only one which is well documented. The local landowner, the Marquess of Breadalbane, did not waste time considering Rhind's first design, which seems to have been unusually economical, but rejected it out of hand. He asked Rhind to provide something better and, as an inducement to higher architectural attainment, offered two hundred pounds towards its cost. To give what was by now a fledgling public building greater credibility in the eyes of the Edinburgh bureaucrats, the local Masons' Lodge and 'Literary Society' were dragged in to give evidence to the effect that they would resort to it frequently. Rhind's design in the baronial manner but here reduced to nonsensical toy fort proportions is appropriately Ruritanian. As so often in Rhind's career the authorities regarded his estimate as wildly optimistic, and legal opinion was taken to establish why a job that had begun as a 'a small prison with four cells' and an estimate of £550 had got so out of hand.

136. Carlowrie Castle, Lothian, 1851–2.

Rhind's difficulties in keeping a check on work in such remote spots is well illustrated by his inspired vision of 1855 that photography would become so very much simpler in the future that:

> I have no doubt that the time is not distant when there
> will be no clerk of works in charge of a building of any
> importance without such a knowledge of the art as will
> enable him to accompany his weekly reports with a
> photographic representation, illustrative of the progress of
> the work under his superintendence.[12]

Rhind was so identified as a designer of public buildings that he never seriously entered the lists as a domestic architect. Nonetheless to Sunlaws — if it is by him — can be added the parallel Knockdolian Castle, Ayrshire which is in a similar Tudor style. His interest in the baronial probably received its greatest stimulus when he turned his attention to Heriot's Hospital while he was preparing his design for Stewart's. It was deep enough for the Institute of Architects in Scotland to ask him to lecture on the architecture of Heriot's Hospital in 1852.[13] Rhind's own brand of the baronial has been dubbed the 'very baronial' by Colin McWilliam. It is scarcely surprising that such an accomplished classical hand should have preferred the style's decadence as displayed at Heriot's and Winton, at a time when the Scottish idiom was in the process of acquiring a Renaissance accent. Unlike Bryce and Playfair, whose approach to the baronial was romantically picturesque, Rhind was attracted by its bold sculptural effects. His finest essay in the style is at Carlowrie, for Thomas Hutchison, a claret baronet and a director of the Commercial Bank. In 1851–2, at a cost of £35,000, Hutchison was provided with one of the most fantastic silhouettes in the revival's *oeuvre*. Unlike Bryce's houses, whose interiors abound in a wealth of old oak culled from Wardour Street, the interior of Carlowrie is modern, with no trace of the curiosity shop, centering on a great top-lit saloon reminiscent of a bank. With his feeling for stone and taste for sculpture, he could occasionally give new life to some of the style's tired quotations. His knotted rope, or rather hauser, above the door into Selkirk Sheriff court has a Laocoön-like thrash which is closer in spirit to Burges than Bryce. Carlowrie, too, exploits the verticality of the style with a skied billiard room approached by scaling a series of staircases, whose thoroughness of application is far from the norm.

It was entirely in keeping with this spirit of fantasy, which frequently spilled over into his estimates, that Rhind's ideal client and the inspirer of his most characteristic work was in fact a corpse. William Henry Miller had succeeded to the Craigentinny estate near Edinburgh in 1799 at the age of ten. The major preoccupation of his life was the creation of that library which is justly celebrated under its subsequent rechristening as the Britwell Court Collection. It was wholly appropriate to these scholarly interests and a certain detachment, which perhaps owed something to his Quaker upbringing, that on his death in 1848 he set his heirs the task of building a monument on the estate, not so much to his own memory but to honour and celebrate the Arts. He stipulated that it should take the form of a facsimile of the Temple of Vesta at Tivoli. Although the estate was far from wealthy and the line of inheritance was unclear, his heirs were not at all hostile to this unusual request. Their organising genius was Samuel Christie, a successful businessman who was

137. The William Henry Miller Mausoleum, Craigentinny,
Edinburgh 1848–67.

Member of Parliament for Newcastle-under-Lyme, and who was a wealthy man in his own right. Rhind was among those architects who wrote in to recommend their services for this attractive archaeological exercise under the direction of one known to be so very rich. Rhind praised the choice of model, and stressed his first-hand acquaintance with the original. It was only when Christie was in possession of more precise details of the dimensions of the Temple of Vesta, which was no diminutive garden ornament, that he became uneasy. If the job which Rhind secured proved more modest than when first advertised, the provision of a tomb which was also an offering to Art was a task for which he was ideally suited. No other Scottish architect had taken such care to give artistic distinction to the enrichment of his buildings. In a compromise, it was decided to recreate an antique tomb. Although William Henry Miller had actually been buried in a deep shaft on the site of the monument some years before construction began, the design takes the form of a PLATE XXXV sarcophagus borne aloft on a handsome base, the whole rising to a height of almost fifty feet. The purely architectural enrichments were modelled by Thomas; the Arts were to be celebrated in sculptured panels inset on each face of the rectangular monument. Christie and Rhind took the placing of this commission with a seriousness appropriate to its lofty aim.

The panels were entrusted to the English sculptor, Alfred Gatley, then resident in Rome. Only two were ever completed, and the modello of the first stopped the

138. Rhind's capriccio of the monuments of Edinburgh.

traffic in Rome. His two panels in white marble depict 'Pharaoh and His Host, overwhelmed in the Red Sea' and 'The song of Miriam'. They are colossal, being no less than twelve feet by six. Rhind, who had followed their progress in photographs took great care over their transportation and insurance. Before they arrived the Mausoleum was consecrated by the Bishop of Edinburgh in March 1860.

Today, the Mausoleum is entirely surrounded, as though washed up by a tide of suburban bungalows. It still holds its own, but this is more on account of its immense size than through any moral authority generated by its artistic embellishments. The unexpected juxtaposition of High Art and the most indifferent speculative building seems poignantly to symbolise the way in which Rhind's own talent was so often diminished in life by the mundane. Now that his Life Association building has been ruthlessly demolished because it could not be accommodated in a uniform town planning scheme, and his glittering constellation of banks have been submerged in a corporate identity, the Craigentinny Mausoleum has become a monument to Rhind's individual genius.

10
ERNEST NEWTON, 1856–1922
Grace Without Style

Richard Morrice

E ARLY IN 1883 W.R. Lethaby, E.S. Prior, Mervyn Macartney and Gerald Call-
cott Horsley met in Ernest Newton's Hart Street rooms in London to found
the St George's Art Society 'for the discussion of Art and Architecture'.[1] This was
expanded in January 1884 and later in the year became the Art Worker's Guild,
'Handicraftsmen and Designers in the Arts', with the aim of a new synthesis of all
the fine and craft arts, following the writings of Ruskin and Morris on the relationship of art to architecture. Because it was so broadly based, the Art Worker's
Guild became the most influential of the groupings promoting the Arts and Crafts
line, while never losing the modest, practical and craft-based ideas of the original
founders. Designing in the light of historical precedent but without archaeological
precision was a constant preoccupation of architects before the turn of the century,
and W.R. Lethaby, amongst others, wrote of the attempts of architects to free
themselves from style. He urged not so much a style-less architecture as one
historically based yet in tune with modern times. For Lethaby the ruling principles
were 'First, the similar needs and desires of men; secondly, on the side of structure,
the necessities imposed by materials and the physical laws of their erection and
combination; and thirdly, on the side of style, nature.'[2] Ernest Newton, too, had
definite ideas about design. 'Building must fall into some sort of style — memory,
inherited forms and ideas. But this must be accepted, not sought. Pass all through
the mill of your mind and don't use forms unmeaningly, like buttons on the back of
a coat.'[3] Newton's use of style can only be understood in terms of what he thought
of tradition.

Ernest Newton was born on the 12th September, 1856, the fourth son of Henry
Newton, the resident agent for the Sturt property in Hoxton, North London. He
was educated at Uppingham College, Leicestershire and seems to have been intended for the architectural profession from the beginning, for though his first entry
into Ewan Christian's office was not successful, he entered Richard Norman Shaw's
office in June 1873, three months before his seventeenth birthday. It was his six years
in that office that settled the line of his early career.

Shaw's office has quite rightly been seen as one source of the Arts and Crafts
movement. However, it was not Shaw's architectural ideas which played the most
important part, but his office policy of fostering a climate in which talent could
develop in its own individual direction. Later nineteenth-century English
architecture was still ruled by the guiding principles evolved for the Gothic Revival
by Pugin and Ruskin, who argued that only by reference to such qualities as truth to
material, honesty of construction and sympathy to locality, both in materials and
position, was a truly rational and modern architecture possible. In other words,

dishonesty was disparaged, but this was problematical at a time when style was a question of revival. Thomas Jackson stated the post-Gothic Revival position when he wrote '... it was not the letter, but the spirit of Gothic architecture which was of use to us: its frank conformity to circumstance, its glorious liberty from the fetters of dogma that oppressed its classic sister, its ready response to the calls of construction, its unaffected naturalism, and its welcome acceptance of fresh ideas and principles'.[4]

139. Detail of a portrait of Ernest Newton by Arthur Hacker R.A.

Shaw and Nesfield, following George Devey, were the first to realise that English vernacular architecture, including modest Stuart and Georgian country buildings, conformed to these criteria, but it was Philip Webb who provided the prototype for the men in Shaw's office, particularly on the question of style. 'Certainly Webb and others', Mark Girouard has noted, 'were thinking in perhaps illusory terms of non-style rather than new style. As Taylor put it to Robson 'You don't want any style, you want something English in character'; and in another letter, 'Style means copyism, the test of good work would be an absence of style'.[5] Although Webb's early works, such as the Red House in Bexley for Morris, were directly influenced by the domestic work of the great Gothic Revival architects (especially G.E. Street who was Webb's master as well as Shaw's), his later work combined features drawn eclectically from many different periods. Smeaton Manor in Yorkshire, 1876, was loosely based on later seventeenth-century prototypes and Standen in Sussex, 1891–94, not only includes within the fabric the pre-existing early eighteenth-century farmhouse, which can still be seen on the court side, but has an interior inspired by seventeenth and eighteenth-century practice and a regular rhythm to the lower central garden-front block. Webb's use of style was without preconceptions, never pedantic or archaeological, and it was his reduction of style to non-style that appealed to Shaw's pupils.

Shaw's devolvement of responsibility on to his pupils allowed them some free-dom to take decisions while working on his commissions, especially in the cases of Newton and Lethaby, who both held the post of Clerk in the office. Andrew Saint's study of the various responsibilities for Shaw's buildings shows how Shaw taught his pupils by gradually increasing their share in works currently being built.[6] The final stage of training was to act as Clerk of Works on a building — and Newton fulfilled his clerkship at Flete, Devonshire, 1878–83, and possibly at Pierrepoint, Frensham, Surrey, 1876–78. Saint also comments on the possibility of design coop-eration between Shaw and his pupils, and though Lethaby's collaborations with Shaw are well known, Newton's are not. As Clerk in the office between 1876 and 1879, Newton was undoubtedly given a modicum of design responsibility and probably had a hand in other aspects of Shaw's work during those three years.

Shaw, characteristic in his generosity, helped Newton set up in practice after he had left the office, with the commission for the House of Retreat and school in Lloyd Square, Clerkenwell, London, begun c. 1883, for the Sisters of Bethany (Newton designed the chapel in 1891). He may also have handed on work on a small artistic suburb of London at Grove Park, north of Bromley, for the Earl of Northbrook. In common with other young architects, Newton experienced a paucity of commis-sions in his early years and in 1882 he published *Sketches for Country Residences* to publicise his practice.[7] This was not his earliest experience of publishing because he had been involved in Shaw's and Adams's *Sketches for cottages and other buildings,* the ill-fated book of designs in concrete of 1878 for which the 1882 book may have been intended as a sequel.[8] Newton was not the only architect represented in his 1882 book — Prior, Maurice B. Adams and E.J. May figure as well — but the most interesting designs are those by Newton. They include two for houses, one in the Midlands and one in a country town, which, although in the Queen Anne style from which Newton moved away after the mid-1880s, show the considered asymmetry in detail and massing which remained one of Newton's hallmarks. His early work at the House of Retreat in Clerkenwell was broadly described at the time as 'Dutch' and designs for Grove Park had a strong Queen Anne feel to them. Despite this, Newton's early buildings were more often Old English, though he varied the style and combined with it Queen Anne elements. For example, Rammels House, Cran-brook, Kent, 1884, by Newton with William West Neve, another pupil of Shaw's, is eclectic although extending just the kind of brick and weatherboarded half-hipped tiled roofed seventeenth-century farmhouse that the Old English style was based on. Indeed, the rear of Rammels House is weather-boarded in sympathy, but the front elevation is rendered with wide red brick pilaster-strips, a three-storey bay to the right and hugely tall, and very plain stacks. Newton chose to illustrate rather less individual houses in his 1890 *Book of Houses,* using a subtle, understated and free version of Shaw's country style.[9] In 1884 Newton built himself a house in Bickley, PLATE XXXVI near Bromley; 8, Bird-in-Hand Lane, a picturesquely asymmetrical tile-hung house with two gables enclosing timbering towards the road. Bromley, like Bickley and Chislehurst to the north-east, was an expanding London suburb in the later nineteenth century. For T.G. Jackson, Bromley, Beckenham and Chislehurst were 'pleasant rural places' in the late 1850s, but in 1858 and 1865 the railway arrived and development began, making the area one of the richest in the country for later Victorian domestic architecture and for Newton's houses in particular.[10]

This Mausoleum designed and erected by David Rhind Arch. Edinburgh – The Bas-Reliefs modelled, and executed by Alfred Gatley. Sculp. Rome

xxxv David Rhind; The William Miller Mausoleum, Craigentinny, Edinburgh, 1847–67.

XXXVI Ernest Newton's own house, 8, Bird in Hand Lane, Bickley, London, 1883.

XXXVII Ernest Newton; Little Orchard, Page Heath Lane, Bickley, London, 1902.

XXXVIII Ernest Newton; Cross Hand, Bickley, London, 1904.

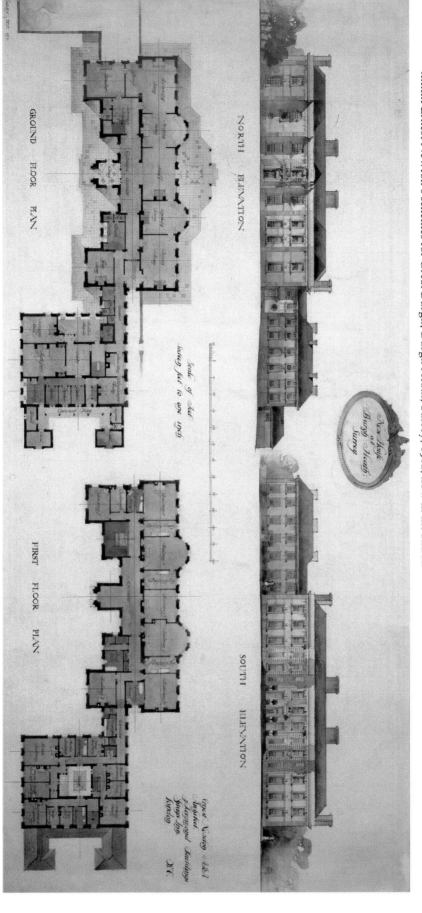

xxxix Ernest Newton's schemes for Great Burgh, Burgh Heath, Surrey, 1912, now in the RIBA.

XL Ernest Newton; Old Castle, Dallington, East Sussex, drawing in the RIBA.

Newton's own house is a simple restatement of Shavian themes, but two omissions are important. Firstly there is little of the hard-edged massing that Shaw had inherited from his master, G.E. Street, and running on from that, little of the romance that Shaw conjured with his piled up roof compositions. These combined, with extraordinary dexterity, a range of motifs: catslides, dormers, huge half-hips

140. 7, The Grange, Wimbledon, London c. 1887.

with gables and overhangs, tall ribbed and grooved oversailing stacks, coves, jetties and so forth. Some of Newton's earlier houses in Bromley, such as 19, Bickley Road, 3, Grasmere Road and 5, Hawthorne Road, take up some of these themes with central gabled and timbered projections, deep roofs and tall stacks but there is a clear subordination of detail to the whole. Stacks, for instance, are plainer and

141. Buller's Wood, Bickley, London, 1888–90.

four-square, the main roof is clearly discernible, with subsidiary cross-gables, and porches tend to be built out. 124–128, Bromley Road, Beckenham of 1884, originally one house, was designed in two parts, the front block to the right more tightly massed with end stacks, large gabled semi-dormers and a strange first-floor bay, jettied out over the entrance with the roof sweeping down over it. This smaller block hides the larger one behind and to the left, a simple ridge-roofed range but one

175

on which Newton began his favourite game of calculated asymmetry, with a shallow two-storey square bay to the left balanced by the more heavily stressed of the two doorways. Gone are the patches of timbering to be replaced by an all-over red brick ground floor and tile-hung first floor. This striving after anonymity and ordinariness became overt at 7, The Grange, Wimbledon, one of Newton's early

142. Buller's Wood, the Drawing Room, decorated by Morris and Company.

masterpieces. The elements have been reduced as far as possible and everything is balanced perfectly; both the proportion of window to wall and the spacing between the windows has now become important.

Buller's Wood, 1888–90, built for the Sanderson family at Bickley, (in fact the extension of an 1860s stucco villa which, true to Arts and Crafts principles, was not clad but left to show on the left-hand return front), was Newton's first commission for a larger house. He immediately took advantage of the site which sloped away sharply to the south and east. Newton later wrote that '... the architect must then study the site, carefully and alone. The general idea of the house will probably float into his mind when he is quietly studying the site. Here aspect is the first and most important consideration. Let no view, however lovely, blind you to the fact that the sun must get into your rooms'.[11] Because of the fall of the site, the house is approached obliquely from the side and Newton gave this view of the house interest by the very deep bays which break up the front, giving tremendous areas of deep shadow to the composition, as well as making good use of the eastern slope by a towering three-storey bay at that end. The bays illustrate Newton's strictures about light, immediately apparent on entering the porch where the huge glazed area gives a greenhouse effect, compounded by the white-painted hall and staircase. Although the exterior is calculatedly free in style, the interior has greater stylistic reference. The decoration of the drawing room was given over to Morris and Company, with

143. Buller's Wood, the staircase.

its painted ceiling and frieze and furniture exclusively designed by Morris. However-er, that room seems atypical, for it is the hall and staircase which were more prescient of Newton's later career. White paint, of course, had been characteristic of artistic interiors for some years, but the Neo-Georgianism of much of the decoration is more indebted to Shaw than to Morris.

The interiors of Buller's Wood relate more to the Queen Anne feel of Shaw's own house 6, Ellerdale Road, Hampstead (1874–76 and 1885–86) than to its near contemporary, Shaw's pioneering work at 170, Queen's Gate, London SW7, with its more archaeological Neo-Georgian decoration. The entrance hall at Buller's Wood, with its Jonesian door-pediments, roll-moulded fireplace and semi-symmetry, (the doorway balancing that to the drawing room has equal visual importance, but leads to a cupboard), shows that where Shaw led, Newton would follow.

144. Redcourt, Haslemere, Surrey, 1894.

Buller's Wood has a thoroughly experimental character, Newton still trying to give external expression to his search for 'non-style'. At Redcourt, Haslemere, 1894, his architecture reached its maturity. Much has been made of its Neo-Georgianism, ('an ominous building with sterile Neo-Georgian just around the corner'), but its importance is rather in the way that Newton managed to draw together stylistic references than in any intention to reproduce later seventeenth or eighteenth-century styles.[12] The entrance front is seventeenth-century in scale and style, a brick version of the gabled vernacular of Wiltshire and Gloucestershire, stripped back to its bones, enlivened by segment-headed sash windows, the small round-headed bay to the right of the porch and by the porch itself. The garden front is more formal, with the balance only disturbed by the roof-zone, where gables and chimneys express the plan below, and by the off-centre first floor bow window with door below. Almost uninterrupted rows of sash windows on two storeys, all with prominent key-stones, and octagonal end bays with parapets compete with the gables to confuse historic references within the general composition. Glebelands, at Wokingham in Berkshire, c.1897, is a good example of Newton's method of designing. The architecture grows out of the plan in the method established by Pugin, and the apparent Elizabethan style of the house, (though Elizabethan with certain provisos), is mirrored in the H-plan which defines the limits of the house. The stacks and the fenestration are the main signs that the plan is irregular, with a double-pile service wing to the right of the entrance, and the hall turning the long axis of the garden-front round through right-angles to that of the drawing-room and the library. The variation of the style, by bracketed cornices, segment-headed dormers and shallow-arched Venetian windows in the gable-ends, is typical of his mid-period houses, where the confusion of historic motifs helped towards greater stylistic freedom.

Newton's architecture, by its firm base in generalised historical reference, its simplification of the Shavian tradition, made its greatest virtue out of its ordinari-

145. Glebelands, Wokingham, Berkshire, c. 1897.

ness. Since Buller's Wood, his commissions had been getting larger and he had been designing with greater breadth. During the 1890s he began to reserve vernacular for smaller, particularly suburban houses, including very free designs for a house at Sutton Coldfield of 1894, High Lands at Burley-in-Wharfedale of 1896 and the houses built for William Willett in Chislehurst around 1900. The turn

146. Steep Hill, Jersey, 1899.

of the century saw Newton's inevitable first venture into symmetrical Neo-Georgian. John Brydon, who had been clerk in the Shaw-Nesfield office, had introduced a symmetrical Neo-Baroque, and his emphasis in the early 1890s on Wren and the architecture of that period as an acceptably English alternative to Gothic for monumental buildings, was bound to influence domestic designers.[13]

179

Newton's first building to be Neo-Georgian in more than spirit was Steep Hill of 1899, in Jersey. Of course, it has elevational symmetry from only one side and the plan is as asymmetrical as might be expected. On the garden front, two hipped wings project forward either side of a curving colonnade, with trellis-work, heavy cornice, shutters and, strikingly, abstracted curving pediments over the ground floor windows. The house, like Redcourt, is L-shaped with a small service-block attached to the rear and with the entrance-front round the corner to the left of the

147. Ardenrun Place, Surrey, 1906, mostly destroyed 1930s, entrance front.

garden front. The emphasis on symmetry on this entrance side is displayed with all Newton's talent for balancing massing and proportion. The rounded and semi-domed porch on a similar colonnade to that on the garden front is flanked to the right by the end of that front and a great curving chimney-breast, and is balanced to the left by the end of the service wing and a hexagonal two-storey bay.

This 'changeful' Neo-Georgian of Steep Hill found further expression around Bickley in the first years of the century, shaping his most formal suburban houses to date.[14] Although Bickley Court, 1904, presents its irregular entrance front to the road, it is almost completely regular to the garden and Ennore nearby, 1903, has a similarly regular garden-front with two canted bays flanking the centre, which is stressed by the blank use of chimney-breast and stack rising up through the centre. Typical of Newton is the placing of two flat-headed dormers square up against that

148. Ardenrun Place, the hall.

stack. Cross Hand, yet again in Chislehurst Road, Bickley, 1904, with its hipped PLATE XXXVIII
projecting wings and square two-storey porch with recessed rusticated quoins, is
only made asymmetrical by the transom and mullion stair window and the arrangement of the stacks. Newton was again achieving an unhistorical effect by his
mixture of motifs, but the houses were no longer free in style. Little Orchard in PLATE XXXVII
Page Heath Lane, Bickley, 1902, was one of his last attempts in a free mixture of
Neo-Georgian and vernacular elements: hereafter his attempts at freedom came in
abstraction rather than combination or confusion of elements. Later works in the
general vein of Steep Hill, such as Triscombe, Somerset, 1904, or Lukyns, Ewhurst,
Surrey, 1906, were generally too regular to be successful and it is the irregularity,
particularly of the bays with balconies and gables over them, which relieves Dawn
House, Winchester, 1907.

This problem — the impinging of a style on Newton's essentially unstyled
designs — also affected Ardenrun Place, at Crowhurst in Surrey, 1906. This was one
of Newton's largest country houses and mostly burnt down in the 1930s. Newton's
houses are notoriously difficult to assess from photographs but it is impossible not
to conclude that the abandonment of his Arts and Crafts principles in designing a

society country house led to a banality and a vapidity which is completely atypical. The house was not actually the pure pastiche of a late seventeenth-century gentry house that it might appear at first glance, and it does have some felicitous touches such as the porch, the craftsmanship and the opulent interior, but the detail and the massing were extraordinarily thin; there was, then, little of Newton's usual genius in evidence. The house was in the same mould as Sennowe Park, Crathorne Hall and Moundsmere Manor, but drained of the passion and panache essential to society Baroque.

Luckley, at Wokingham, Berkshire, 1907, shows the reverse of that coin; an architecture born of reticence. Since Redcourt, Newton's architecture had been simple, but it had never been stripped down as far as it was at Luckley, where dullness is only avoided by perfection of proportion and the judicious use of materials and decoration in a thoroughly Arts and Crafts way. The style of Luckley, and later Feathercombe and Logmore, has been called Neo-Georgian, but is essentially without style in the sense that Lethaby seemed to be calling for the rejection of style. Luckley probably has more in common with some of his smaller buildings and

149. Luckley, Wokingham, Berkshire, 1906.

its telling similarity with Ludwick Corner will be considered later.

Two other works in Bromley justify attention; Molescroft in Hill Brow, 1899, and 107, Plaistow Lane, 1902. These were among Newton's first essays in rough-cast, and, like Voysey's work, they show his realisation that the material compelled the use of an architecture less rich in detail but with greater stress given to massing and proportion. Newton's later vernacular houses tend to be roughcast, perhaps because the medium forced him to think rather more in abstract terms than brick and tile or stone would have done. Roughcast was also a more generalised material in terms of locality and its use in Bromley, Hampshire, Hertfordshire and the West Midlands enabled him to move away from the strictest Arts and Crafts line on local materials.

Four Acre, at West Green in Hampshire, c.1902, perhaps Newton's masterpiece, shows him on the path to these more abstracted vernacular houses. Built of brick with some diaperwork and raised decoration, its interest arises from the subtle relationship of proportions such as the blank centre to the garden-front recess with triple stack rising from it, flanked by a pair of identical gabled cross-wings, or from

150. Feathercombe, Hambledon, Surrey, 1910.

the standard features, like sash windows for the reception rooms playing against casements elsewhere. Newbies at Baughurst in Hampshire, also of 1902, is very similar in its lowish irregularity to Four Acre, though the roughcast has reduced the detail, and on the garden front the house resembles nothing so much as a row of

151. Four Acre, West Green, Hampshire, c. 1902.

early nineteenth-century cottages with semi-dormers and oversize stacks. The style, with gabled weatherboarded dormers, segment-headed casement windows and tall stacks, is almost identical to that of Molescroft and 107, Plaistow Lane, though the latter has a triple-gabled garden front with a deep central two-storey bay.

The later roughcast houses were even more stripped down, Scotsman's Field at Church Stretton in Shropshire, 1908, and Brand Lodge at Colwall, Hereford and

Worcester, 1910, both being rather too large for the style, their tall gabled wings appearing gawky and their major importance lying in the high quality of the detail, particularly the lead-cladding of the window bays. Ludwick Corner at Welwyn Garden City, 1907, though essentially very similar, is far more successful. The flatness and abstraction of the composition are emphasised more consistently without being boring; the windows of the gable-ends, for instance, project on two storeys in the flattest of flat bays.[15] The simplicity both of the material and the massing works much better in a smaller building, a point more fully appreciated by Voysey. Though smaller, Ludwick Corner is a restatement of Luckley. The flatness of fenestration, the straightforwardness of massing, and even details such as the semicircular porch-hood on columns and the oculi flanking the porch are similar, Newton here demonstrating the ultimate interchangeability of vernacular and Neo-Georgian, almost reducing thereby the question of style to irrelevance. As we have

152. Ludwick Corner, Welwyn Garden City, Hertfordshire c. 1907.

seen, Luckley was regarded as Neo-Georgian in style, but by comparing Luckley and Ludwick Corner, one concludes that Newton achieved the functionalism through traditional practice, for which Lethaby was searching, by using craft principles and local materials. In fact Luckley and the very similar Feathercombe of 1910 and Logmore of 1913, as well as Ludwick Corner, were less a new architecture or a return to first principles, than a simple solution to the problems of building unpretentious smaller country houses.

PLATE XXXIX In the last years before the First World War, Newton received commissions for his largest houses. At Kingswood, Great Burgh, both 1912, and Abbotsbury 1913, replacing an earlier house that had burnt down, the style used was broadly eighteenth-century classical, while the Flint House at Goring Heath, Oxfordshire and the never to be finished Jouy-en-Jouas in France, both 1913, were gabled Jacobean; all very low key. Massing and detail were subdued to the total design, and it is Newton's attitude to tradition and excellence in materials which give interest to these houses, 'houses', according to Lethaby, 'which were really homes, while graceful and dignified as well'.[16] These houses were all, perhaps, rather too large for

153. Flint House, Goring Heath, Oxfordshire, 1913.

Newton's reticence in design, which was far better suited to restorations and alterations to older buildings while respecting their historic fabric. This had been shown in his treatment of a framed house at Upton Grey in Hampshire, 1909, and his rambling additions to Old Castle at Dallington in Sussex, 1912, which, with PLATE XL extraordinary virtuosity, becomes almost symmetrical while dropping down on the

154. Flint House, the porch.

west side to form a tall stop to the building, similar in feeling to the eastern end of Buller's Wood, some twenty-five years before.

Although domestic work formed the great majority of his practice, Newton did a small amount of church work; his chapel at the House of Retreat, Lloyd Square of 1891, and his two churches in Lewisham, c.1881 and c.1890–95, showed his ability

155. Old Castle, Dallington, East Sussex, extended 1912.

to design with restraint and modesty. They were typical Edwardian churches, works of the late Gothic revival, of grace and elegance in a free Curvilinear or early Perpendicular style, with excellent fittings and craftmanship, all features favoured by church architects like Nicholson and Moore, Bidlake and Tapper. The only example of full-blooded revival in his church work was the west tower and spire for St George's Church in Bickley of 1905–06, which was an addition to an earlier Victorian church already in a Decorated style.

Newton's very last works, apart from a design of 1920 for a monastery in Caen, Normandy, were for the War Memorial Shrine and Memorial Hall at Uppingham School, where he had been a pupil. The shrine was designed as an adjunct to the chapel, and Newton's stripped Curvilinear style suits perfectly the sombre mood of the panels of the fallen. Newton based the Hall on the courtyard elevation of the hall block at Kirby Hall in Northamptonshire, its Jacobean style giving the main fronts their grids of pilasters and transom and mullion windows, abstracting the later Victorian school or university hall, (typified by Jackson in his Examination Schools at Oxford, 1877–82, or the Big School at Cranbrook, Kent, 1883–84). It is interesting to compare Newton's Memorial Hall, so formal and monumental, with Ernest Gimson's School Library at Bedales School of the same date, a more thorough-going Arts and Crafts building with structural timber-framing. The Memorial hall has a timeless quality that makes it a fitting end to Newton's career.

156. St Swithun's Church, Lewisham, London, c. 1890–5.

Ernest Newton died on January 25th, 1922. The First World War interrupted his practice in the later years of his life, years which he devoted to work in connection with the registration of the issue of building licences. In 1914 he became President of the Royal Institute of British Architects and in 1918 was given the Royal Gold Medal; he was admitted a Royal Academician in 1919 and was awarded the CBE in 1920, all this official recognition reflecting the esteem of his contemporaries. It was appropriate that his cremation was attended by E. S. Prior and W. R. Lethaby, two of his colleagues in the foundation of the Art Workers' Guild some thirty eight years before.

Newton's architecture, then, was based on reticence; his characteristic style and his own cast of mind did not lend themselves to the more mannered vernacularism of some of his contemporaries. It is obvious that Newton was influenced initially by Shaw, and in his suburban work at Bromley he followed Webb's ideas on the reduction of style in reducing and simplifying Shavian Old English. He remained one of Shaw's closest friends in the architectural world and was always valued for his advice. Indeed, in the second of the Alliance Assurance offices in Pall Mall, Shaw was offered the choice of partnership with either Lutyens or Newton. Shaw chose Newton, though one supposes that Newton's influence was primarily on the interior, combined with the Clerk of Works role.[17] After Shaw's death, his family turned to Newton in order to realise Shaw's idea of a family tomb modelled on an eighteenth-century chest tomb in Fairford churchyard.[18]

Lethaby's influence on Newton's architecture began with Buller's Wood, and he remained a friend, drawing some of the perspectives of that house. Lethaby's two

187

157. Uppingham School, Leicestershire, 1919, The Memorial Hall.

earliest houses, Avon Tyrrell and The Hurst at Four Oaks near Birmingham, (1891–93 and 1892 respectively), were very similar to Newton's work of this period, The Hurst in particular prescient of Redcourt, a gabled brick house with tall parapeted bays, tall stacks and thin segment-headed sashes used only for the main reception rooms. There was, of course, the common source of Philip Webb, but it is interesting to speculate how much the two influenced each other. Certainly Lethaby's ideas on decoration, expounded in his book *Architecture, Mysticism and Myth* of 1891, would seem to have been the source for the abstract designs that Newton used to give interest to the elevations of his roughcast houses, and the decoration of Four Acre, particularly the band over the ground floor in the garden front recess, was probably related to the bands used by Lethaby at High Coxlease, near Lyndhurst in Hampshire, 1900–01. Lethaby's ideas for 'a developing structural art satisfying the special requirements of the time by experiment' were central to the Arts and Crafts movement, The Art Workers' Guild and the free style, and it is probable that this emphasis on architecture and experiment rather than style was the reason for the lack of stylistic development in the traditional sense among Arts and Crafts architects, including Newton.[19] Lethaby commented that Newton was 'aiming rather at sound and expressive building than at style imitations'.[20] Working within a complex set of ideals, Newton made an original and considered contribution to architecture.

ABBREVIATIONS

AEB	Architect's, Engineer's and Building Trades' Directory	LB	London Borough
BL	British Library	NMR	National Monuments Record
BN	The Architect and Building News	NMRS	National Monuments Record Scotland
Br	The Builder	*Pevsner*	Relevant volume in *Buildings of England* series by Sir Nikolaus Pevsner
CL	Country Life		
cons.	consecrated		
CRO	County Records Office	PRO	Public Records Office
dem.	demolished	RA	Exhibited at the Royal Academy
DRO	Diocesan Records Office	RIBA	Royal Institute of British Architects
Eccl	The Ecclesiologist	RIBA obit	Obituary in proceedings of RIBA
f	folio	RL	Royal Library, Windsor
fs.	date of laying of foundation stone	RO	Records Office
HMC	Howard Colvin *A Biographical Dictionary of British Architects,* London, 1978. An indispensable work of reference for these essays.	SDD	Scottish Developments Department, Historic Buildings Section
		SRO	Scottish Record Office
		V&A	Victoria and Albert Museum
ILN	The Illustrated London News	WAM	Westminster Abbey Muniments

Counties

Avon Avon	*Leics* Leicestershire
Beds Bedfordshire	*Lincs* Lincolnshire
Berks Berkshire	*Mers* Merseyside
Bucks Buckinghamshire	*Middx* Middlesex
Cambs Cambridgeshire	*Nflk* Norfolk
Ches Cheshire	*Northants* Northamptonshire
Clev Cleveland	*Northld* Northumberland
Corn Cornwall	*Notts* Nottinghamshire
Cumb Cumbria	*Oxon* Oxfordshire
Derbs Derbyshire	*Salop* Shropshire
Devon Devon	*Som* Somerset
Dors Dorset	*Staffs* Staffordshire
Dur Durham	*Sflk* Suffolk
Esx Essex	*Sry* Surrey
Glos Goucestershire	*E Ssx* Sussex, East
GL Greater London	*W Ssx* Sussex, West
GM Greater Manchester	*T & W* Tyne and Wear
Hants Hampshire	*Warwicks* Warwickshire
Herefs Hereford & Worcester	*W Mids* West Midlands
Herts Hertfordshire	*Wilts* Wiltshire
Humb Humberside	*N Yorks* Yorkshire, North
IOW Isle of Wight	*S Yorks* Yorkshire, South
Kent Kent	*W Yorks* Yorkshire, West
Lancs Lancashire	

NOTES

1 SIR ROGER PRATT

The author wishes to thank Mr E R M Pratt of Ryston Hall, Norfolk, for allowing access to both the Pratt collection of manuscript material, and to Ryston Hall itself.

1 Pratt Collection: MS E.
2 Pratt Coll. MS L.
3 Evelyn to Lord Cornbury, 20th January, 1665/6. *Diary ... of John Evelyn*, W. Bray, ed. iii. 166–8.
4 De Beer ed., *Diary of John Evelyn* 14 July 1655, iii, 153.
5 Pratt Coll. MS L.
6 *Ibid.*
7 *Ibid.*
8 R T Gunther, *The Architecture of Sir Roger Pratt,* Oxford, 1928, 9. Gunther reproduces a letter written by Edward Pratt to Lord Horace Townshend (Gunther 132–4. Pratt Coll. MS F). Gunther mistakenly assumed the 'Sir Roger' of the letter to have been Sir Roger Pratt, rather than Sir Roger Townshend, father of Horace, and builder of Raynham Hall.
9 Both essays in Pratt Coll. MS L.
10 *Ibid.*
11 Pratt Coll. MS A.
12 J Summerson, *The Classical Language of Architecture,* 1978, 8.
13 Pratt Coll. MS L.
14 PRO PRO B. 11/207, 41.
15 Sir Mark Pleydell's *Common Place Book,* 63. Currently in the possession of Miss K Pleydell-Bouverie.
16 J Bold, *John Webb,* University of Reading PhD thesis 1979, 202.
17 Pratt Coll. MS L.
18 *The Journeys of Celia Fiennes,* London, 1983, 42.
19 Pratt Coll. MS A.
20 N Pevsner and J Newman, *Dorset,* 1972, 311.
21 Pratt Coll. MS M.
22 H Colvin and J Newman eds. *Of Building; Roger North's Writings on Architecture,* Oxford, 1981, 123.
23 *Ibid.,* 124.
24 Proceedings of the Cambridge Antiquarian Society x li 1948, C E Parsons, *Horseheath Hall and its Owners,* 32.
25 De Beer ed., *The Diary of John Evelyn,* 21 July 1670, iii, 553.
26 De Beer ed., *The Diary of John Evelyn,* 2 May 1666, iii, 436.
27 *Of Building ... op. cit.* 61.
28 *The Poems and Letters of Andrew Marvell,* ed. H M Margoliouth 2 Vols, Oxford, 1971, 1, 143–7.
29 Clarendon, *The Life of Edward Earl of Clarendon ... in which is included a Continuation of His History of the Grand Rebellion.* Clar. 1358. Vol. ii, 588.
30 Vide 'Wren Society' xiii, Oxford, 1936 13–19.
31 De Beer ed., *The Diary of John Evelyn,* 27th August 1666, iii, 449.
32 De Beer ed., *The Diary of John Evelyn,* 2nd September 1666, iii, 450.
33 N Pevsner, *North-West and South Norfolk,* 1977, 299.
34 Pratt Coll. MS D.
35 Pratt Coll. MS L.
36 Pratt Coll. MS H.

2 JAMES LEONI

1 *The Architecture of A Palladio, Revis'd, Design'd, and Publish'd by Giacomo Leoni, a Venetian: Architect to his most Serene Highness, the Elector Palatine,* 1715.
2 Rudolf Wittkower, *Giacomo Leoni's Edition of Palladio's 'Quattro Libri dell' Architettura',* Arte Veneta, 1954, 310–6.
3 Lionello Puppi, *Andrea Palladio,* 1975, 351, no 84, discusses the Villa Valmarana at Lisiera di Bolzano Vicentino, citing the relevant articles.
4 Leoni's alterations of Palladio's plates are demonstrated in Note 77.
5 Rudolf Wittkower, 'English Neoclassicism and the Vicissitudes of Palladio's *Quattro Libri*', in *Palladio and English Palladianism,* 1974, 88–90.
6 The bibliographical history is described by Wittkower, in *Arte Veneta, loc. cit.*
7 *Idem,* and Wittkower, in *Palladio and English Palladianism, cit.,* 88
8 James Leoni, *The Architecture of Leon Battista Alberti,* 3 vols, 1726 (2nd edition, 1739, 3rd edition, 1755). The 1955 edition is a facsimile of the 3rd (1755) edition: but it omits some of the plates and the section devoted to Leoni's own work, and it adds 'The Life of Leone Battista Alberti by Raphael du Fresne' from the 2nd (1739) edition. It is titled *Ten Books in Architecture by Leone Battista Alberti ...* edited by Joseph Rykwert. It was reprinted in 1965. It supplies a summary bibliographical history on page iv.
9 Nathaniel Lloyd, *A History of the English House,* 1931. Reginald Blomfield, *A Short History of Renaissance Architecture* in England, 1901.
10 Lloyd, *op. cit.,* 127.
11 John Summerson, *Architecture in Britain 1530–1830,* 1953, 190.
12 Timothy Hudson, *'A Venetian Architect in England', CL,* CLVII, 3 April 1975, 830.
13 Gervase Jackson-Stops, 'The Cliveden Album: drawings by Archer, Leoni and Gibbs for the 1st Earl of Orkney', *Architectural History* 19, 1976, 5. However, he found that his newly discovered drawings were an exception to his observation, being 'an

unusual example of his adherence to Palladian rhythm and classical austerity'.

14 *HMC*, 513.

15 Stanley Boorman, 'Lord Burlington and Music', and Clive T Probyn, 'Lord Burlington and Literature', both in *Apollo of the Arts: Lord Burlington and his Circle*, 1973. (Catalogue of an exhibition held at Nottingham University Art Gallery.) Timothy Connor, 'Burlingtonian Publications', in *Lord Burlington and His Circle (Papers Given at a Georgian Group Symposium on 22 May 1982)*. H M Colvin ed, *The History of the King's Works*, volume V, 1660–1782, *passim*, but especially 88–9.

16 G L M Goodfellow, 'Colen Campbell', *Architectural Review*, August 1966, 145, and correspondence, Feb 1967, 94. G L M Goodfellow, 'Colen Campbell's Last Years', *Burlington Magazine*, CXI, April 1969, 185. H M Colvin, 'A Scottish Origin for English Palladianism?', with a note by T P Connor on 'Colen Campbell Abroad', *Architectural History* 17, 1974. T P Connor 'The Making of *Vitruvius Britannicus*', *Architectural History* 20, 1977. T P Connor, 'Colen Campbell as Architect to the Prince of Wales', *Architectural History* 22, 1979.

17 A C Edwards, *The Account Books of Benjamin Mildmay, Earl Fitzwalter*, 1977, 64.

18 *Ibid*, 53.

19 *HMC cit.*, 512.

20 T P Hudson, 'Moor Park, Leoni, and Sir James Thornhill', *Burlington Magazine*, CXIII, Nov 1971, 661, note 26.

21 *HMC cit.*, 512, note 1.

22 *Idem*.

23 Edwards, *op. cit.*, 190. And it was Leoni who bought for Lord Fitzwalter 'a little horizontal sundial made at Paris' (although by an Englishman, 'one Butterfield').

24 Sheffield City Library, *Wharncliffe MSS*, WhM 58/49.

25 Edwards, *op. cit., passim*.

26 For instance, in a letter to Peter Legh quoted below (see note 30) he wrote 'fews days'.

27 Edwards, *op. cit., passim*

28 Leoni's signature exists on 7 letters, concerning: Lyme Park (University of Manchester, J.R. Rylance Library, *Legh of Lyme MSS*), on a bill of work at Shardeloes (Bucks. CRO *Drake MSS* D/DR/S/1), on a drawing for Thorndon (Essex CRO Petre MSS), on a drawing and letter relating to Clivedon (National Trust, Hughenden Manor, Bucks), and on a volume of drawings for 21 Arlington Street (in the possession of Colonel R Fleetwood-Hesketh).

29 See note 8.

30 *Legh MSS, cit.*

31 See note 1.

32 Victoria History of the Counties of England, *Buckinghamshire*, Vol. 4, 1927, 96.

33 Richard Hewlings, 'Wortley Hall', *The Archaeological Journal*, 137, 1980, 397.

34 *Legh MSS, cit.*

35 Lady Newton, *The House of Lyne*, 1917, 291 (note).

36 *HMC cit.*, 319.

37 Newton, *op. cit.*, 368.

38 Burke's *Peerage, Baronetage and Knightage*, 1953, 492 (Cork and Orrery).

39 *Ibid*, 492 (Cork and Orrery), and 1729 (Queensberry).

40 *Ibid*, 492 (Cork and Orrery), and 1222 (Lansdowne).

41 *Ibid*, 492 (Cork and Orrery), and Sir Bernard Burke, *Dormant, Abeyant, Forfeited and Extinct Peerages*, 1883, 70 (Boyle — Viscount Shannon).

42 Burke's *Peerage …, cit.*, 492–3 (Cork and Orrery).

43 *Ibid*, 493 (Cork and Orrery), and John Burke and John Bernard Burke, *Extinct and Dormant Baronetcies*, 1841, 581 (Worsley, of Appuldurcombe).

44 *Survey of London*, xxxii, 455.

45 *Ibid*. 456 and 460, and pl 77b.

46 *HMC cit.*, 129, 217.

47 *Ibid*. 217, note 2.

48 T P Hudson, *The Origins of English Palladianism*, unpublished PhD dissertation presented to the University of Cambridge, 1974, 256–8.

49 Leoni's motifs with the number of times used. Even an exhaustive list has its limitations as a stylistic guide. It excludes attributions, even strong possibilities such as the post-Thornhill work at Moor Park, thereby limiting the probable range. The appearance of 3 designs (Shardeloes, Mansion House, and 4 Whitehall Yard) is not known. 2 (Bath House, and 4 New Burlington Street) are known only as plain exteriors. 2 (Wrest and Thorndon) are only known in plan. 2 designs (Burton and Wortley) are only known from one elevation each. One (Wycombe House) is only known from one elevation, and viewed indistinctly from a distance. Only 5 interiors survive, and stucco ornament which may be the stuccadors' design has to be discounted. Finally, enumeration of motifs can give a distorted view of an architect's style; the commonest motifs are sometimes common to other architects as well, and the most idiosyncratic motifs may only be used once. The panelled pediment at Clandon, for instance, was not repeated. But it appears also not to have been used by more than one other English architect at that date, so it is more significant than this analysis makes it appear.

Despite these limitations, it provides the

basic critical tool. For Leoni did work in a recognisable style, and it helps to identify its features. Elevations which break forward twice towards the centre, for instance, were nearly unique in England at that moment: but Leoni designed seven.

1 Elevations with one break forward (17)
2 Giant orders (14)
3 Rusticated ground floors or basements (12)
4 Two main storeys (12)
5 Skyline sculpture (10)
6 Giant orders with basement (9)
7 Two storeys of equal height (9)
8 Single-storey orders (9)
9 Chimneypieces and overmantels proud of wall plane (8)
10 Elevations of two storeys alone (8)
11 Explicit giant orders with basement (7)
12 Double breaks forward in elevation (7)
13 Staircases of equal status flanking hall (7)
14 Basement kitchens (7)
15 Two-storey halls (7)
16 Chapels (7)
17 Niches with figures (7)
18 Doric entrance doors (7)
19 Elevations which break forward in the centre and at the ends (7)
20 Elevations of 3.3.3 bays (7)
21 Perrons (6)
22 Porticos in antis (6)
23 Pedimented windows used as sub-accents (5)
24 Implied single-storey orders (5)
25 Giant orders without basements (5)
26 Explicit giant orders with half-storey basement (4)
27 Explicit single-storey orders (4)
28 Attic storeys (4)
29 Rectangular stair halls, with stairs on three sides (4)
30 Essential articulating elements continued around all elevations (even where these are astylar) (4)
31 Elevations of 1.5.1 bays (4)
32 Giant porticos (3)
33 Windows without architraves, but with cornices on brackets (3)
34 No visible roof (3)
35 Pediments above eaves line (3)
36 Blocked rustication (3)
37 Perrons without porticos (3)
38 Perrons with porticos (3)
39 Explicit giant orders with full-storey basement (3)
40 Attic storeys over giant orders (3)
41 Libraries (3)
42 Galleries (3)
43 Kitchens in offices (3)
44 Ground floor kitchens (3)
45 Elevations of 1.1.3.1.1 bays (3)
46 Porticos in antis known only in plan (3)
47 Giant porticos in antis (2)
48 Kitchens under the courtyard of a town house (2)
49 Staircases in the hall (2)
50 Staircases of different status flanking the hall (2)
51 Elevations of 2.1.3.1.2 bays (2)
52 Square stair halls, with stairs on all four sides (2)
53 Implied giant orders with basement (2)
54 Two-storey elevations with attics and basements (2)
55 Cavettos on upper side of cornice (2)
56 Doric entablatures with central triglyph overlaid by upward break from below (2)
57 Serlianas (2)
58 Round-arched windows on the ground floor (2)
59 Pediments with boys on (2)
60 Broken pediments (2)
61 Semi-circular projections to the rear (2)
62 Vase-shaped balusters (2)
63 Drawing rooms (2)
64 Porticos or frontispieces with arched sides (1)
65 Porticos with Villa Trissino columniation (1)
66 Single-storey porticos in antis (1)
67 Attic storeys over single-storey orders (1)
68 Panelled pediments (1)
69 Brackets below ground floor windows (1)
70 Broken pediments with both swan's neck and segmental elements (1)
71 Mansard roofs (1)
72 Cornices above parapet (1)
73 Elevations of two storeys with basement (1)
74 Elevations of two storeys with mezzanines (1)
75 Elevations of two storeys with attics (1)
76 Billiard rooms (1)
77 Family wings (1)
78 Staircases of Coleshill-type plan (1)
79 Dog-leg staircases (1)
80 Staircases directly behind the hall (1)
81 Side elevations with projections at either end (1)
82 T-shaped arrangement of hall and saloon (1)
83 Gateway flanked by scrolled consoles (1)
84 Porte-cochères (1)

50 Wittkower, in *Arte Veneta, cit.,* 311 (note 1).
51 Giuseppe Mazzotti, *Palladian and other Venetian Villas,* 1958, pl 115.
52 *Ibid,* pls 241 and 290.
53 Wittkower, in *Arte Veneta, cit.,* 310.
54 *Ibid,* 310, and 311 (note 2).
55 Peter Collins, 'The McGill Leoni', *Journal of the Royal Architectural Institute of Canada,* XXXIV, 1957.
56 Jörg Gamer, *Matteo Alberti,* 1978, for this and the following account of Alberti's life.

57 For instance, the Baroque Villa Giovanelli at Noventa Padouana [Mazzotti, *op. cit.*, pls 381–3], and, more monumentally, the Villa Maffei della Quercia, at Vallegio sul Mincio, near Verona (1692, by the Vicentine Vincenzo Pallesina [*ibid.*, pl 395]).

58 For instance the Villa Piovene da Porto at Castelgomberto, near Vicenza, illustrated in *ibid*, pl 344.

59 *Ibid*, pl 408.

60 William Kent, *Designs of Inigo Jones*, 1727, Vol 2, pl 40 (Palace consisting of five courts), and plate 50, (Design of a Building with Porticos).

61 *HMC, cit.*, 601.

62 *Ibid*, 340.

63 James Gibbs, *A Book of Architecture*, 1728, pl 27.

64 *Legh MSS, cit.*,

65 Gamer, *op. cit.*, pl 85.

66 Deborah Howard, *Jacopo Sansovino, Architecture and Patronage in Renaissance Venice*, 1975, 107, pl 75.

67 *Ibid*, 83, pl 63.

68 Gamer, *op. cit.*, pl 92.

69 Deborah Howard, *The Architectural History of Venice*, 1980, 189, pl 98.

70 Howard, ... *Venice* ..., *cit.*, 198, pl 105.

71 *Ibid*, 195, pl 103.

72 *Ibid*, 200, pl 107.

73 Puppi, *op. cit.*, 395, discusses this drawing and illustrates (pl 559) another version of it.

74 *Legh MSS, cit.*

75 Gamer, *op. cit.*, pl 157.

76 Bay Rhythms: Leoni

One break forward in the centre:

2.1.2 Lyme (courtyard: west side)	(1)
1.3.1 Clandon (south elevation)	(1)
2.3.2 *Alberti*, 'House in Town' design (garden elevation)	(1)
3.3.3 Lyme (courtyard: N and S sides)	
3.3.3 Carshalton (end elevations)	
3.3.3 Clandon (entrance elevation)	
3.3.3 Bold	(6)
3.3.3 Alkrington	
3.3.3 Cliveden Design 2 (main elevations)	
5.3.5 Carshalton (main elevations)	
5.3.5 Lathom (garden elevation)	(2)
1.5.1 No. 7, Burlington Gardens	
1.5.1 *Alberti*, 'Another house in Town' design (garden elevation)	
1.5.1 Cliveden: Design 1 (right side)	(4)
1.5.1 Cliveden: Design 2 (right side)	
3.5.3 Cliveden: Design 1 (main elevations)	(1)
8.5.8 *Alberti*, 'Design after Andrea Palladio' (garden elevation)	(1)

Two breaks forward toward the centre:

1.1.3.1.1 Cliveden: Design 1 (left side)	
1.1.3.1.1 Cliveden: Design 2 (left side)	(2)

2.1.3.1.2 Moulsham (N. elevation)	
2.2.1.3.1.2.2 Moulsham (W. elevation)	(2)
2.2.3.2.2 Moulsham (E. elevation)	(1)
3.2.3.2[irregular] Wrest (side elevations, butting against the old house)	(1)
5.3.3.3.5 *Alberti*, 'Design after Inigo Jones'	(1)
6.1.5.1.6 Thorndon (both plans)	(2)

One break forward in the centre, and breaks forward at either end:

1.1.3.1.1 Wortley	(1)
1.2.3.2.1 Lathom (entrance elevation)	(1)
4.2.3.2.4 Wrest	(1)
3.3.3.3.3 Lyme (S. elevation)	(1)
1.4.3.4.1 Burton	(1)
3.1.5.1.3 *Alberti*, 'Design after Andrea Palladio' (entrance elevation)	(1)
1.3.1.5.5.5.1.3.1 *Alberti*, 'Design after Inigo Jones' (entrance elevation)	(1)
	TOTAL (33)

77 Bay Rhythms: Venetian Villas c 1500–1700. The sample was taken, *in toto*, from plates of Guiseppe Mazzotti's *Palladian and Other Venetian Villas*, 1958, which show villas falling within the approximate date range 1500–1700. The total number is 80, of which 47 are earlier than 1600, and of these, 21 are by Palladio.
Commonest examples:
Over the whole period

2.3.2.	(23)
1.3.1.	(14)
1.5.1.	(11)
3.5.3.	(6)

Before 1600:

1.3.1.	(13)
2.3.2.	(11)
1.5.1.	(9)
3.5.3.	(3)

The sharpest decline in popularity occurred to 1.3.1 (with 13 examples before 1600, and only 1 thereafter) followed by 1.5.1. (with 9 examples before 1600, and only 1 thereafter).

78 Bay Rhythms: English Country Houses c. 1600–1728. Taken from Colen Campbell illustrated in Colen Campbell's *Vitruvius Britannicus* and Gibbs's *Book of Architecture*. Both include unexecuted projects; Campbell's is more of a historical survey, so some early buildings and conversions have been omitted as being inappropriate (Longleat, Hampton Court and one elevation of Cholmondeley Castle). Buildings other than houses were excluded from both. Two houses have been added, Jones's Prince's Lodging, Newmarket and Chiswick Villa, as they are both considerable omissions from *V.B.* The total number is 110, of which 83 are in *V.B.* alone.
Commonest examples over all:

2.3.2.	(15)
1.3.1.	(14)
3.3.3.	(13)

1.2.3.2.1. (10)

In *Vitruvius Britannicus* alone

2.3.2. (9)

1.3.1. (8)

1.2.3.2.1. (7)

3.3.3. (7)

79 R T Gunther, *The Architecture of Sir Roger Pratt*, 1928, 9–11, 135–66.

80 Gibbs, *op. cit.*, pl 122, for instance.

81 Gibbs, *op. cit.*, pl 80.

82 William Kent, *Designs of Inigo Jones*, 1727, Vol. I, pl 27.

83 Puppi, *op. cit.*, 308–10, pls 122–35 (Villa Badoer), 352–3, pls 171–5 (Villa Emo), 297, pl 385 (Villa Arsiero).

84 Margaret Whinney, 'John Webb's Drawings for Whitehall Palace', *Walpole Society*, 31, 1942–3, pl XXI.

85 For Heythrop, see John Woolfe and James Gandon, *Vitruvius Britannicus* V, 1771, pls 82 and 85. For St John, Smith Square, see W A Eden, in *CL*, CXXXI, 1 March 1962.

86 Kerry Downes, *Hawksmoor*, 1959, 167–70, pl 53a.

87 Victoria History of the Counties of England, *Essex*, Vol. IV, 1956, 30.

88 Arthur Oswald, 'Kimbolton Castle, Huntingdonshire — IV', *CL*, CXLIV, 26 Dec 1968, 1696–8.

89 For Sudbrook, see Gibbs *op. cit.*, pl 40. For Witham, see Colen Campbell, *Vitruvius Britannicus* II, 1717, pls 91–2. For Adderbury, see Mary Cosh, 'Two Dukes and their Houses', *CL*, CLII, 13 July 1972, 80.

90 In addition to Sudbrook, he illustrated two anonymous porticos *in antis*, pls 46–7, and pl 59.

91 Harris and Tait, *op. cit.*, plates 66 and 67.

92 Kerry Downes, *Vanbrugh*, 1977, 102–6. The plan is illustrated in Campbell, *Vitruvius Britannicus*, III, pl 20.

93 For instance, those illustrated in *Catalogue of the Drawings Collection of the Royal Institute of British Architects: Inigo Jones and John Webb*, 1972, pls 36, 40, 41, 66, 67, and 162. Or Kent, *op. cit.*, pls 63–5.

94 I am indebted to Miss Juliet Allen for this information.

95 *Cat ... of RIBA: Jones and Webb, cit*, pl 154.

96 Kent, *op. cit.*, vol 2 pl 17. For the attribution to Webb, I am indebted to Dr John Bold.

97 *Ibid* vol 1 p 127.

98 *Ibid* vol 1 pl 6.

99 *Ibid* vol 2 pl 26.

100 *Cat ... of RIBA: Colen Campbell* 1973; 10 (Nos 7/16–18), figs 38–40; and 15(No30/1) fig 120.

101 Pl 20 (design dedicated to the Duke of Argyll), pl 24–25 (Wanstead 2), and pl 54 (design dedicated to Lord Islay).

102 Pl 83–4 (design dedicated to Sir Robert Walpole), and pl 86 (design dedicated to Lord Stanhope).

103 Pl 23–4 (Burlington House).

104 *Cat ... of RIBA Colen Campbell, cit.*, 17 (No 37), fig 132; 17 (No39/2), fig 134; and 19 (No 74/4), fig 166.

105 Puppi, *op cit.*, 314–8 and pls 144–58 (Villa Barbaro), and 261–4, and pls 318–23 (Villa Thiene).

106 *Cat ... of RIBA: Colen Campbell, cit.*, 16 (No 36/1), fig 130; and 17 (No 1), fig 138.

107 John Harris, 'Inigo Jones and his French sources', *Metropolitan Museum of Art Bulletin*, 1961, 253.

108 Christopher Hussey, *English Country Houses, Early Georgian*, 1955, pls 73 and 75.

109 Marie P G Draper and W A Eden, *Marble Hill House and its owners*, 1970, pls 24, 34, 36, and 37.

110 Cosh *op. cit.*

111 Hussey *op. cit.* 72–86.

112 Draper and Eden *op. cit.* pls 11, 27, 28, and 29.

113 Hussey, *op. cit.* 187 ff.

114 Collins, *op. cit.* (see note 55).

115 Goodfellow in *Architectural Review, loc. cit,* (see note 16).

116 Wittkower, in *Arte Veneta, loc. cit.*, 310. But see also *HMC*.

117 Colvin, *Architectural History*, 17, *cit.*, 6.

118 As regards Leoni's known craftsmen full documentation survives at Moulsham Hall among the Fitzwalter papers, so the craftsmen are known, as follows:-

Surveyor: Mr Pullen (Nov 1728, paid Nov 1729)

Measurers: Mr Burningham from London (Oct 1729: Mar 1732)

Thomas Chadbourne (Jan 1733: Nov 1735: Dec 1737: Oct 1739)

Stonemasons: Anthony Goude of Chelmsford (Sept 1729. Died 1741)

Thos Hunt sub-contracted stable coping from Goude (Feb 1736)

William Cooley replaced Goude (1741-Nov 1744)

Bricklayers: Richard Eves (April 1731. Discharged May 1734)

John Middleton replaced Eves (May 1734)

Carpenters: John Bagley (Apr 1731)

Robert Bernard (Sept 1732)

Bishop of Bedfordshire (July 1737)

George Gainge (stables)

Joiner: George Gainge (Nov 1728)

Sawyer: William Sullen (Feb 1732)

Painter: Robert Mason of Chelmsford (March 1730-Sept 1734)

Glazier: John Blatch replaced Mason, September 1734

Plasterers: William Mantle (Nov 1729)

William Fearnley replaced Mantle

Robert Dawson (April 1745)

Bagutti (Dec 1730 — agreement made with

Bagutti, but Artari sub-contracted busts and figures
Artari (April 1746)
Carvers: John Boson of Greenwich
John and James (Iame) Dowyer
G. Murray (Oct 1745)
Mr Richards (Mar 1746)
[A C Edwards, *The Account Books of Benjamin Mildmay, Earl Fitzwalter*, 1977].

119 E Twycross, *Mansions of England*, 1 1847, 51, calls him Concilio.

120 P Leach, *The Life and Works of James Paine*, unpublished D. Phil. thesis presented to the University of Oxford, 1975, 249, and Ivan Hall, 'A neoclassical episode at Chatsworth', *Burlington Magazine*, CXXII, June 1980, 403.

121 Edwards, *op. cit.*, 29, 34, 39, 72.

122 *Survey of London* xxix, 90–1 (addendum); but, for the architect, see *HMC, cit.*, 732.

123 Christopher Hussey, 'Culverthorpe — II, Lincolnshire', *CL*, LIV, 22 Sept 1923.

124 *Survey of London*, xxxii, 458.

125 *Ibid*, xxix, 90–1 (addendum).

126 Edwards, *op. cit.*, 34, 63, 76, 112.

127 *HMO*, 561.

128 John Cornforth, 'Lyme Park, Cheshire — III', *CL*, CLVI, 19 Dec 1974, 1932.

129 Lindsay Boynton, 'Newby Park, Yorkshire', in H M Colvin and John Harris (eds) *The Country Seat*, 1970, 97–105.

130 HMC, 512 (note 2).

131 *Idem*.

132 Puppi, *op. cit.*, 406–8.

133 *Catalogue of … the RIBA: Jones and Webb, cit.*, 16 (Nos. 52–4), and figs. 48–55.

134 Oswald, *op. cit.* Ilaria Toesca, 'Alessandro Galilei in Inghilterra', in Mario Praz, *English Miscellany*, iii, 1952.

135 R D Middleton, 'The Abbé de Cordemoy and the Graeco-Gothic Ideal' *Journal of the Warburg and Courtauld Institutes*, XXV, nos. 3–4 (1962), XXVI (1963).

3 HIORN BROTHERS

I wish to acknowledge the kindness of the owners of the various houses mentioned in this essay in allowing me such ready access to their houses and their papers. I am especially grateful to Mrs A Wrigley for allowing me to quote from the Delbury papers, to the Earl of Aylesford for Packington, to Lord Leigh and the Stoneleigh Abbey Preservation Trust Ltd for Stoneleigh, to Mr F H M FitzRoy Newdigate for Arbury, to the Sotheby Trustees for Ecton; to Messrs Hoare & Co for the use of their archives, to the archivists of the Shakespeare Birthplace Trust, Kidderminster Public Library and the County Councils of Northamptonshire, Oxfordshire, Warwickshire, Wiltshire and the County of Hereford and Worcester for the use of material

within their care, to Bodley's Librarian, to the Curator and staff of the RIBA drawings collection; and for endless encouragement to Howard Colvin and John Harris.

1 Lilian Dickins & Mary Stanton eds., *An Eighteenth-Century Correspondence*, 1910, 316; Anthony C Wood, *The Shire Hall, Warwick* Warwick, 1983, *passim*; Anthony C Wood & William Hawkes, *Sanderson Miller of Radway*, Banbury, 1969, 93 & 108; William Hawkes, 'The Gothic Architectural Work of Sanderson Miller' in *A Gothick Symposium*, Georgian Group, London, 1983, 109–135.

2 John Summerson, *Architecture in Britain 1530–1830*, Harmondsworth, 1953, 222.

3 *HMC* 419: a cottage built by John Hiorn in 1680 survives. The family name was spelt in a variety of ways unusual even in the 17th and 18th centuries — Hiorn, Hiron, Hiorne, Hiorns being the forms most commonly met with ('Irons', which appears occasionally in second-hand reports, must arise from mishearing): I have adopted the form normally used by William and David in signing documents or drawings. A family pedigree through three generations is in the Warwick CRO (556/630/86(a)). But numerous other Hiorns, who may or may not have been related, muddy the picture — in particular an apparently illiterate William Hiornes who turns up among the Stoneleigh accounts in 1734–8 as plumber and glazier (Shakespeare Birthplace Trust RO, DR 18/5/1738): he may be the same as the 'William Hyron of Warwick' who in 1699 agreed to do a third of the glazing in St Mary's church (Warwick C R O, Warwick Corporation order book: CR 1618/W.21/3) and as the William Hyrons who did plumbing at the court house in 1725–6 and (as William Hiornes) in 1729 (*ibid* Warwick Corporation accounts). William and David had one younger brother, John, who was a glazier and lived on at Great Tew. A recent scion, F R Hiorns, returned to the family trade and rose to be architect to the LCC between the wars. He wrote a note on the family in *CL*, 18th August 1923.

4 Oxford CRO, Dil. I/p/1i; copy of the will in Warwick CRO.

5 David's date of birth is not known, but the pedigree puts him after William, and William's name regularly appears first in joint documents; the Shire Hall accounts, however, refer to David Hiorn & Co.

6 Kirtlington accounts: copy in History of Art Library, Oxford. Altogether payments to the Hiorn brothers from William Smith's account at Hoare's bank amount to £4,210 between 1742 and 1747 — all but about £650 to

William. (Hoare's bank archives).

7 Bodleian Library, Oxford, Eng MS. f 556, ff 26–8. The best joinery at Kirtlington was in the hands of the experienced and trusted George Eborall.

8 Leigh papers (Shakespeare Birthplace Trust DR/18/31/459; miscellaneous Stoneleigh vouchers 1764–7). One might have expected the Hiorns to pick up at Edgcote, but the summary accounts (at the house), though leaving the masons anonymous, make no mention of them, and the carpentry was the work of Abraham Swan & Co: several craftsmen then or later associated with the Hiorns were however at Edgcote after Smith died and William Jones became the executive architect.

9 For Charlecote see Warwick CRO, Lucy papers L.6/1102-5, 1476. The proposed elevation for Stanford is at the house.

10 At one time it seemed to me possible that the now lost elevational drawing of the main front of Ditchley illustrated by Christopher Hussey in *English Country Houses: Early Georgian*, 2nd edn. 1965, 67 and wrongly described there as 'original', might be a drawing-out by one of the Hiorns of amendments proposed by Flitcroft. The drawing certainly incorporates Office of Works features, most notably the cupolas worked out by Kent for Badminton (Gloucester CRO, Beaufort drawings, 4.2–5); and I am now inclined to think that it was probably by Flitcroft himself.

11 Wood and Hawkes, *op cit.* 1969, 94 n. 34. But a John Hiorn (the brothers' father?) was in 1747–9 paid for mason's work on the tower (designed by Miller) at Wroxton church (Lord North's account book, Bodleian Library MS North c.59); and so perhaps it was he who earlier had been altering Radway.

12 See Hawkes, 1983, 113 and pl. 6; Warwick CRO, Newdigate papers (CR 125B/V.156). The first payments came to the Hiorns in 1748, for a plan and for woodwork in the 'rotonda'. Payments to D Hiorn may have been for carpentry or simply in the absence of his brother.

13 Michael McCarthy, *Architectural History*, vol. 16, 1973, 29–34. Newdigate was an uncommonly proficient architectural draughtsman, and the story told in Miller's diary (quoted by Hawkes, 1983, 113) of his needing to be taught to draw gothic arches strikes me as tall.

14 Parts of an older house may be incorporated into the back of the building of 1752, and Mr Eric Mercer suggests that two diapers on the entrance front imply walling which long antedates the Hiorns. The brickwork however appears to be continous, and the accounts (at the house, with a copy at the Shrewsbury CRO) seem to suggest an entirely new building. The estimate and contract unfortunately have not been found.

15 Four Oaks was pulled down in c.1900: it is illustrated in Peter Reid, *Burke & Savill's Guide to Country Houses*, vol. 2 146; for Guy's Cliffe, see *ibid.*, 149f.

16 See RIBA Drawings, Hiorn 18–23; *ibid.*, *Catalogue*, G-K, pl 76–7. The Hiorns' drawings for Rococo decoration are themselves things of great beauty

17 Rode (built from Randle Wilbraham) is a long way beyond the Hiorns' known geographical range: the evidence (other than stylistic) for their authorship is a plan at the house which appears to be in David's hand: they may of course not have been the builders, but if so it is the only known case of their making a design for others to work from.

18 See Shakespeare Birthplace Trust, DR. 10/1518. The house is illustrated in Geoffrey Tyack, *Warwickshire Country Houses in the Age of Classicism*, Warwick, 1980, pl 11, and in Strong, Binney & Harris, *The Destruction of the Country House*, 1974, pl 78.

19 Building accounts are at Worcester CRO (BA.4707/4). See also Hussey, *op. cit.*, 219ff. Again the contract was by the great, though the owner was, as was commonly the case, expected to dig the foundations and find the scaffolding; at Kyre he must also have made the bricks.

20 The diaries are now in Kidderminster public library: see especially that for 1759 (000294). In 1766 he ordered chimneypieces from Mr Hayward (*ibid.* 000285) — perhaps the same Hayward who made others for Stivichall and worked at Arbury. Also in 1766 there are numerous unexplained payments to Coplestone Warre Bampfylde, the amateur architect from Taunton. But the accounts are hardly clear. A lot of building was evidently going on in the 1780s with, for the most part, a new generation of craftsmen (the mason was Thomas Wise), though Blockley is still there and the plasterer Joseph Rose, who has already appeared likewise in the Stivichall and Compton Verney accounts. Possibly these payments relate to Knight's other house of Lea Hall nearby, which was destroyed in 1945.

21 See Wood, *op. cit.* 1983, 11, 15, 18. Further confirmation comes from Francis Hiorn's elevation and plan drawn and engraved in 1768 within his father's lifetime: the elevation (reproduced in Wood, *ibid.*, 16–17) carries the legend 'Gul^s et David Hiorn strux" — not 'Inven^t'. Miller's subscription plan to pay for the Shire Hall was not very successful, and eventually a rate had to be levied. Already by

January 1755, a year after the start of building, Lord Guernsey was regretting that 'poor David Hiorn must be kept so long unpaid'. (Dickins & Stanton, *op. cit.*, 248).

22 At the other end of the Bodleian notebook already referred to (see above, n. 7) either D or W Hiorn has written out many pages of careful tabulated instructions for the orders, paraphrased from Chippendale and other contemporary manuals.

23 Marcus Whiffen, *Stuart and Georgian Churches Outside London* 1947–8, 43.

24 Note also the lack of a visible roof. A shabby economy was practised on the north (and once less easily seen) side, where, except at the angles the order has been left out altogether, and the wall looks bare and mean.

25 These derive in fact direct from the Doric order shown in Chippendale's *Director*, pl 2. The columns incidentally are plastered wooden shells hiding octagonal stone ones. It looks as if W Hiorn came back to Daventry in 1769: the façade of the Moot Hall is surely his, with its ingenious series of interlocking Venetian openings (the Hiorn-like staircase is now at Welton Manor nearby); the Saracen's Head, with a similar staircase and more Venetian windows is of the same year; and so might well be the Tavern, a rambling castellated fantasy with a Batty Langley doorcase.

26 A drawing of the church as originally built is reproduced in Whiffen, *op. cit.*, pl 79.

27 Or was: each section of the house was raised and a somewhat bland homogeneity introduced in the early 19th century: for the original state see Wolfe and Gandon, *Vitruvius Britannicus*, vol. 5, pl 46.

28 Delbury has a 'three-bay' version of this plan which William Adam and other Scottish architects used frequently on a small scale, though it seems rare in England. The mid-18th-century Fonthill (Wolfe and Gandon, *op. cit.*, vol. 4, pl 83) is perhaps the nearest (though not very near) to Foremarke. The eighteenth-century range at Thame (attached of course to a surviving older house) is a single pile pure and simple. Wolverley of course is a double pile, as the unaligned front and back bays indicate. The Foremarke plan has been interestingly likened to a section of a London terrace, with a three-bay house between pairs of two-bays ones, the stacks always being in the party walls — a comparison I owe to Anne Riches. Foremarke was a much more expensive house than Delbury. The summary accounts (Burdett papers, Wiltshire CRO) suggest a total cost of £4,236 — evidently to include the carcase, internal carpentry, decorations, materials and some out-buildings. Hiorn's share was

£3,019: unfortunately his craftsmen are not named. The portico, incidentally, was a late addition to the estimate, costing in itself £139.

29 Both in Northants. The quiet sensible office wings at Gopsall were, in the mysterious words of the historian Throsby, 'through a misunderstanding ... built by Mr. Hiorn'. They contrast favourably with the solecisms of Westley's clumsy facades. See, eg, John Harris, *The Palladians*, 1981, pl 98.

30 The amounts come to at least £1,620 (Hoare's bank ledgers and accounts at Packington, with copies at Warwick CRO, z.488). Lord Guernsey, a close friend of Sanderson Miller, succeeded as fourth Earl of Aylesford in 1757. The Hiorns' presence at Packington is apparently another instance of their stepping into the Smiths' shoes. Francis Smith had provided chimneypieces in 1731 and was, it seems, highly enough regarded for his patron to own his portrait: in 1739 the steward's account includes an item for 'framing Mr Bromley's and Fra. Smith's pictures'. William Bromley, Speaker of the House of Commons, was another of Smith's clients.

31 Bird's-eye views of the house and outbuildings (not quite as executed) survive in the fourth earl's hand.

32 At Packington; copies at Warwick CRO, z.306/2.

33 Sir Edward Turner, writing to Miller on 20th January 1749/50, said 'Guernsey grumbles because he had no opportunity of hearing your Lecture during the Holidays, upon intended Stables at Packington.' (Dickins & Stanton, *op. cit.*, 161).

34 *Cf* the immense square at Houghton, built probably 1730–4.

35 There is thus no need, as Pevsner (*The Buildings of England: Warwickshire*, 1966, 299) proposes, to go to Joseph Bonomi for the neo-classicism of the Packington portico. Morris, who was the popularizer, if not the inventor of pyramid-capped corner towers, puts thermal windows into their attics: his design is decidedly more nervous than the Hiorns'.

36 In Wolfe and Gandon's basement plan of Foremarke (*op. cit.*, vol. 5, pl 31) an outline to the west of the house, corresponding to the kitchen block to the east, is marked 'Space not built on'. Perhaps a new stable court was intended.

37 Respectively RIBA Hiorn 24 (ill. Rowan, *Garden Buildings*, 1968 pl 12); 15, 29–31; 33 (ill. RIBA *Catalogue G–K*, fig 78); 38 (Rowan, pl 17); 39 (Rowan, pl 15); 35 (Rowan, pl 12); 36. James Paine adapted the second rotunda design for one that was built at Gopsall and survives (Rowan, pl 13). The Chinese designs are related to rails illustrated in Chippendale's

Director (first published in 1754), but the boathouse, orangery and a summer-house had already been built by 1749 when John Grundy made a survey plan of the park (also at the RIBA).

38 RIBA, Hiorn 34 reproduced in Rowan, *op. cit.*, pl 22. But there is nothing specially distinctive about this clearly professional but unsigned drawing, and it may not be correctly attributed. The design derives closely from Batty Langley and would by the 1750s have been within the competence of a number of provincials. It also bears comparison with the gothick bookcase shown on pl 100 of the 1762 edition of the *Director*.

39 The Ecton drawings are Northampton CRO Maps 2151–3. There is a curious tie-up between Ecton and Farnborough, whose exquisite oval pavilion depends closely on an early 17th-century one at Ecton. Work on the house at Farnborough started in the late 1740s (Benjamin King was there in 1749); again it is claimed for Miller, though stylistically there is nothing beyond the Hiorns' range even then (certainly not the skirted and pedimented architrave on the south doorcase, identical with three on the Packington elevation); and William was certainly employed there later. The pavilion is undated, but its Rococo plasterwork is very like that in the house, which was done by the York stuccador William Perritt, who was paid in 1750 and perhaps unlikely to have come a long distance on another occasion for a separate, fairly small job. Keene of course, with an at least equal liking, Dr Mowl tells me, for skirted architraves, was already working for and with Miller in 1749 on the drawings for Hagley. An additional north-east range at Ecton was never built: it would have contained a circular dining room with a large hemispherical dome. The house is now, alas, derelict.

40 *Cf.* Roger White in the *Gothick Symposium, op. cit.*, 86.

41 A suggestion I owe to Bruce Bailey. This would be yet another example of a return to a Smith house.

42 The house, which used to be the rectory, has a distant link with Shenstone, whose uncle and guardian, Thomas Dolman, was rector till his death in 1745 — certainly too early for the rebuilding, which was presumably done for his successor. Or was Broome a squarsonage, and would Shenstone have inherited it with the rest of Dolman's estates?

43 *Op. cit.*, 421.

44 His bill (Shakespeare Birthplace Trust, Stoneleigh vouchers 1764) is endorsed by Lord Leigh: 'Mr. Hiorn, You are acquainted that my servants are never allow'd to take any money as vails, acknowledgements, or presents. Upon discovery of bribes both tradesman & servant will be turn'd off.' Whatever the occasion and intention of this, Hiorn's name does not appear subsequently in the Stoneleigh accounts.

45 Since this paper was written I have examined again the elegant stable block at Delapré Abbey, Northampton, probably built for Charles Hardy in 1749–50 (it was described as newly built in the sales particulars of 1756): simple but most stylishly proportioned. The projecting central block with thermal window and cupola is entirely in the Hiorn manner, and an attribution to them is supported by a plan of the house among the Bouverie papers in the Northamptonshire Record Office which may be in their hand. The orangery immediately east of the house might also be theirs, but the south range, sometimes also given a mid-18th-century date, appears to be somewhat earlier. The plan referred to and a photograph of the stables are reproduced in Joan Wake and W A Pantin, *Delapré Abbey,* published in 1959 for the Northamptonshire Record Society.

4 JOHN VARDY

This essay is based on research carried out at Oxford in the mid 1970s under the supervision of Howard Colvin and, as all such writing on this period of English architectural history must, it takes as its basic text the entry in Mr Colvin's *Biographical Dictionary of British Architects 1600–1840.* It has also benefited greatly from discussions over the years with John Harris of the RIBA Drawings Collection and John Hardy of the V&A Department of Furniture and Woodwork.

1 Howard Colvin, 'Lord Burlington and the Office of Works', in *Lord Burlington and his Circle*, (Georgian Group Symposium, 1982.)

2 This and the following biographical facts are found in the parish registers of St Mary-le-Bow and St Mary-the-Less, Durham, published by the Durham and Northumberland Parish Register Society at Newcastle in 1912 and 1908 respectively.

3 Another possibility might be Daniel Garrett, another Burlington protégé, who in the 1730s was building up a practice in Durham, Northumberland and Yorkshire. It is also worth noting that Vardy's Office of Works contemporary William Robinson came of a Durham family.

4 H M Colvin and others, *History of the King's Works,* V 74.

5 V&A, Department of Prints and Drawings 3436.199. See Harold Barkley, 'A Kent-Vardy Collaboration', (*CL* 13 Oct 1960).

6 *History of the Kings Works* V 427.

7 This still exists, with a battlemented third floor added in 1768 (*History of the King's Works* V 244). In 1761 Vardy exhibited a design, possibly more ambitious than that executed, which he had made in 1748.

8 V&A 3317. The drawing is not signed or identified in any way and could as easily be a design for a country house — a supposition supported by the fact that a carriage could not have passed through the arches at the centre of the composition.

9 *History of the King's Works*, V, 436–440; *Survey of London*, XVI, 11–14.

10 V&A 3318.

11 *History of the King's Works*, V, 425–430, and pl 64 A–B.

12 John Harris, *A Catalogue of British Drawings for Architecture, Decoration, Sculpture and Landscape Gardening 1550–1900 in American Collections*, 1971.

13 There exist two Vardy designs for chimneypieces (V&A 137a and British Museum Print Room 1962-7-14-68) which incorporate royal crowns into their swan-neck pedimented overmantels, but there is no indication of the date or intended location of these; they may relate to the fitting up of the Treasury.

14 Minutes of the Standing Committee of the Trustees of the British Museum, 26 February 1754 and 3 April 1756. See also J Mordaunt Crook, *The British Museum*, 1972, 51. The Vardy drawing, which he exhibited at the Society of Artists in 1761, was formerly in the collection of Mr Simon Houfe.

15 See John Summerson, 'The Society's House: an Architectural Study' (*Journal of the Royal Society of Arts*, cii, 1954, 920–33).

16 1745 is the date given by E Hargrove's *History of Knaresborough* (4th ed. 1789, 286–7), although a reference, in a letter from James Collins to Arundell after a visit to Allerton in March 1752 (Nottingham University Library, Galway Papers 12, 210/38), to the effect that 'the Flagging of the Church is not done', may indicate that work dragged on. The Allerton drawings (not individually numbered) are in Leeds Archives Department, Acc.1493. The handwriting on them can be compared with that on the Hackwood drawings. The composition and stylistic mix of the west front may be compared with Vardy's unthatched lodge design for Hackwood (see below), which combines open pediments, a large quatrefoil oculus, and round-arched window with Gothic tracery, set within a round-headed rusticated arch.

17 V&A 3312, inscribed 'J:V 1746, for Mr. Arundell'. What is possibly an intermediate design, half-way between Holkham and the

V&A drawing, is in the Ashmolean Museum (uncatalogued 'Kent' drawings, inscribed 'Arundell').

18 V&A 3313.

19 Greater London RO, Westminster DD 5408.

20 The elevation and first-floor plan were exhibited at the Society of Artists in 1764. The client, or at least the first occupant, was George Wade, Lt. Colonel in the 3rd Regiment of Dragoon Guards (died 1799).

21 The attribution to Ware was made by John Harris, initially in 'English architectural drawings in some American collections' (*Connoisseur*, April 1961, 219), and subsequently in 'Clues to the 'Frenchness' of Woodcote Park' (*Connoisseur*, May 1961, 241–250). It is disputed by the present author in 'Isaac Ware and Chesterfield House' (*A Rococo Symposium*, Georgian Group Symposium 1984).

22 RIBA, G4/14. The design for the stables and terrace was exhibited in 1764.

23 Westminster Reference Library, ratebooks of the parish of St George Hanover Square. Vardy's design of 1761 for the overmantel in 'Lady Milton's Dressing Room' (RIBA G4/10) probably relates to Dorchester House rather than Milton Abbey.

24 James Joel Cartwright ed., *The Travels through England of Dr. Richard Pococke*, 1888–9, ii, 143.

25 RIBA G4/15.

26 RIBA G4/11^1.

27 Chambers's letter book, British Museum, Add. MS 41133.

28 Hereford CRO Hanbury Papers.

29 See Roger White, 'The Influence of Batty Langley' (*A Gothick Symposium*, Georgian Group 1983).

30 Royal Library, Windsor Castle, R L 17461.

31 Formerly in the collection of Fello Atkinson, and inscribed in a later hand 'Elevation & Plan of the Bath House designed by J: Vardy 1754'. At the Society of Artists in 1764 Vardy exhibited 'the inside view of a bath designed for a gentleman in Suffolk'; this may be identifiable with the plan and sections of a bath house illustrated in John Harris's *Catalogue of British Drawings ...*, which displays knobbly banded rustication, rocaille stuccowork in the ceiling cove, and extraordinary pendant four-centred Tudoresque arches.

32 V&A 3320.

33 Hackwood Park archives. Vardy's account for the work for the Duke of Bolton at Hackwood and elsewhere is in Hampshire CRO, 11.M.49. What may be a more grandiose scheme for the south front, with a giant colonnade and pedimented portico, is RIBA G4/7^2.

34 Soane Museum.

35 RIBA G4/1.

36 Guildhall Library, Joiners Company archives MSS 8052/5 (Apprentice bindings 1724–42) and 8051/5 (Freemen admissions 1750–1804).

37 Vardy's Hackwood furniture is discussed by Anthony Coleridge in 'John Vardy and the Hackwood Suite' (*Connoisseur* May 1962, 12). Two further side tables for the Duke of Bolton, made to another Vardy design in the RIBA (G4/4^3) are now at Bolton Hall, North Yorks.

38 V&A E3143–1938; a related design is 3436–392.

39 Lord Spencer, 'Spencer House', (*CL* 30 Oct 1926).

40 Soane Museum and RIBA.

41 The room scheme is signed by Vardy and dated 1755 (Greater London RO, Westminster DD 5393). The design for the chimneypiece was endorsed by Gray on 24 Nov 1755 (Soane Museum).

42 See Peter Thornton and John Hardy, 'The Spencer Furniture at Althorp' (*Apollo*, March 1968).

43 I am indebted to John Hardy for pointing this out. Anthony Coleridge (*Chippendale Furniture*, 1968, 49) suggests that Vardy's table looks forward to the early 19th century antique designs of Percier and Fontaine.

44 PCC 239 Rushworth.

5 HENRY KEENE

It gives me special pleasure to thank Valerie Barnish, Mrs H J Bicknell, Brian Earnshaw, Robin Gard, Andor Gomme, Charles Hind, Nicholas Kingsley, Patricia Lancaster, Christopher Lyster, N H MacMichael, and Roger White for their help.

1 V&A, Print Room, A.189. The drawings were acquired in 1921 and reattributed to Keen in 1954. Their provenance is not recorded.

2 *HMC*, 481.

3 Drawing E919.

4 Miller's correspondence in the Warwicks. CRO CR 125B/350.

5 Terence Davis, *The Gothick Taste*, 1974, 56–60, 64 and note 17 for Miller's contribution to Arbury and his bout of insanity.

6 Miller's diary in the Warwicks. CRO, CR 1382/1, 26 October 1749.

7 *Ibid.*, 15 June 1750.

8 For the attribution of the Museum to Keene and its probable date of construction see Timothy Mowl, 'The Case of the Enville Museum' in *Journal of Garden History*, Vol. 3, 2, 134–43.

9 Bodleian Library, MS Top. Gen. b.55, ff

29–34.

10 Drawing E882.

11 Thenford House, Northants, has been attributed to Keene by Arthur Oswald (*CL* 4, 11 October 1946). The case for the attribution is stylistic but the likeness between Thenford and the V&A designs is remarkable. The central block has Keene's old fashioned high hipped roof, a thin central pediment with a Rococo cartouche and blind balustrades below the central windows. The Palladian side pavilions are in Kent's style as often drawn by Keene and they are linked to the main house by the strongly emphasised arcading which Keene favoured.

12 There is a drawing for the cupola of the Guildhall in the V&A, E877.

13 This theory was first put forward by Arthur Bolton in 1922. An elevation in Keene's hand with a giant hexastyle portico survives at Bowood and, though Lord Shelburne rejected this particular scheme, it is likely that Keene's revised scheme for the remodelling included giant pillars intended for the hexastyle portico which were then used by Adam in a modified form.

14 *CL,* 15 October 1953.

15 There is a drawing for the fireplace in the V&A, E903.

16 Marian Evans was born on the Arbury estate and immortalised the house in 'Mr Gilfil's Love Story' which appeared in *Scenes of Clerical Life,* 1857.

17 Sir Robert Newdigate's accounts for 1779 state that Keene had been unable to pay his workmen in full for the work at Newdigate's London house and as a result 'became insolvent'. (*CL,* 15 October 1953).

6 JAMES ESSEX

I would like to thank the staff of the British Library, the Cambridge University Library, the Cambridge colleges of Christ's, Emmanuel, St John's and Trinity, and the Cambridgeshire, Essex and Lincolnshire Record Offices for their assistance in my research. I am also grateful to Professor M McCarthy and Ms Y Jerrold for discussing Essex with me.

1 Schemes for a new court at Corpus came to a head in 1747–8, when Essex and Masters produced their rival plans. (W M Fawcett ed., *Journal of a Tour through part of Flanders and France in August 1773*, Cambridge Antiquarian Society vol xxiv, 1888 ix-xiii). In October 1773 Tyson was 'in great hopes' that the building would start the next spring, (J Nichols, ed. *Literary Anecdotes of the 18th Century,* 1812–15, viii, 608).

2 Cole considered the expense of the St John's building 'preposterous' (R Willis and J W Clark, *The Architectural History of the*

University of Cambridge, 1886, II, 318 n. 2).

3 Willis and Clark, *op. cit.* II 745 n. 1.

4 Willis and Clark, *op. cit.* III 70: drawings of the two schemes are in BL Add MS 6776 ff 94–5.

5 Willis and Clark, *op. cit.,* III 62 n. 2.

6 The building was intended to be the N. range of a new court E. of the Chapel, with the 17th-century library range in the S. being rebuilt to match.

7 BL Add MS 5832 f 85v.

8 The elder Essex was responsible for the joinery of the Caius lantern but the designer was Burrough, who was fellow and, eventually, Master of Caius. The Clare lantern was presumably planned before Burrough's death but it was certainly executed by Essex, who may have altered its detailing.

9 BL Add MS 5868 f 76.

10 *Common Day Book of Corporation of Cambridge,* 1770–86, 253: Essex refused the honour.

11 T Ruddock, *Arch Bridges and their Builders 1735–1835,* 1979, 35.

12 The contract for its erection, mentioned in Willis and Clark, *op. cit.* I 214 n. 2, cannot be traced in the Trinity Hall archives. There is one engraving of the bridge, after Robert Leach.

13 CC Babington, *Ancient Cambridgeshire,* Cambridge Antiquarian Society vol xx, 1883, 8.

14 The BL drawings are Add MSS 6776 f 83–4: the RIBA drawing is G3–11.

15 St John's Conclusion Book 1730–1786 f 221r.

16 Willis and Clark, *op. cit,* II 41–2.

17 The elder Essex died intestate in February 1750, (the Old Style year of 1749 was misleadingly printed by Fawcett, *op. cit.,* p. viii). His estate must have been worth about £500 since representatives had to stand surety for a bond of £1000, a sum by convention about twice the value of the estate. (I owe this information to the kindness of Dr Leedham Green). No inventory survives.

18 The street frontage of the Hartshorn was only 26 feet and the annual rental 38/4d and a 'well-fed pike': original lease from Corpus Christi College to James Essex snr, 20 March 1744.

19 Extract from lost account book of Essex, quoted by Fawcett, *op. cit.,* xxv.

20 The figure is based on the documents giving probate to Essex's estate (like his father, he died intestate); (Cambs RO, Probate R 70/46. His daughter Meliscent's two-thirds share of the money available in 1784 was £14,700, so the total must have been over £20,000.

21 There are notes relating to masonic ritual in BL Add MS 6760 ff 39–48.

22 St John's College muniments D 103, 338.

23 Willis and Clark, *op. cit.,* II. 606.

24 Trinity Junior Bursar's Account Book 1757–64, f 59v.

25 Fawcett, *op. cit.* xx–xxi.

26 W S Lewis, ed., *Horace Walpole's Correspondence,* 1937–80, I 338 n. 7.

27 BL Add MS 6772 f 94v.

28 E.g. Corpus Christi College Act Book, 10 March 1769: 'tiling on Master's Lodge to be repaired as the Bursar and Mr Essex think proper' and St John's College Conclusion Book 1730–1786 f 276, 23 October 1782, 'passage doors be put up under the direction of Mr Essex'.

29 Essex's father-in-law, William Thurlbourn, sometimes appears in the same accounts as Essex's e.g. at Trinity Hall, Emmanuel and the University itself, for supplying books, and he published Essex's unexecuted design for a whole new river range at Queens' in his *Cantabrigia Depicta* in 1763.

30 E.g. 28 January 1772 when Essex and Tyson ate their mutton with Cole; J Nichols, *Literary Anecdotes,* VIII 578.

31 A summary of the original scandal is given in Fawcett, *op cit.,* pp xi–xiii and references to its unwitting revival by Gough in 1780 in W S Lewis, *op. cit.,* II, 242–3.

32 W S Lewis, *op. cit.,* II, 151–2.

33 W S Lewis, *op. cit.,* I, 214.

34 BL Add MS 5842, 333.

35 A design by Essex for a tower at St Clement's is recorded in a note to J Nichols, *Literary Anecdotes,* I, 712 as being in BL Add MS 5173 but that volume has been missing from the British Museum for over a century. It is possible that the present tower of 1821/2 (formerly with a spire) by Charles Humfrey reflects Essex's design. Humfrey's father worked for Essex at St Edward's Church in 1784 and may have had access to his papers after his death.

36 Quotation from Cole's will in W M Palmer, *William Cole of Milton,* 1935, 29.

37 W S Lewis, *op. cit.,* I, 92.

38 Letter from Essex to Dean and Chapter of Lincoln of 16 December 1779; Lincoln Chapter archives, on deposit in Lincolnshire County Record Office, A/4/16 item 26.

39 W S Lewis, *op. cit,* I, 190–2, 203–6.

40 Both men wrote journals of the tour. Nothing is known of Tyson's but Essex's was published by the Cambridge Antiquarian Society in 1888 (see full reference in note 1); the original MS is lost.

41 There is a list of Essex's publications in Fawcett, *op. cit.,* xxxiii–xxxiv.

42 BL Add MS 6772 ff 97–111.

43 BL Add MS 6771 f 204v.

44 BL Add MS 6771 f 200v.

45 BL Add MS 6772 f 267.

46 *Ibid* f 273.

47 BL Add MS 6772 ff 260, 265: the roof was restored to its original form in 1800.

48 *Ibid* f 5.

49 BL Add MS 6762 f 16v.

50 *Ibid*.

51 *Ibid*.

52 BL Add MS 6768, 63: in 1750 the W. front of the cathedral had been rebuilt with 'round balls and other such vile ornaments' to the irritation of Bishop Lyttelton: BL Add MS 5841, 57.

53 Lincoln Chapter archives, A/4/13 item 11.

54 *Ibid*, item 7.

55 Lincoln Chapter archives, A/4/16 item 3. Lumby's estimate for the new vestry furnishings was £23–12–6d.

56 Lincoln Chapter archives, A/4/13 item 9.

57 Lincoln Chapter archives, A/4/15 items 12 & 13.

58 J Perkins, *Westminster Abbey, Its Worship & Ornaments* (Alcuin Club Collections), 1938–52, I, 135–42.

59 BL Add MS 6776 ff 58, 65–6.

60 A copy of the printed Advertisement of 1756 is at BL Add MS 6772 f 2. In 1771 Essex was alarmed lest Thomas Sandby forestalled him but it was discovered, via Cole and Horace Walpole, that Sandby only wanted illustrations of the chapel for his Royal Academy lectures on architecture: (W S Lewis, *op. cit.* II, 208, 211.) The King's book was still being considered in 1782; (J Nichols ed. *Illustrations of the Literary History of the Eighteenth Century*, 1817–58, VI 292–3.)

61 W S Lewis, *op. cit.*, I, 184 for the letter for 3 August 1769 from Cole to Horace Walpole forwarding Essex's request for help from Walpole in planning such a work and *idem* I, 190–2 for Walpole's reply suggesting how a collaborative history of Gothic might be organised.

62 BL Add MS 6771 f 121.

63 BL Add MS 6771 ff 1, 197

64 *Ibid* f 197.

65 The only full analysis of Essex's treatise so far attempted is the unpublished thesis by Y Jerrold, *A study of James Essex of Cambridge, Architect and Antiquarian*, Cambridge University, School of Architecture, 1977.

66 BL Add MS 6771 f 198v.

67 Fawcett, *op. cit.* xxiv/xxv.

68 J Nichols, *Literary Anecdotes*, VIII, 610.

69 W S Lewis, *op cit.*, I, 340. Cole is characteristically sharp: Essex's writings, even when not polished for publication, show no great lack of grammar or powers of expression.

70 W S Lewis, *op cit.*, XXXII, 322.

71 J Nichols, *Literary Anecdotes*, VI, 625.

72 A C Pugin, *Specimens of Gothic Architecture* (the literary part by E J Willson), 1821–3, pp xvi–xvii.

73 Willis and Clark, *op. cit*, III, 545 & 543.

74 *The Architects' and Builders' Journal*, 31 December 1910, 22.

75 N Pevsner, *Some Architectural Writers of the 19th Century*, 1972, 2–8.

7 THOMAS HOPPER

1 *Br* vol xiv 1856, 481.

2 Sir John Summerson, *Architecture in Britain 1530–1830*, 1953, 297.

3 Quoted in 'Thomas Hopper' by Charlotte Fell Smith, *Essex Review*, Vol xxiii 1914, 145.

4 Information from Mr J Smith, Essex County Library, Southend.

5 *The Diary of Joseph Farington*, March 12th 1810.

6 Faulkner, *History of Fulham*, 1812.

7 For a fuller description of Hopper's work at Melford see G Jackson-Stops, 'Thomas Hopper at Melford and Erddig' in *National Trust Studies 1981*.

8 The catalogue for the sale of the estate in 1921 gives the date of the conservatory as 1831. There is a copy of the catalogue in the NMR, London.

9 For Hopper's work as a prison architect see Robin Evans, *The Fabrication of Virtue*, CUP 1982.

10 Essex RO: Q/SBG 605/51.

11 John Vivian Hughes, *Margam Castle*, 1981.

12 *Gentleman's Magazine*, August 1836.

13 Atlas Fire Assurance Co Directors Minutes are in the Guildhall Library, London.

14 Robin Evans: *The Fabrication of Virtue — English Prison architecture 1750–1840*. CUP 1982.
Robin Fedden: Neo-Norman in *Architectural Review* Dec 1954.
John Vivian Hughes: *Margam Castle* 1981.
G Jackson-Stops: Thomas Hopper at Erddig and Melford in *National Trust Studies* 1981.
T Mowl: Neo-Norman — unpublished Oxford doctoral thesis.
Arthus Searle: Thomas Hopper, *Essex Journal* vol v Oct 1970.
Charlotte Fell Smith: Thomas Hopper, *Essex Review* vol xxiii 1914.

8 SAMUEL TEULON

The author gratefully acknowledges the help of: Peter Allen, David Isherwood, Paul Joyce, Mrs Marjorie Levy, Chris Pickford and Treve Rosoman. A number of the designs in the two RIBA Sketchbooks are unidentified. A Market Cross design for an unspecified location was exhibited at the RA 1844. Sir John Summerson possesses an original drawing executed by Teulon of 'A Villa now erecting for a Gentleman' in Surrey exhibited at the RA in 1834 at a time when Teulon was employed by George Porter. The Archives of Jesus College, Cambridge contain an undated plan for reseating and repaving the nave of the College Chapel credited to Teulon.

1 H S Goodhart-Rendel, *Rogue Architects of the Victorian Era*, RIBA Journal, Vol. 56, 1949, 251.

2 S Smiles, *The Huguenots,* 1905.

3 For a short biography of William Teulon, see article by Charles E Lee in the *Camden History Review,* 1977. He lived 1823–1900.

4 Will, 1872 (2) 387 (Somerset House).

5 Gavin Stamp, 'Sir Gilbert Scott's Recollections' in *Architectural History,* Vol 19, 1976, 55.

6 *HMC.*

7 Beds. CRO R4/4140 etc.

8 *Eccl.* 1856, 79.

9 James Stevens Curl, *The Life and Work of Henry Roberts,* Phillimore 1983.

10 Peter Allen, dissertation, University of Newcastle upon Tyne, January 1981.

11 Treve Rosoman, Vol. 31, 1980, of *Transactions of the London and Middlesex Archaeological Society.*

12 Matthew Saunders, *The Churches of S S Teulon,* The Ecclesiological Society, 1982.

9 DAVID RHIND

The author is especially grateful to David Walker who, with characteristic generosity, placed his biographical notes on Rhind at the author's disposal. The catalogue of works attached to this essay is wholly his. For particular help the author is indebted to Richard Emerson and Duncan Bull. Colin Johnston of the Scottish Record, Maurice Berrill of The Company of Merchants of the City of Edinburgh, John Gifford of the Buildings of Scotland Research Unit and Joe Rock all entered into pursuit of Rhind with an enthusiasm which deserves special mention. The author is grateful to the following scholars for their specialist guidance; Mrs Alexandra Wedgwood, Dr James Macaulay, Dr David Blissett and Dr Rory O'Donnell. The author has also to thank the staff of the following institutions, owners of Rhind houses and guardians of archives for their help and kindness:

— John G Dunbar, Catherine Cruft, Janet Christie and Christopher Campbell of the Royal Commission on the Ancient and Historical Monuments of Scotland.

— Mr & Mrs Wilson Marshall of Carlowrie and Sir Peter Hutchison Bt.

— John Christie-Miller for so generously allowing me to quote from his unpublished family history with its details of the Craigentinny Mausoleum.

— Miss Craig-Brown for information about Ettrick Lodge.

— Dick Peddie & McKay Architects, Edinburgh.

— Joanna Mundy and Dr Walter Makie of the City of Edinburgh District Council.

— Elizabeth Brady, Tristram Clarke and B G Dale of the Episcopal Church of Scotland.

— Miss Ierne Grant.

— Dr David Howarth.

— Mr J Innes of The Life Association of Scotland.

— Charles McKean of the Royal Incorporation of Architects in Scotland.

— The Company of Merchants of the City of Edinburgh.

— Dr Lindsay Errington and James Holloway of the National Galleries of Scotland.

— Professor Alistair Rowan.

— Christina Hunter Robertson and Mr I Morton of The Royal Bank of Scotland.

— George Bryden of The Royal Society of Edinburgh.

— Elizabeth Beaton and Aonghus MacKechnie of the Scottish Development Department Historic Buildings Section.

— Hugh T Stevenson.

1 A portrait of Rhind was exhibited at the 1907 Edinburgh Architectural Exhibition, 214 in the catalogue.

2 David Williamsom Robertson Ewart. (Information from John Gifford). The use of Williamson in the Rhind family as a christian name probably recalls the family's connection with Lord Balgray.

3 SRO GD/224/508/1/57. I am indebted to Colin Johnston for directing me to this source.

4 However as John Gifford has pointed out, Smith was interested in architectural education as the publication of his *Elements of Architecture* in 1827 shows.

5 The elder Pugin's establishment may have been more in the nature of a school than a conventional office. Information from Rory O'Donnell.

6 John Christie-Miller, *'The Miller Inheritance',* unpublished 1982.

7 Dr James Macaulay tells me that James Gillespie Graham had a villa at Seafield called 'Viewfield'. Although it has not been identified it is of interest that the Grahams and the Rhinds were neighbours.

8 It is just possible that Playfair acted as a mentor to Rhind. David Walker has suggested that Rhind's design for Stewart's Hospital is indebted to Playfair's preliminary schemes for Donaldsons's Hospital.

9 Robert Strathern Lindsay, *History of the Masons Lodge of Holyrood House, St Luke's No*

44, 1935. I am indebted to Joe Rock for drawing this to my notice.

10 Extracts from Rhind's speech are published in the *Building Chronicle* 1st Jan. 1855.

11 Christopher Christie, *The Institute of Architects in Scotland,* Exhibition catalogue to *Mr David Bryce* University of Edinburgh 1976, eds. Valerie Fiddes and Alistair Rowan. The papers quoted by Christie are in SRO GD224/510/3/3. In the Playfair Letter Book 7 deposited in Edinburgh University Library there is on 8th January 1841 a copy of Playfair's letter to Rhind enclosing his subscription to the Institute. For the refounding of the Institute see *The Builder,* Nov 30th 1850.

12 *Building Chronicle* 1st January 1855.

13 *Transactions of the Architectural Institute of Scotland,* Second Session 1851–52 No VIII, 'On the Respective Claims of Inigo Jones, Dr Balcanquall Dean of Rochester; William Wallace, — to have been the Designer of Heriot's Hospital by David Rhind Esq, Architect FRSE and FAIS' (The lecture was in reply to an earlier paper by David Laing).

Although Rhind's family papers and drawings were available in 1907, when the organisers of the Edinburgh Architectural Association drew on them for their exhibition, unfortunately no trace of the collection can be found today. Rhind died in London at 19 Selwood Terrace, Onslow Gardens on the 26th of April 1883. The house is listed in London Directories as belonging to Mrs Watson. Obituaries appeared in *The Scotman* on the 1st May 1883 and *The Builder* of 12th May 1883. The principal source of information on Rhind's family is his Testament SRO SC/70/1/254. After the death of his brother McDuff there is an additional Testament SRO SC/70/1/254. McDuff's death certificate of 1st October 1885 and Testament SRO SC 70/1/215 contain useful supplementary information on the family. Their father's Testament of 1833 has the reference SRO SC/70/1/48.

In 1969 Hugh T Stevenson now of Glasgow Museums and Art Gallery, Kelvingrove, wrote an undergraduate thesis on David Rhind for the University of Edinburgh. The author greatly regrets that he was unable to consult Mr Stevenson's thesis during the preparation of this essay but there is now a copy in the library of the National Monuments Record of Scotland.

Rhind's practice was run from the following addresses: 1834–5, 6 Forres Street; 1836–38, 11 Abercromby Place; 1839–40, 24 Duke Street; 1841–42, 12 Dublin Street; 1834–48, 24 Northumberland Street; 1849–1877, 54 Great King Street; 1878–1880, 19 Hill Street. His pupils included John Alex Hamilton, Robert Morham,

H J Blanc (inf. from David Walker) and John Peddie (inf. from Richard Emerson).

10 ERNEST NEWTON

Since going to print it has come to the author's attention that Philip Webb's interesting relationship with classicism is at present being explored by Sheila Kirk, who presented some of her discoveries at an exhibition at the Cleveland Art Centre, Middlesbrough in May 1984, reviewed in *Building Design* May 25th 1984 by Mark Swenarton.

1 E S Prior, 'The Origins of the Guild', Lecture to the Guild, 6 December, 1895, in H J L J Massé, *The Art Worker's Guild 1884–1934,* Oxford, 1935, 6.

2 W R Lethaby, *Architecture, Mysticism and Myth,* republished London, 1973, 3.

3 Quoted from Newton's notebook in W G Newton, *The Work of Ernest Newton RA,* London, 1925, 16.

4 Basil Jackson ed. *Recollections of Thomas Graham Jackson,* London, 1950, 121.

5 M Girouard, *Sweetness and Light,* Oxford, 1977, 18. Warrington Taylor and E R Robson, later architect to the London School Board, were members of the circle around Morris and Webb in the 1860s.

6 A Saint, *Richard Norman Shaw,* 2nd ed., London and New Haven, 1983, 185–191.

7 Ernest Newton, *Sketches for Country Residences,* London, 1882.

8 R N Shaw, *Sketches for cottages and other buildings,* London, 1878.

9 Ernest Newton, *A Book of Houses,* London, 1890. Newton published one later book, *A Book of Country Houses,* London, 1903.

10 Basil Jackson, *op. cit.,* 37.

11 W G Newton, *op. cit.,* 15.

12 I Nairn and N Pevsner, *The Buildings of England: Surrey,* London 1971, 301.

13 *Br* Vol. 56, 147, 168, for the lecture that Brydon gave to the Architectural Association in February, 1889, entitled 'The English Renaissance'.

14 Ruskin stressed changefulness as the second characteristic of Gothic architecture in his chapter 'The Nature of Gothic' in *The Stones of Venice,* first published in 1851.

15 Ludwick Corner was originally intended to be of diapered brickwork on the first floor.

16 Written by Lethaby in his obituary of Newton in the *Architectural Review.*

17 A Saint, *op. cit.,* 371–74.

18 A Saint, *op. cit.,* 398–99.

19 W R Lethaby, *Philip Webb and his work,* reprinted London, 1979; quoted in introduction by G Rubens, v.

20 Lethaby, Newton obituary, *Architectural Review.*

LIST OF WORKS

1 SIR ROGER PRATT

1650S GARDEN PAVILION, RMCS Beckett Hall, Shrivenham, Oxfordshire. Attributed.

*c.*1657/8–*c.*1662 COLESHILL HOUSE, Oxfordshire. Gutted by fire in 1952 and subsequently demolished. 4 pairs of gate piers and a dovecote (possibly contemporary) remain.

*c.*1660s WARWICK HOUSE, Warwick House Street, London. Attributed. Dem. 1827
LORD ALINGTON'S HOUSE, Bloomsbury, London. Attributed. Restoration work.

1663–1665 KINGSTON LACY, Dorset. Greatly altered by Sir Charles Barry in 1835–46. Acquired by The National Trust in 1982. Since then much archaeological investigation has taken place in the house. The author wishes to acknowledge the advice of Antony Cleminson concerning the 'pergolo'.
HORSEHEATH HALL, Cambridgeshire. Dem. late 18th century. No remains above ground.

1664–1667 CLARENDON HOUSE, Piccadilly, London. Dem. 1683. No remains.

1669–1672 RYSTON HALL, Norfolk. Altered beyond recognition by Soane (*c.*1788) Further alterations made early this century.

2 JAMES LEONI

1715 WREST PARK, Silsoe, Bedfordshire for Henry Grey, 1st Duke of Kent (1671–1740). Three signed drawings by Leoni survive [Beds CRO, *Lucas and Dingwall MSS*], comprising one of two proposals for rebuilding the house, prepared shortly before July 1715, when the Duke sent them to his son, the Earl of Harrold, then Grand-Touring, to solicit the opinions of the 'best Architects and Judges'. Harrold, and his tutor, Mr Gerard, showed them to Filippo Juvarra on reaching Turin in Oct. Juvarra was critical, and sent a version of his own. Gerard's report to the Duke of Oct 20 contains Juvarra's criticisms in detail, and is very instructive. In the event the Duke used neither proposal, and the house was probably unaltered. It was an irregular courtyard house of mediaeval origins, with an imposing 19-bay Palladian front of Pratt/North type, applied in the 1670's. Leoni's first proposal retains the 1670s front, but replaces the irregular early buildings with modern apartments built around 2 courtyards. Juvarra's comments indicate that the other proposal was of half-H plan, the main block linked to the wings by open 'porticos'. The house was pulled down and replaced in 1834 [*CL*, 25 June, 2 July 1970]. It now houses the National Institute of Agricultural Engineering. Further drawings by Leoni in the same collection include 7 designs for arcades to flank the south parterre at Wrest, 2 alternative designs for a Keeper's Lodge, and 1 for an obelisk (among a number of obelisk designs which the Duke solicited from various architects), also presumably intended for Wrest. [Timothy Hudson, 'A Ducal Patron of Architects', *CL*, 17 January [1974].

1719 TRIUMPHAL ARCH, Hyde Park, London, for General James Stanhope, 1st Earl Stanhope. Leoni published his designs in his *Alberti*, from which all surviving information is known. The patron was apparently Stanhope, then Secretary of State, and owner of Chevening, where he employed Nicholas Dubois, Leoni's collaborator (as translator) on the edition of *Palladio* [HMC, 276]. The arch was intended 'to the Immortal Memory of George I', then still alive, so its political intent and iconography are doubtless richer than is now apparent. The plate in *Alberti*, on the other hand, was dedicated to Algernon Seymour, Earl of Hertford. [James Leoni, *The Architecture of Leon Battista Alberti*, 1726, pls 1–2].

*c.*1722. 7, BURLINGTON GARDENS, Westminster, London, for John Bligh, created Lord Clifton in September 1721, and subsequently Viscount Darnley (1723), and Earl of Darnley (1725). Sometime in 1722 Clifton surrendered the still unfinished house, which was held on a building lease from Lord Burlington, to Charles Douglas, 3rd Duke of Queensberry, who took out another lease from Lord Burlington on 4 March 1723. Leoni published his designs in some detail in his *Alberti* (1726) [pls 14–15], and this evidence is supplemented by John Bligh's (as he then still was) agreement with his builder, the bricklayer John Witt, to follow 'the plans now drawn and designed by Ja. L.', which dates Leoni's designs to shortly before 12 April 1721. The Duke of Queensberry was first cousin to Lord Burlington, and a good draughtsman himself. He had met with Kent in Italy even before Lord Burlington. The Duke and Duchess were significant patrons of the arts, famous in particular for their support of Gay, who died at 7 Burlington Gardens in 1732. In 1725 they inherited Amesbury House, Wilts (designed by John Webb), and began improvements, but to the designs of Flitcroft, rather than Leoni [information from Miss Juliet Allen]. The house was unfinished when sold to the Duke, and Witt entered into an agreement with him to complete it. The details of this show that little had to be done to the exterior, but that the interior, including floors and stairs, was scarcely started. Unfortunately none of Leoni's interior details survive, as the house was extended and internally altered in 1785 by John Vardy the younger for the 1st Earl of Uxbridge. In 1855 it became a branch of the Bank of England, and was further altered by Philip Hardwick. In 1878, it was partly gutted to provide the present large banking hall, designed by P C Hardwick. It now houses the Royal Bank of Scotland. [*Survey of London*, XXXII, 455–66].

1723 ARGYLL HOUSE, Kings Road, Chelsea, London, for John Pierene. Leoni published his designs in his *Alberti* [pls 20–2], which dates it and names the patron [p. 4v]. The date is confirmed by two rainwater heads on the garden front, stamped P 1723 , and the patron J A appears (as John Perrin) in the ratebooks as the householder from 1724 to 1740. Beyond this nothing is known about him. The house, which still exists, is a suburban villa, whose accommodation is described by Leoni in *Alberti* [4v]. It owes its name to the rather brief occupancy of John, 4th Duke of Argyll, from 1769 to 1770. [*Survey of London*, IV, 82–3 and pls 84–99].

1722/3–27 CARSHALTON PARK, Surrey, for Thomas Scawen. Leoni published his designs in his *Alberti*, where they are dated 1723 and 1727. Thomas Scawen inherited the estate and manor of Carshalton from his uncle, Sir William Scawen, 'a great merchant who ventured almost all his property in the cause of William III' [Victoria County History, *Surrey: Hundred of Wallington*, 183]. Sir William bought it in 1696, and died in 1722, leaving instructions in his will that Thomas was to build the house 'as neare to and agreeable to the Modell I now have as may be' [*HMC*, 513]. We could assume that the model followed Leoni's design; if so, the design cannot be later than 1722, and both generations of Scawens were Leoni's patrons, for he was certainly employed by Thomas. On the other hand, Thomas may have ignored his uncle's will, favouring Leoni in preference to an earlier architect. Three letters sent by Leoni to Peter Legh of Lyme between Sept 1725 and Sept 1726 [John Rylands University Library of Manchester, *Legh of Lyme Muniments*] convey Scawen's service to Legh and suggest that Leoni was occupied at Carshalton over that period. One is actually written from Carshalton, on 7 Sept 1725, and says explicitly that 'The Workmen ... are now in ye highth of their bussiness, ... much forwarder than I could have expected'. So it was evidently begun, although nothing survived into the present century other than some gate piers [Hudson, 'A Venetian Architect in England', *cit.*, fig. 5], and since there are no known views

or descriptions of the finished house, it was probably not finished. Scawen's son James disposed of the estate in 1781. The house was Leoni's largest country house, and his most intriguing design.

1725–40 LYME PARK, Lyme Handley, Cheshire, for Peter Legh. Building accounts [Stockport Central Library] document the chronology from 1727 to 1738, but do not mention Leoni. Letters from Leoni to Legh [*Legh Muniments, cit.*], however, prove Leoni's responsibility for the design of the W. front (May–June 1725), the S. front (in draft Oct 1725; finished drawings sent Aug 1726), and the courtyard (draft Aug 6 1726; queried by workmen Aug 26 1726). Leoni's letters also show that he sent finished drawings for stables (Apr 1740), which were probably never built, as Lewis Wyatt sent another set in 1818 and the present stables were built by Alfred Darbyshire in 1863. In April 1740 Leoni was also being consulted about the terraces, and walls to the ponds. In addition 12 unsigned and undated drawings are almost certainly in Leoni's hand; 6 are full scale drawings for the workmen; 3 are finished drawings for those parts of the building which the letters prove were designed by Leoni; 1 is a drawing for stables, probably the drawing discussed in his letter of April 1740; 2 are finished drawings in Leoni's hand, of the courtyard, and of a section of the hall, suggesting that Leoni was responsible for this last also. The letters reveal that Peter Legh introduced Leoni to a number of other Cheshire gentlemen, notably Sir William Meredith of Henbury (an amateur architect), Edward Wright of Stretton (the author of a book of continental travels), and Sir Richard Grosvenor of Eaton. Lyme was a 16th century courtyard house of considerable magnificence, which had already been much improved in the late 17th century by the Platt family of mason-architects. The house was further altered by Lewis Wyatt in 1815–8, and by Philippe Amadée Joubert in the early 20th century. [John Cornforth, 'Lyme Park, Cheshire', *CL*, CLVI, 5, 12, 19 and 26 Dec 1974).

*c.*1726 WYCOMBE HOUSE (now Wycombe Abbey), High Wycombe, Buckinghamshire, for Henry Petty, 1st Earl of Shelburne. A letter from J Watson to Peter Legh of Lyme [*Legh Muniments, cit.*], conveying Leoni's terms to Legh, explains 'says he I have 15 guineas when I go but as far as Wickham to my Lord Shelbourn, wch is 27 miles + stay out but two nights'. The date of this letter is 5 April 1726, and it suggests that whatever Leoni was doing for Lord Shelburne, it had already been designed by that date. The unidentified activity was probably the building of

Wycombe House; for a 3 storey, 7 bay early Georgian house on this site is illustrated in Harrison and Co, *Picturesque Views of the Principal Seats of the Nobility and Gentry in England and Wales*, c.1788. Lord Shelburne was the son of the famous Sir William Petty, and was married to Lady Arabella Boyle, Lord Burlington's aunt [Burke's *Peerage* ..., 1953, 492 (Cork and Orrery), and 1222 (Lansdowne)]. He bought the estate and manor of Loakes, High Wycombe in 1700 and 'considerably enlarged and improved' the manor house [Lysons, *Magna Britannia*, I, 1806, 676]. He was MP for Wycombe, and was raised to an Irish peerage in 1709. He died in 1751, leaving his estates to the Hon John Fitzmaurice, son of his sister Anne by Thomas, 1st Earl of Kerry. Fitzmaurice was created Viscount Fitzmaurice in 1751, and Earl of Shelburne of the second, and present creation in 1753. His son, William, was Prime Minister, and was created 1st Marquess of Lansdowne in 1784 [Burke, *op. cit.*]. Lord Lansdowne entertained his famously intellectual circle at Wycombe, and the house was praised for its beauty by Wesley in 1775 [*Victoria County History, Buckinghamshire*, III, 114]. He sold it in 1798 [High Wycombe Public Library, C9.SM 188, Sale Particulars of Shelburne Estate, 13 and 14 Aug 1798], and it was rebuilt by James Wyatt for the 1st Lord Carrington between then and 1806 [Lysons, *op. cit.*]. Lord Carrington re-named it Wycombe Abbey, and his successor sold it to Wycombe Abbey School in 1896. Although the archaeology of the present house indicates that Wyatt's work incorporates an earlier building, there is no evident trace of work of Leoni's period.

1727 CLIVEDEN HOUSE, Taplow, Buckinghamshire, for Lord George Hamilton, Earl of Orkney. A portfolio among the Cliveden architectural drawings contains 5 drawings which together comprise 2 alternative proposals for a country house. One is signed by Leoni, and dated 1727; the others demonstrably accompany it. It has been suggested [Gervase Jackson-Stops, 'The Cliveden Album: drawings by Archer, Leoni and Gibbs for the 1st Earl of Orkney', *Architectural History*, 19, 1976, 5] that these were proposals for rebuilding Cliveden House. They were not, however, submitted at the same time as Leoni's other proposals for Cliveden (*q.v.*), and could be for any country house. Since an alternative location has not occurred to me, I have referred to them (in the text) as 'Cliveden 1' and 'Cliveden 2'. Cliveden was, in the event, not rebuilt until 1851, by Barry [*HMC*, 92].

1728 SHARDELOES HOUSE, Amersham, Buckinghamshire, for Montagu Garrard Drake. Leoni supplied designs for a new house, which was begun, but probably left off almost immediately owing to the death of Montagu Garrard Drake in 1728 [Burke's *Landed Gentry* ..., 1965, I, 212] (Tyrwhitt-Drake, formerly of Shardeloes). His bill [Bucks CRO *Drake MSS*, D/DR/5/1] specifies sketches of 4 new fronts, made on January 10 1728, four days surveying the old house on February 13, seven drawings of a new proposal (2 plans, 4 elevations, and 1 section) on February 29, larger scale drawings for the workmen on March 9, moulding profiles on March 14, and directing the workmen beginning the new house on March 16. The bill is addressed to Drake as if he were still alive, so it could be that Leoni's responsibilities were always intended to end at this point. Or it could have been addressed to him fictionally, but destined for his widow. Leoni, among other creditors, had to sue for its settlement, in 1732. Shardeloes, seat of the Drakes since the time of Queen Elizabeth, was a 17th century house; but an 18th century view of it shows a modern office and stable courtyard on its north side, which are probably those which still survive. It is possible that these were Leoni's design, but it does not sound like what he billed for. They may instead be the 'new building' erected by Francis Smith of Warwick in the two years before Leoni's arrival [*Drake MSS, cit.*, D/DR/9, 31]. The house was eventually replaced, after the minority of Drake's son, William, but to the designs of Stiff Leadbetter in 1758 [*HMC*, 509]. It is now divided into flats.

1728–45 MOULSHAM HALL, Chelmsford, Essex, for Benjamin Mildmay, 1st Earl Fitzwalter. Lord Fitzwalter had to buy his family seat from his sister-in-law, the dowager Lady Fitzwalter, in May 1728. Three weeks later Leoni visited, and on 15 July was paid £21 for plans. Work began immediately, and Lord Fitzwalter laid the first brick later that month. As completed, it was a courtyard house [*Vitruvius Britannicus* IV, 1767, 30–1], and the accounts reveal that it was built one range at a time: it seems likely therefore that its predecessor was also a courtyard house, demolished one range at a time. In Oct 1729 the S. front was roofed, and the family moved in in May 1730. In Sept 1729 the first pin was driven into the E. front, and in Nov 1730 the plasterers were at work on its interior. In May 1732 the old west front was pulled down, by autumn the shell of the new one was complete, and in Aug 1733 joinery in the west range was finished. Before the final side was begun, ten years later, new stables were built, between summer 1735 and July

1737, and a brewhouse, dairy, wash house and laundry were completed (foundations laid April 1735: complete by Sept 1740). The foundations of the north side were laid in May 1743, and Artari was paid for plasterwork in the Great Room in 1745–6. Leoni was repeatedly paid for plans, for supervision, for setting out foundations and for other more specific tasks. It is clear that he was the architect for all of the above. Leoni was evidently confident that he was to be retained as architect of Moulsham, and borrowed money in advance. When he was ill, Lord Fitzwalter supported him. He also worked for Fitzwalter's step-son, the 4th Earl of Holderness, and may have done more (as yet unidentified) work for this family. The house was demolished in 1816. [A C Edwards, *The Account Books of Benjamin Mildmay, Earl Fitzwalter*, 1977].

After 1724 MOOR PARK, Rickmansworth, Hertfordshire, for Benjamin Styles, after 1724. The exterior and most of the interior were completed, unambiguously to the design of Sir James Thornhill, by June 1728, when Thornhill and Styles went to law. But there is a persistent attribution to Leoni, dating from 1806 [Britton and Brayley, *Beauties of England and Wales*, 7, 1806]. And, when Thornhill quarrelled with Styles, his paintings in the hall were taken down and replaced by Amigoni's more classical works; while in 1732 Sleter was engaged to paint the staircase. Both Amigoni and Sleter were friends of Leoni, and Leoni's son was probably apprenticed to Sleter [*HMC*, 512, n. 2]. There may therefore be some truth in this old attribution. Possibly Leoni advised Styles after Thornhill's dismissal in 1728, but this is only a guess, and it is not possible to say what, if anything, Leoni designed. Styles had made a fortune in South Sea Company stock, and had bought Moor Park, a very large house built in 1680–4 for the Duke of Monmouth, possibly to the design of Hugh May [*HMC*, 545]. The house was subsequently altered by Gibbs (1730), Brettingham (1751–4), Adam (1763–5), Cundy junior (1830), and William Burn (1879) [*HMC*, 343, 136, 52, 246, and 166], and now belongs to Moor Park Golf Club. [T P Hudson, 'Moor Park, Leoni and Sir James Thornhill', *Burlington Magazine* CXIII, Nov 1971, 657].

1731–8 BOLD HALL, Prescot, Merseyside, for Peter Bold. A panel in a corridor of Bold Hall was
inscribed P $\overset{B}{\underset{1731}{A}}$. The attribution to Leoni was made in E Twycross, *Mansions of England*, III, 1847, 27–8. No further documentation survives to confirm or deny these facts, except that, among the papers of the carver Henry

Watson of Bakewell is a design dated 1738 for a chimneypiece, annotated 'This design was made by Mr Leoni, the ornaments I performed in wood for Peter Bold, Esq'. [Rupert Gunnis, *Dictionary of British Sculptors 1660–1851*, 1951, 414]. On Bold's death in 1762, Bold Hall passed first to the Pattens of Bank Hall, Warrington, thence to the Hoghtons of Hoghton Tower. It was eventually sold in 1858 to William Whitacre Tipping, an eccentric and millionaire Wigan cotton-spinner, whose heirs sold it c.1899 to a colliery company, Bold Hall Estate Ltd. Shortly thereafter the house was demolished, and the property now belongs to the National Coal Board. [Victoria County History, *Lancashire: Hundred of West Derby*, 406–7].

CLANDON PARK, West Clandon, Surrey, for Thomas Onslow, 2nd Lord Onslow, ?1731–3. Horace Walpole first attributed Clandon to Leoni ['Visits to Country Seats', *Walpole Society* XVI, 61], but no documentation has so far been discovered to corroborate this. Manning [*History of Surrey*, 1809–14] and Neale [*Views of Seats*, 2nd series, III, 1826] both gave a date of 1731, and two rainwater heads are dated 1733. Family tradition has it that Frederick, Prince of Wales, was entertained to dinner there in 1729, and Defoe described it as being 're-edified' before 1724 [*Tour ...*, I, 1724, addenda], but it has been argued that this must refer to an earlier house, as Leoni would have surely included an illustration of it in his *Alberti*, had it been designed before 1729. [Although the publication date of *Alberti* is 1726, some of the plates are dated 1729] [John Cornforth, *Clandon Park, Surrey*, National Trust Guidebook, 1979, 15]. On the other hand the same could be said of Lyme or Moulsham, designed in 1725 and 1728 respectively. So an earlier date is possible. Some small alterations were made to Clandon by the 4th Lord Onslow after 1776, and in 1876 the 4th Earl Onslow replaced the entrance steps with a *porte-cochère*. In 1956 the house was given to the National Trust. [H Avray Tipping 'Clandon Park, Surrey', *CL*, LCII, 10, 17 and 24 Sept 1927].

1732 MONUMENT TO DANIEL PULTENEY, East Cloister Walk, Westminster Abbey, London. The monument is signed by Leoni (architect), and Rysbrack (sculptor), but no further documentation is known. Daniel Pulteney was first cousin to William Pulteney, created Earl of Bath in 1742, famous largely for his opposition to Walpole. He died on 7 Sept 1731, and was originally buried in St James, Piccadilly. His remains were removed to the site of the monument on 17 May 1732, and Leoni's design may therefore precede this date [*Dictionary of National Biography*, 1975,

(Compact edition), 468].

1733–42 THORNDON HALL, West Horndon, Essex, for Robert James Petre, 8th Lord Petre. 3 plans, comprising between them 2 alternative proposals for re-modelling Thorndon Hall, exist among the Petre papers. They are evidently a set; 2 are dated 1733; 1 is signed by Leoni. A certain amount was done, for a MS note on the back of one plan records that in 'the year 1734–5: Robert James, Lord Petre, began pulling down the East side which he rebuilt (according to the plans within this) adding the new East wing to the old West one, with a Portico in the center, which was never put up tho' finished ready, his death occasioned by the smallpox 1743 prevented the works from being compleated'. After a minority of 20 years, the next Lord Petrre pulled the house down and built a new house 1½ miles north to the designs of James Paine. Tradition has it that Paine used the cut but unused stones of Leoni's projected portico for the new house. The portico has fluted columns of huge dimensions, quite characteristic of Leoni. Thorndon Hall was a splendid house of 1575, built by John Petre, the son of a leading Tudor civil servant. [J C Ward, *Old Thorndon Hall*, 1972].

1735 THE MANSION HOUSE, London, for the Corporation of the City of London. On March 15 a Committee appointed to build a mansion house for the Lord Mayor invited Gibbs, John James and Leoni to attend. On May 8 Gibbs and Leoni submitted drafts of plans, and on Dec 18 a total of 5 architects had by now submitted finished schemes. On 27 July 1736 the Committee eventually recommended George Dance's proposals. On 3 March 1737 the unsuccessful competitors received premiums, Gibbs 100 gns, James 75 gns, Leoni 50 gns, and Batty Langley 20 gns. Leoni's drawings cannot be located. [S Perks, *A History of the Mansion House*, 1922, 165–73].

1735 THE OCTAGON TEMPLE, Cliveden House, Taplow, Buckinghamshire, for Lord George Hamilton, 1st Earl of Orkney. 9 drawings from the Cliveden collection, all apparently in Leoni's hand, show proposals and working details for this garden building. A letter of 20 June 1735 from Leoni to Lord Orkney proves that he was engaged on an unspecified building for his lordship. As the letter mentions drawing the framing of a cupola, it probably refers to the Octagon Temple, the only domed building on the Cliveden estate. A contract drawing for it, signed by Lord Orkney and Edward Vickers, was witnessed by Leoni. The letter suggests that the Temple was under construction already; the drawing shows that the contractor was Edward Vickers. The Temple still stands in this spectacular river-side garden, now belonging to the National Trust. [Jackson-Stops, *op. cit.*].

THE BLENHEIM PAVILION, Cliveden House, Taplow, Buckinghamshire, for Lord George Hamilton, 1st Earl of Orkney, c.1735. This garden seat has been attributed to Leoni since its mention in sale particulars in 1818. 4 drawings from the Cliveden Collection, all apparently in Leoni's hand, show the Blenheim Pavilion as built. A letter of 20 June 1735 from Leoni to Lord Orkney proves at least that Leoni worked for him, almost certainly designing the Octagon Pavilion (*q.v.*), whose contract drawing Leoni witnessed. Strictly speaking, the Blenheim Pavilion can only be attributed to Leoni, although the draughtsmanship evidence supports the attribution. The Pavilion still stands in this spectacular river-side garden, now belonging to the National Trust. [Jackson-Stops, *op. cit.*].

1735. 4, NEW BURLINGTON STREET, Westminster, London, for Henry Worsley, 1735. A letter from Leoni to Lord Orkney dated 20 June 1735 reveals that he was 'obliged to attende Mr Pulteny and Governor Worsley in order to begin their Buildings'. [Jackson-Stops, *op. cit.*]. Governor Worsley was Henry Worsley, MP, younger brother of Sir Robert Worsley, 4th Bart, of Appuldurcombe House, Isle of Wight. He had been, in 1714, envoy to the court of Portugal, and, in 1721, Governor of Barbados [... Burke, *Extinct and Dormant Baronetcies*, 1841, 581 (Worsley, of Appuldurcombe)]. His 'Building' was No 4 New Burlington Street, leased from the Burlington estate, whose building agreement, signed with the contractors William Grey and Richard Fortnam, bricklayers, dates from just over a month after this letter, 1 Aug 1735. Perhaps it was complete by 20 Dec, when Worsley signed a lease with Gray, Fortnam and Burlington as lessors. It was demolished in 1912, and rebuilt by the architects Niven and Wigglesworth. A photograph of 1898 shows the N. side of New Burlington Street, including No 4. Nothing is known of its interior. [*Survey of London*, XXXII, 451, 552–3].

1735. 82, PICCADILLY, Westminster, London, for William Pulteney, later Earl of Bath. A letter from Leoni to Lord Orkney dated 20 June 1735 reveals that he was 'obliged to attende Mr Pulteny and Governor Worsley in Order to begin their Buildings' [Jackson-Stops, *op. cit.*]. As Daniel Pulteney had died in 1731, and Henry Pulteney might be expected to be styled General, this must refer to William Pulteney, the famous politician, created Earl of Bath in 1742, whose career is well-known. His 'Building' was 82 Piccadilly, later called Bath House, and the letter indicates that it must have been begun in the summer of 1735. It was demolished in 1821, recorded only in a water colour view. [A I Dasent, *Piccadilly*, 1920, 72].

1735–7 ALKRINGTON HALL, Middleton, Lancashire, for Sir Darcy Lever. A copy of the *Builder's Dictionary* (1734) in the Metropolitan Museum of Art, New York, contains the words 'Architect — Leoni' against Alkrington Hall. The words 'Darcy Lever LLD, 1735' are carved on the lintel of the basement door. The keystone of the north door is dated 1736, but this must be Old Style, as it is carved with a knight's helmet, and Lever only received his knighthood in January 1737 [W J Smith, 'Sir Ashton Lever of Alkrington and his Museum, 1729–88', *Transactions of the Lancashire and Cheshire Antiquarian Society*, 72, 1962, 61]. Alkrington Hall still stands, divided into flats. [Peter Fleetwood-Hesketh, 'Alkrington Hall, Lancashire', in H M Colvin and John Harris (eds), *The Country Seat*, 1970, 139–44].

After 1735 MONUMENT TO SIR RICHARD PIGOTT, THOMAS PIGOTT AND LETTICE PIGOTT, Quainton Church, Buckinghamshire, for John Pigott. Sir Richard Pigott, of Doddershall House in the parish of Quainton, died in 1685. He was succeeded by his nephew Thomas, who died in 1704, and the latter's widow Lettice. Lettice died in 1735, and the property passed to a cousin, John Pigott, second son of Robert Pigott of Chetwynd, Shropshire. The monument, which is a collective memorial to John Pigott's benefactors, must therefore have a *terminus post quem* of 1735. It is signed by Leoni. [Victoria Country History, *Buckinghamshire*, 4 (Hundred of Ashendon), 96].

1738. 21, ARLINGTON STREET, Westminster, London, for Field Marshal Richard Boyle, 2nd Viscount Shannon. A volume of 14 drawings (8 plans, 4 sections, and 2 elevations) for this house is signed by Leoni and dated 25 May 1738 [in the possession of Col Roger Fleetwood Hesketh]. The house was built to Leoni's designs with the exception of the proposed 3 bay arcade between hall and staircase, which, as built, was a solid wall with a door at one end. Chambers made some alterations in 1769 for the 3rd Viscount Weymouth [*HMC*, 208], perhaps the front elevation, which is not quite as Leoni designed it. Some early 19th century chimneypieces were installed; otherwise it is much as designed. It now belongs to the National Association of British and Irish Millers Ltd.

1738 BURTON PARK, Barlavington, West Sussex, for Richard Biddulph, 1738. J P Neale [*Views of Seats*, 2nd series, 1, 1824] attributed Burton Park to Leoni. A drawing in the British Museum [Add MS 5674, f. 50] shows the date 1738 in the tympanum sculpture. No further documentation has so far come to light. Burton belonged, since the time of Henry VIII, to the Gorings of Goring, Sussex. On the death of Sir William Goring, 3rd Bart, in 1725, it passed to his sister, Anne, who married Richard Biddulph of Biddulph Grange, near Congleton, Staffordshire, a member of a Papist family [Christopher Hussey, 'Burton Park, Sussex', *CL*, 11 July 1936], and perhaps an acquaintance of Peter Legh of Lyme. The house was burned down in 1826, and rebuilt for John Biddulph by Henry Bassett [*HMC*, 96]. The gatepiers alone appear to remain from Leoni's time.

1738. 4, WHITEHALL YARD, Westminster, London, for Robert Darcy, 4th Earl of Holderness. The house, which was erected out of a ruinous part of the former Palace of Whitehall, by Lord Holderness' father, the 3rd Earl, some time after acquiring it in 1718, was sub-divided by the 4th Earl in 1738. [*Survey of London*, XIII, 152–3]. Leoni was paid £260 'on account' by Lord Holderness in 1740, probably for this work of sub-division [*HMC*, 514]. Lord Holderness was the step-son of Earl Fitzwalter of Moulsham Hall, by whom he had been brought up. He was also the owner of Hornby Castle, near Richmond, North Yorks, and Aston Hall, near Rotherham, South Yorks and it is possible that these payments refer to his other properties [Burke's *Peerage*, 1975, 726, (Darcy de Knayth)]. No 4 Whitehall Yard was acquired by Michael Angelo Taylor, son of the architect Sir Robert Taylor, in 1788, and in 1793 was described as 'scarcely habitable'. In that year Taylor pulled it down, and rebuilt it [*Survey of London, loc. cit.*].

c. 1740 STOWE HOUSE, Stowe, Buckinghamshire for Richard Temple, 1st Viscount Cobham. Two gateways flanking the forecourt on the north side of the house were attributed to Leoni by Seeley, author of the Stowe guidebook, as early as 1744 [B Seeley, *Stowe: A Description of the House and Gardens*, 1744]. Although there appears to be no other documentation, it is difficult to disagree with an attribution made only four years after the event. The east gateway survives, the west one was replaced by school buildings in this century.

c. 1740 LATHOM HOUSE, Lathom, Lancashire, for Sir Thomas Bootle, c. 1740. The date of building is taken from Daniel Defoe's *Tour of England* [Vol III, 1742, 225]. In *Vitruvius Britannicus* IV, 1767, it is illustrated by four plates [plates 94–8]. Two are inscribed 'Leoni Arch', one 'J Leoni', but the fourth is inscribed 'B Leoni'. The same publication has an illustration of Moulsham [pl 31] inscribed 'Battista Leoni'. And, according to Colvin [*HMC*; 512, n. 1], a Battista Leoni occurs in the Westminster Rate Books. His identity has not been established. Lathom was an ancient seat of the Earls of Derby, sold by the Earl to Sir Thomas Bootle, Chancellor to Frederick, Prince of Wales. The Bootles became Bootle-Wilbraham, and subsequently Lords Skelmersdale and Earls of Lathom. The 1st Earl employed T H Wyatt to aggrandise it in 1862. The 3rd Earl had it pulled down in 1929 [*HMC*, 514].

1743 WORTLEY HALL, Wortley, South Yorkshire, for Edward Wortley Montagu, 1743. A pencil draft of the south front of the house almost exactly as it is today is among the Wharncliffe MSS, inscribed on the back 'Rough Draught of the Upright of Wortley by Sigᵣ Leoni, Apr 1743', in the distinctive hand of Edward Wortley Montagu [Sheffield City Library, *Wharncliffe MSS*, Wh M 58/49]. Edward Wortley Montagu, husband of the famous Lady Mary, unsuccessful Whig politician of George I's reign, ambassador to Turkey, and millionaire coal-owner, inherited Wortley Hall from his father Sidney Montagu, who was a younger son of the Earl of Sandwich and who had acquired Wortley by marrying the natural daughter of the last of the Wortley baronets. Only late in life, and long after his separation from his wife and estrangement from his son, did he consider rebuilding his house. At first he employed George Platt of Rotherham, who died almost at once, leaving his business in the hands of his 14 year old son and his widow. Leoni superseded Platt, but the Platt firm continued to act as contractors. The building was added to by Matthew Brettingham (1757–9), John Platt again (1788), John Carr (1800), Peter Atkinson (1800), William Burn and Hugh Stannus. It descended with Wortley-Montagu's family, subsequently Earls of Wharncliffe, until the present earl sold it to Labour's Home for Rest. [Richard Hewlings, 'Wortley Hall', *The Archaeological Journal*, 137, 1980, 397].

3 DAVID & WILLIAM HIORN

1742–52 KIRTLINGTON PARK, Oxfordshire, W Hiorn as clerk of works and master-mason to William Smith, 1742–7, probably in charge thereafter; D Hiorn as master-carpenter. Kirtlington Accounts, History of Art Library, Oxford; Hoare's Bank archives.

1744 ST ANDREW'S CHURCH, Rugby, Warwickshire: monument to Thomas Crossfield. Gunnis, *Dictionary of British Sculptors*.

1747 ST MICHAEL'S CHURCH Coventry, West Midlands, altarpiece by 'Mr Hiorne of Warwick'. [*HMC*].

1748–56 ARBURY HALL, Warwickshire, W Hiorn as principal mason and executant architect to Sir Roger Newdigate; D Hiorn as carpenter. Warwicks CRO: Newdigate papers.

1749–51 ST BARTHOLOMEW'S CHURCH, Birmingham, By W & D Hiorn. Destroyed 1941. [*HMC*].

1749–? FARNBOROUGH HALL, Warwickshire, Reconstructed for William Holbech, possibly to designs by D Hiorn; W Hiorn known to have been employed later. G Jackson-Stops: *Farnborough Hall*; accounts at house.

1749 STONELEIGH ABBEY, Warwickshire, W Hiorn in charge of completion of internal work for 2nd Lord Leigh, following the death of William Smith. Shakespeare Birthplace Trust.

1749–50, DELAPRÉ ABBEY, Northampton: stables and orangery, for Charles Hardy. Stylistic attribution supported by surviving plan of the house probably in William Hiorn's hand.

*c.*1749–52 WOLVERLEY HOUSE, Hereford and Worcester for Edward Knight. Stylistic attribution supported by Knight's knowledge of the Hiorns.

*c.*1749–60 GOPSALL HALL, Leicestershire for Charles Jennens. Offices & garden buildings. RIBA drawings collection.

*c.*1750 COURTEENHALL HALL, Northamptonshire: stables for Sir William Wake. Stylistic attribution.

1751 ACTON SCOTT, Salop: monument to Edward Acton, designed by William Baker. Baker's account book.

1751–2 EDGBASTON HALL, West Midlands, internal alterations for Sir Henry Gough. [*HMC*]

1751–6 DELBURY HALL, Salop, for Captain Frederick Cornwall. Accounts at house.

1752 KING EDWARD'S SCHOOL, Birmingham, library. [*HMC*]
RODE HALL, Cheshire. Plan at house.

1752-8 HOLY CROSS CHURCH, Daventry, Northamptonshire. W Baker's account book; Peterborough DRO.

*c.*1752 LEE PLACE, Charlbury, Oxfordshire, reconstructed for Lord Litchfield. Stylistic attribution, supported by previous connexion with Smiths.

1753 ST MARTIN'S CHURCH, Birmingham, spire repairs & alterations. Removed. [*HMC*].

1753–6 KYRE PARK, Hereford and Worcester, remodelled for Edmund Pytts. Worcs CRO.

1753–65 PACKINGTON HALL, Warwickshire, various work for 3rd & 4th Earls of Aylesford, including internal alterations, stables & other offices. Accounts at house; Warwicks CRO.

1754 GREAT HOUGHTON CHURCH, Northamptonshire. [*HMC*].
WALTON HALL Warwickshire, unidentified work for Sir Charles Mordaunt. Destroyed. Bill at Worcs CRO.
KNOWLE HALL, West Midlands, unidentified work for Benjamin Palmer. Destroyed. Bill at

Worcs CRO.

1754–8 SHIRE HALL, Warwick, to designs of Sanderson Miller. Warwicks CRO; Anthony C Wood, *The Shire Hall, Warwick*.

1755 CHARLECOTE, Warwickshire, bridge for George Lucy; by D Hiorn. Warwicks CRO: Lucy papers.

c.1755 STANFORD HALL, Leicestershire, alterations for Sir Thomas Cave. Unexecuted. Drawings at house.

1755–6 COUNTY JAIL, Derby, Destroyed 1823. [*HMC*].

ECTON HALL, Northamptonshire, for Ambrose Isted. Drawings at Northants CRO.

1755–8 STIVICHALL HALL, West Midlands, for Arthur Gregory. To design by Henry Flitcroft. Shakespeare Birthplace Trust.

1759–61 FOREMARKE HALL, Derbyshire, for Sir Robert Burdett. *Vitruvius Britannicus;* Wilts CRO, Burdett papers.

1762 ST MARY'S CHURCH, Nottingham, rebuilding of E. end. Destroyed 1843. [*HMC*]

1762–5 CHARLECOTE, Warwickshire, internal alterations for George Lucy. Warwicks. CRO.

1763–4 HOLY TRINITY CHURCH, Stratford-Upon-Avon, tower & spire, perhaps to design by T Lightoler. [*HMC*].

1764–6 STONELEIGH ABBEY, Warwickshire, chimneypieces & other internal fittings for 2nd Lord Leigh. Shakespeare Birthplace Trust.

1766 OVER WHITACRE CHURCH, Warwickshire. Stylistic attribution.

1769 MOOT HALL, SARACEN'S HEAD, THE TAVERN, Daventry, Northamptonshire, Stylistic attributions.

In addition the following undated stylistic attributions:

ABINGTON HALL, Northamptonshire, entrance lobby & doorcase.

BIGGIN HALL, Northamptonshire, remodelling and enlargement.

BROOME HOUSE, Hereford & Worcester.

FOUR OAKS HALL, West Midlands, remodelling. Destroyed *c*.1900.

HARLESTONE HOUSE, Northamptonshire, stables.

TRYSULL, Staffordshire, The Red House.

A recent inspection of Horace Walpole's account book for the building of Strawberry Hill (now at Chetham's Library, Manchester) has turned up the following entries:

6 June 1749: Pd Hierons £26–6–0
22 Feb 1754: Pd Hierons for 2 vases in ye garden £50–0–0

William Hiorn? His skill as a carver is proved by the two documented monuments at Rugby (1744) and Acton Scott (1751) as well as numerous chimneypieces. Twickenham is outside his normal geographical range, but

individual pieces might have been sent down from Warwick; possibly Walpole met him through Roger Newdigate.

4 JOHN VARDY

c.1745–46 ALLERTON MAULEVERER CHURCH, Nr Knaresborough, North Yorkshire. Attributed. Rebuilt for the Hon Richard Arundell. Design for new house for Arundell, 1746, unexecuted.

1748 ROYAL PALACE, Whitehall, London. Vardy's unexecuted design, exhibited in 1761, is not known to survive.

1748–9 ST JAMES'S PALACE, London. Rebuilt façade at N-E. corner.
State bed for King George II, 1749.

1750–9 THE HORSE GUARDS, Whitehall, London. Erected under Vardy's supervision, but probably mainly to Kent's designs. Vardy's unexecuted design for the Whitehall gate is dated 1753.

1750–2 SHOBDON CHURCH, Hereford and Worcester, attributed, for Lord Bateman.

1751 SOCIETY OF DILETTANTI, Cavendish Square, London. Unexecuted, design for new headquarters on north side of square.

c.1751 MILTON (later DORCHESTER) HOUSE, Park Lane, London. For Joseph Damer, Baron Milton and 1st Earl of Dorchester, begun *c*. 1751 but completed 1769–71 by Sir William Chambers. Dem. 1849, but Vardy's stable block, for which he exhibited a design in 1764, was retained by Vulliamy.

1753–5 MILTON ABBEY, Dorset. Remodelling for Joseph Damer, but left unfinished and rebuilt by Chambers, 1771–6.

1750s WOODCOTE PARK, Epsom, Surrey, attributed. Refronting of house for Frederick Calvert, 6th Lord Baltimore; undated, but probably early 1750s. Burnt in 1934 and rebuilt by Mewes & Davis.

1753 COLONEL WADE'S HOUSE, Whitehall, London for Colonel George Wade. Dem. 1875.

RUTLAND HOUSE, Knightsbridge, London, for 3rd Duke of Rutland. Dem *c*.1834. Vardy's plan and elevation (V&A 6821/4), dated 1763, may only be a survey drawing and does not necessarily indicate that he designed the house.

NEW STONE BUILDING, Palace of Westminster, London. Accommodation for the King's Bench Records and Exchequer Bill Offices, designed 1753, central section built 1755–8; extended 1766–70, completed by Soane in 1821, and demolished in 1883 after completion of the Strand Law Courts.

1754–6 PARLIAMENT OFFICE, Old Palace Yard, London, attributed, for the Clerk of the Parliaments.

1754 THE BRITISH MUSEUM, London, unexecuted. Vardy's designs were conceived for a site in Old Palace Yard.

ST MARY ABBOTS CHURCH, Kensington, London, unexecuted. Vardy submitted a design (not known to survive) for rebuilding the tower of the church.

WINDSOR GREAT PARK, Berkshire, unexecuted. Design for boat house for William Augustus, Duke of Cumberland. Two elaborate maps of the park were drawn by Vardy in 1750. (PRO and British Museum).

A BATH HOUSE IN SUFFOLK. In 1764 Vardy exhibited a design of the inside of a bath house 'for a gentleman in Suffolk'. His plan and elevation for a bath house, dated 1754, was apparently bought in the 1950s at a sale at Lilias Rider-Haggard's house near Bungay on the Suffolk-Norfolk border.

LEES COURT, Kent. Design for dining room overmantel (RIBA G4/2) and possibly other internal alterations, for Lewis Watson, 1st Lord Sondes. Lees Court was gutted by fire c.1913.

1755 HOWLETTS, near Bekesbourne, Kent. Unexecuted design for mansion for Sir Thomas Hayles.

HOLLAND HOUSE, Kensington, London, attributed, thatched Gothic lodge, for Henry Fox, Lord Holland; dem. 19th century. This very early example of a cottage orné lodge may have been designed by Vardy, who in 1761 was commissioned by the 5th Duke of Bolton to reproduce it at Hackwood Park. In 1752 Vardy drew a general view of Holland House for Fox, who had been the Hon Richard Arundell's successor as Surveyor of the Works in 1737–43. Hugh Honour asserts (CL December 10 1953) that Vardy worked on Fox's mansion at Kingsgate, Kent, but there is no documentary evidence for this.

1755–60 SPENCER HOUSE, St James's Place, London. For John, 1st Earl Spencer. Vardy completed the exterior and ground floor rooms (together with furniture now at Althorp and elsewhere), but was superseded in the decoration of the first floor rooms by James 'Athenian' Stuart.

c.1757 FONTHILL GIFFORD, Wiltshire, attributed, gateway to Fonthill Splendens. The house at Fonthill was begun for Alderman Beckford, apparently by a City of London builder called Hoare.

c. 1760 AMISFIELD HOUSE, Lothian, attributed, temple. Isaac Ware's Amisfield House was built for Francis Charteris in 1756–9.

c.1761–3 HACKWOOD PARK, Hampshire. Remodelled S. front and interior for Charles, 5th Duke of Bolton. Vardy's work was destroyed in the further remodelling by Samuel and Lewis Wyatt in 1805–13. Vardy also supplied designs for a pair of pier tables and mirrors which are still in the house, and for the following: a pair of lodges for the Basingstoke gate (1761, apparently executed but since dem.); 'a Cottage … for a man to Open the Park Gate' (1761, possibly not executed); a thatched lodge copied from that at Holland House (1761); a park feature combining prospect tower and stables; a garden temple; a sofa, organ case, and fire grates for the house. In addition Vardy apparently carried out work on the Duke's houses in Winchester (probably in 1761–2 when he was mayor of the city), Ealing and Grosvenor Square (qv).

c.1761 37, GROSVENOR SQUARE, London. Work for 5th Duke of Bolton. Vardy was paid £7,000 for repairs to the house, where the Duke committed suicide in 1765. A design for a candle bracket is dated 1761, and the side tables bearing the Duke's arms, now at Bolton Hall, North Yorkshire, may have been designed for Grosvenor Square. A design for an overmantel and wind-dial (Cooper-Hewitt Museum of Design, Smithsonian Institution) for the Duke of Bolton, formerly attributed to Gibbs, is probably another Vardy contribution to the refitting of this house. Dem. 1934.

1761 FULHAM PARISH CHURCHYARD, London. Monument to Thomas Sherlock, Bishop of London (died 1761).

1762 DRUMMOND'S BANK, Charing Cross, London. Drummonds' own accounts indicate extensive building work on their premises in 1762–3, with payments in 1762 to Vardy for plans and to Thomas Vardy for carving. Dem. 1877.

1763 DURHAM YARD, Strand, London. Vardy was paid 12 guineas for 'plans and planning' by the 3rd Duke of St Albans in 1763. Durham Yard was leased in 1769 to the Adam brothers, who redeveloped the site for their Adelphi scheme.

1763–5 STANMORE HOUSE or PARK, London, for Andrew Drummond, unfinished at Vardy's death and completed by Chambers in 1766–9. Dem. 1938.

5 HENRY KEENE

c.1749–50 THE FLESH MARKET, Westminster; dem. 1805. Designs in the Westminster Abbey Muniments (P) 733, 733 A-B, 734 (elevations and ground plans) and 24887 (survey dated 12 October 1749). For views of the Market see William Capon, Views of Westminster, London Topographical Society 1923–4.

HARTLEBURY CASTLE, Hereford and Worcester. Remodelling of the chapel, probable refenestration of the castle, addition of a Gothick cupola and design of a Bishop's throne which survives in the Library at Worcester Cathedral for Bishop Maddox. There is no concise contemporary

documentation of Keene's work at
Hartlebury, but he walked in the park there
with Sanderson Miller on 21 Aug 1750,
(Miller's diary, Warwicks. CRO 1382/1) and a
manuscript reference in the Hurd papers at the
castle dated 1796 states that 'Bishop Maddox
fitted up the Chapel, and put a new roof to it.
The Architect was Mr Keene of London'. This
traditional attribution is accepted by E H
Pearce, *Hartlebury Castle*, 1926. *CL*, 23 Sept
1971.

1749 HAGLEY HALL, Hereford and Worcester.
Designed in collaboration with Sanderson
Miller dining room chimney piece and
furniture for the sham castle for the 1st Lord
Lyttelton. Miller's correspondence in the
Warwicks. CRO 125B/350.

c. 1750 NELMES, Hornchurch, London. Repairs for
Godfrey Webster under the direction of
Miller. Miller's diary (Warwicks CRO
1382/1).

c. 1750–2 ENVILLE HALL, Staffordshire. The
Museum for the 4th Earl of Stamford.
Attribution made by Timothy Mowl in 'The
Case of the Enville Museum' in *Journal of
Garden History*, Vol 3, no. 2, 134–43.

1750. 4, SOUTH SQUARE, Gray's Inn. Designed in
conformity with nos. 2–3, already built. R J
Fletcher ed., *Records of Gray's Inn*, ii, 263, 268.

WORCESTER CATHEDRAL. On 18 May 1750 the
Dean and Chapter ordered 'That Mr. Kean or
some other skilfull Architect be applied to for a
draught of a proper Ornamental Portico in the
Gothick Stile & order to be erected over the
great Gate of the Cathedral instead of a mean,
deformed covering now over the Gate falling
into Ruins.' Worcester Cathedral Muniments,
A 78: Chapter Acts Book, 1747–79, f 19. It is
not known if this was erected.

1751 CHART PARK, Surrey. Designs in
collaboration with Miller for a greenhouse for
Henry Talbot. L Dickins & M Stanton eds.;
An Eighteenth Century Correspondence, 1910,
138; Bodleian Library, MS North d. 19, f 68.

1752–9 TRINITY COLLEGE, Dublin. Provision of
plans and working drawings based on
Theodore Jacobsen's designs for which Keene
and his collaborator John Sanderson were paid
£74 11s 8d. *Journal of the House of Commons in
the Kingdom of Ireland* vi, 1757–60. Appendix.
cclxiii, no xxxv.

1753–5 HARTWELL CHURCH, Buckinghamshire.
For Sir William Lee, Bart. Fell into ruin in
1951. H Smythe, *Addenda to the Aedes
Hartwellianae*, 1864, 20–1. Alternative designs
for the project are in the Bodleian, MS Top
Gen b. 55, ff.29–34 and stylistically linked
drawings are in the V & A, A 189, nos. E882 &
904.

*c.*1755, EALING GROVE, Middlesex. For Joseph
Gulston; altered by J Yenn *c.*1780,

subsequently dem. An elevation for the east
front signed by Keene is in the Northld. RO,
ZBU 5/6 (28).

1755 HIGH WYCOMBE CHURCH, Buckinghamshire.
Addition of a Gothick cornice, parapet and
pinnacles to the tower (the projected spire was
omitted) for the 1st Earl of Shelburne.
Accounts at Bowood House. Keene also
designed a Gothick pew for Lord Shelburne, a
drawing for which is reproduced by F Skull in
Records of Bucks, ix, 1908, but whose
whereabouts is unknown. The pew is shown
in its original position above the chancel screen
in Addleshaw & Etchells, *The Architectural
Setting of Anglican Worship*, 1948, pl 5. The
pew is now in the assembly hall of Wycombe
Abbey School.

LOAKS, High Wycombe. Designs for a new
seat for the 1st Earl of Shelburne. Keene's
scheme for Loaks was rejected and he was
limited to supervising alterations at the house
in 1758–9. Accounts at Bowood.

1755–7 HANOVER SQUARE, London. Alterations
and additions to house for the 1st Earl of
Shelburne. Accounts at Bowood.

THE GUILDHALL, High Wycombe. For the 1st
Earl of Shelburne. Accounts at Bowood.

1755–60 BOWOOD HOUSE, Wiltshire. Alterations
and additions for the 1st Earl of Shelburne,
including service block, rebuilt in 1761–4 by
Robert Adam as the Diocletian wing, and
alterations to the original Orlando Bridgeman
house subsequently modified by Adam. Main
house dem. 1955–6. Keene also designed a
'Principal Lodge' for Bowood which does not
appear to have been executed. Accounts at
Bowood. For illustrations of Keene's W.
front see A T Bolton, *Architecture of R and J
Adam*, 1922, i, 204–15. *CL* 6 Sept 1913.

1756–7. 17–18, CAVENDISH SQUARE, London. For
Thomas Bridges and William Lloyd.
Drawings and building accounts in the Middx
CRO, 85/223–64.

1759–60 CORSHAM COURT, Wiltshire. Designs for
Sir Paul Methuen for the provision of a Picture
Gallery and Library which were unexecuted.
Eleven of Keene's drawings are preserved at
Corsham and he was paid thirty guineas for
them in 1760. F J Ladd, *Architects at Corsham
Court*, 1978, 41–5 and pls 27–39. Keene may
also have been responsible for a
Rococo-Gothick scheme for the Library as an
unidentified drawing at Corsham is close in
style to one of the V & A drawings for a
Gothick pavilion (E901) — see Ladd,
Architects, 51–4 and pls 44–6.

1759–63 HARTWELL HOUSE, Buckinghamshire.
Rebuilt the S. and E. fronts and remodelled the
interiors for Sir William Lee. Keene also
designed a bridge in the park which has since
been destroyed (illustrated in Smythe,

Addenda, 21). Keene's bills and estimates for the work sold at Sotheby's on 8 March 1939, lot 665. Drawings relating to the work in the Bodleian, MS Top Gen b. 55. For illustrations of the interiors see *CL,* 14–21 March 1914.

*c.*1760 HALSWELL HOUSE, Somerset. Gothick garden building known as Robin Hood's Temple for Sir Charles Kemys Tynte Bart. There is an inscribed design for the temple in the V & A, no E892. It was altered in execution and is now (Spring 1984) in ruins. It is shown in the distance in a view of the house given in J Collinson, *History and Antiquities of Somerset,* 1791, 81.

1760 GOATHURST CHURCH, Somerset. Tynte Pew for Sir Charles Kemys Tynte. The churchwardens' accounts record the date of construction but give no architect. Keene is likely to have designed the pew (a small S. transept) when he was working on Robin Hood's Temple as it bears unmistakable marks of his eclecticism. The plaster barrel vault has pseudo-Jacobean strapwork and the Gothick cornice has intricate cusping and sexfoils entwining *papier-mâché* heraldic shields.

1762–76 ARBURY HALL, Warwickshire. Assisted Sir Roger Newdigate Bart. in remodelling the house in Gothick style. Keene first mentioned in the accounts for 1762, again in 1771, and finally after his death, in 1779. He probably designed and supervised the erection of the vault in the Parlour and the chimney piece in that room is sufficiently close to that at University College, Oxford to confirm his authorship. The accounts for 1771 specify payment for 'Front and Hall etc.' confirming his authorship of the Dining Room with its three bay oriel. Refs. from the accounts and illustrations of Arbury are given in *CL,* 15 Oct 1953.

1763 SPRING GARDENS, London. Repairs and alterations to house for Sir Roger Newdigate, dem. *c.*1882. (Warwicks. RO, Newdigate family papers).

1766 UNIVERSITY COLLEGE, Oxford. Remodelled interior of Hall in Gothick style. Destroyed in 1904 but the chimney piece survives behind panelling. A Wood, *Colleges and Halls,* ed. Gutch, 1786, Appendix, 236; fireplace design in the V & A, no. E903.

1766–7 CHRIST CHURCH COLLEGE, Oxford. Designed the Anatomy School (later Chemical Laboratory) and enclosed and fitted up ground floor of the Library in 1769–72. W G Hiscock, *A Christ Church Miscellany,* 1946, 70–1, 210, for illustrations of Keene's work in the Library see *CL,* 4 April 1947.

1767–8 SHELDONIAN THEATRE, Oxford. Inserted sash windows, replaced in 1959. University Archives, Theatre Account, 1767–9.

1768 HAREFIELD CHURCH, London. Designed and supervised the erection of a new chancel arch and Gothick plaster vault in the chancel for Sir Roger Newdigate. (Warwicks. RO, Newdigate family papers). Keene may also have been responsible for the Gothick stalls and plasterwork in the chancel of ASTLEY CHURCH, Warwickshire carried out for Newdigate at this time.

MAGDALEN COLLEGE, Oxford. Provision of a plan for repaving the ante-chapel which is preserved in a volume of drawings in the College Library (f 26). Keene mentions this work in a letter to Sir Roger Newdigate of 16 June 1768 (quoted in *CL,* 15 Oct 1953). Keene is said to have been 'engaged at Magdalen College for about 20 years' and the President's lodgings are said to have been altered by him in 1769 [*HMC* 484].

1768–9 BALLIOL COLLEGE, Oxford. The Fisher building; N. side refaced 1877 and 1963, S. side refaced and altered by Waterhouse in 1870. J Nichols, *Literary Anecdotes* 1812–15, viii, 248.

1769 WESTMINSTER ABBEY. Remodelled the interior of the Jerusalem Chamber in Gothick style (WAM, 24836 — Workmans' Bills), designed two sets of Cloister Gates (WAM 24836) and Gothick choir-stalls, pulpit, reading desk and parclose screen in 1775 (WAM, Register 46, ff 170v–172v). Keene's plasterwork in the Jerusalem Chamber has been destroyed, his Cloister Gates survive *in situ* and his choir furniture was removed in 1847 by Blore; its fate is unknown, but the pulpit is now in Trottiscliffe Church, Kent. For an illustration of the choir furniture see J P Neale & E W Brayley, *The History and Antiquities of the Abbey Church of St Peter, Westminster,* 1823, ii, pl 30. Keene is also likely to have designed the Gothick doorcase to the Deanery and a tripartite Gothick doorway in Dean's Yard.

1770 WESTBOURNE CHURCH, West Sussex. Timber Gothick spire for the Earl of Halifax. The inscription 'Henry Keene Architect 1770' is painted on a beam inside the spire. H Woodyer removed the decorative details in 1865.

1772 SPELSBURY CHURCH, Oxfordshire. Monument to the 3rd Earl of Litchfield (died 1772), signed 'H. Keene Archs. invt. W Tyler sculpt.'

THE RADCLIFFE OBSERVATORY, Oxford. Begun to Keene's designs but in March 1773 the Trustees adopted James Wyatt's scheme which Keene carried out until his death in 1776. Keene's son took over then and the building was completed in 1794. Bodleian, MS. Minute Books of the Radcliffe Trustees. For the public criticism of Keene's designs see Edward Tatham, *Oxonia Explicata et Ornata,* 1773, for an illustration of Keene's ground floor storey see H M Colvin, *Unbuilt Oxford,* 1983, pl 82.

1773–6 WORCESTER COLLEGE, Oxford. The

Provost's Lodgings. Keene also completed the north range of the College, of which he built the central portion and the two staircases to the W., repeating the design of the two staircases to the E. erected by Dr Clarke's trustees between 1753 and 1759. *Victoria County History: Oxfordshire*, iii, 308–9. See also *CL* 5 Nov 1948.

1774 UPPARK, West Sussex. The Vandalian Tower for Sir Matthew Fetherstonhaugh, *CL*, 21 & 28 June 1941.

6 JAMES ESSEX

Since Essex's practice fall into two distinct parts, his work at Cambridge and that elsewhere the catalogue has been arranged alphabetically by place. Within this, his Cambridge work has been listed according to building type.

AMPTHILL, Bedfordshire. Cross erected for 2nd Earl of Upper Ossory on site of Ampthill Castle in memory of Catharine of Aragon. Designed 1771, erected 1773; extant.

AUDLEY END, Essex. Consulted about new chapel at Audley End, 1768. Survey of farm house at Littlebury, Essex, 1771.

Cambridge, Colleges:

CHRIST'S Internal face of First Court ashlared and regularised in stages 1758–75; extant although in part altered.

CLARE New chapel and ante-chapel, designed by Burrough 1763 but erected by Essex 1764–69; extant.

CORPUS CHRISTI Design for new court, prepared for Rev R Masters, 1747; engraved, not executed.
Minor works, 1769–71, 1777.
Design for new court, 1773; engraved, not executed.

DOWNING Designs prepared for new college, 1771; not executed.

EMMANUEL Survey of college grounds, c.1745.
Hall repaired, re-faced and re-fitted, 1760–64; extant.
Design for rebuilding W. range of Chapel Court, 1769–70; engraved, not executed.
New W. range of Chapel Court to revised design, 1771–75; extant.

GONVILLE AND CAIUS Internal face of Gonville Court ashlared and N. range rebuilt, presumably to design and under supervision of Burrough, 1749–54: extant in part.

JESUS Combination room re-fitted, 1762–63; extant.
(?) Rebuilding of cloister arches, 1762–65; extant.
Alterations in Principal Court, perhaps re-arrangement of rooms at SW. angle, 1784.

KING'S Restoration of chapel roof and supervision of restoration of masonry, 1750–56.
Design for new reredos in chapel, 1766; rejected.
New reredos in chapel designed and installed, 1770–75; removed 1897.
Ante chapel re-paved, 1774–76; extant.
Alterations to gardens to W. of Gibbs's building, 1771–72, 1775–77.

PEMBROKE Minor works and repairs in N. range of Ivy Court 1768.

QUEENS' Timber bridge constructed 1749–50 to design of W Etheridge. Rebuilt 1867 and 1904 to original design.
Design of new W. range, parallel to river: southern part only executed (Essex building), 1756–60: extant.
(?) Office range built on N. side of gallery of President's Lodging, 1761; extant
Chapel 'entirely taken to pieces and new modelled', 1773–75. All Essex's work removed in restorations of 1845 and 1858–61.
Room over butteries fitted as temporary chapel, 1773.
Rooms over butteries altered and re-panelled, 1779; extant.

ST CATHARINE'S Survey of houses adjoining Trumpington Street, 1745.
(?) Formation of library in W. part of N. range, 1755–58; extant.
Addition of 'Ramsden building' at E. end of S. range, 1757–c.1760; extant.
(?) Screen of railings and gate piers closing E. side of court, c. 1780; extant.
Survey of additions to college 'according to Mrs Ramsden's will', 1765.

ST JOHN'S S. range of First Court heightened and re-faced, 1773-75; extant.
Combination Room altered and refurnished, 1777–78; destroyed 1863.
Arch between library and W. range of Third Court altered and foundations of range repaired, 1777–78; extant.
Repair of library roof, 1783.

SIDNEY SUSSEX (?) Assisted Burrough in refitting of Hall and new entrance gateway, 1749–53; extant.
Designed and built summer-house in Fellows' garden, 1775; destroyed.
3 designs for new chapel, March-July 1775, unexecuted.
New E. range of S. court, including chapel and library, 1776–82; library and staircase extant but altered, chapel extended and completely re-fitted c.1920, S. front re-faced in Gothic style, c.1833.

TRINITY Reconstruction of Nevile's Court to modified version of original design, 1756–60; extant.
Passage formed and new panelling in Master's Lodge, 1757-8.
Designed and built 'Cycloidal' bridge, 1763–5;

extant.

New building at S. end of W. range of Great Court, including Combination Room, 1771–4; extant though altered internally.

TRINITY HALL Drew Burrough's plan for total rebuilding of college; engraved 1745.

Garret Hostel bridge rebuilt at expense of Trinity Hall, 1769; replaced by iron bridge, 1837.

University

LIBRARY Creation of 'Dome Room' in SW. angle of Schools building, probably to design by Burrough, and furnishing of it with cases for MSS, 1750–1; room extant but cupola and cases removed.

Drew Burrough's design of 1752 for new University Library, engraved before 1764

W. facade of SENATE HOUSE, 1766–8; extant.

Design of LECTURE ROOM for Professor of Botany in former Botanic Gardens, 1783; not executed.

Cambridge Churches

ST CLEMENT's Design of W. tower in accordance with will of William Cole, c.1783; tower erected in 1821 by Charles Humfrey, possibly following Essex's design; extant.

ST EDWARD's Alterations to interior and·to doorways, 1784; removed in 19th century.

GT ST MARY's Construction of pews in nave (for the parish) and Doctors' Gallery, 'Golgotha', (for the University) in chancel, the latter to a design by Burrough, 1752–6; removed 1863. Alteration of aisle windows c.1766, 1776; Clearance of houses from W. end of church and 'making good' of church, 1768. (?) Supervised repair of tower, 1777. Repair of nave roof and its covering by a new roof above, 1782/3.

Corporation

BRIDGE Rebuilding of Great (Magdalene) Bridge in stone 1754; dem. 1823.

Advice on improvement of Clayhithe-Littleport Navigation, 1779.

GUILDHALL Designed and built new Guildhall, 1782; altered and enlarged 1865, the whole dem. 1933.

Domestic

Designed and built Randall (now Kenmare) House, Trumpington Street, 1768; extant though altered internally.

Design of picture gallery for W H Ewin, c.1780;? executed.

CANTERBURY Kent. Advice on new roof of cathedral, 1776.

DEBDEN, Essex. Designed timber and lead steeple and (?) W. facade of church; steeple erected 1786; dem. 1930.

ELY Cambridgeshire, Survey of cathedral, 1757.

Restoration of cathedral, including

(i) Rebuilding of lantern over Octagon and E. wall of presbytery, 1757–8; lantern rebuilt to different design c.1860.

(ii) Repair of Galilee, 1762.

(iii) Renewal of presbytery roof 1768.

(iv) Removal of choir to E. end, with medieval stalls retained and repaired but new reredos and organ screen, planned 1759, decided 1768, executed 1770–1; choir again removed and Essex's work destroyed 1851.

(v) ? Design of tablet and ossuary in bishop West's Chapel for bones of Saxon 'Kings' discovered in demolition of old choir, 1771; extant.

Reconstruction of Bishop's Palace, with Sir Robert Taylor, 1771, extant.

ENFIELD, London. Design and construction of chimney piece and Gothic window, with stained glass, together with advice on other alterations to Gough Park, home of Richard Gough, 1778–80; destroyed.

LINCOLN Survey of cathedral, 1761.

Second survey of cathedral, 1764.

Restoration of cathedral, including

(i) Reconstruction of chapter house roof to lower pitch, 1761–2; original pitch restored 1800.

(ii) Repair of roofs and gutters, 1763–5.

(iii) Reredos and screens behind high altar, 1769; extant; but tracery added in 1857.

(iv) Rebuilding of original apse of St Mary Magdalene's (now St Hugh's) chapel in transept 1772; extant.

(v) Cresting and corner pinnacles on central tower, 1775–6; extant.

(vi) Survey of screen wall across W. end of nave, 1775.

(vii) Refashioning of screen openings in Gothic style, 1776; extant.

(viii) Formation and furnishing of canons' vestry off S. transept, 1776; extant.

(ix) Erection of bishop's throne, 1778; extant, but enriched c.1880 by Pearson.

(x) Repair of W. front, begun 1778.

(xi) Designs for ornamental screens incorporating tie beams in E. transept, 1779–81; cresting on beams added by W Lumley c.1781.

(xii) Repaving of cathedral, 1780–3; extant in part.

MADINGLEY Cambridgeshire: Re-erection at Madingley Hall of former E. gateway of Schools building as Gothick entrance to stable court, 1758; extant.

Alterations to Madingley Hall, including new dining room, c.1758; extant in part.

MILTON, Cambridgeshire: Milton Lodge (now House) entrance/stairhall and bow windows added and interior altered for Rev William

Cole, 1768–9; extant though enlarged.

SALISBURY, Wiltshire. Survey of cathedral, probably of a roof, 1758.

STOWLANGTOFT, Suffolk; (?) Work on Stowlangtoft Hall for Sir Walter Rawlinson, c.1780.

SWAFFHAM PRIOR, Cambridgeshire: (?) Alterations to Swaffham Prior House for Dean Allix of Ely, c.1750.

(?) Alterations to Swaffham Prior Hall, c.1770,

THAXTED, Essex. Alterations to church, including repair of windows on N. side (c.1760) and new Gothic altarpiece 1765–7; destroyed.

THRIPLOW, Cambridgeshire. Alterations to property of Master and Fellows of St John's College, Cambridge, (now Thriplow Manor and St John's College Farm) 1781/2: extant in part.

TWICKENHAM, London. Designs for Horace Walpole at Strawberry Hill;
  (i) Gothic gatepiers for gateway in garden, 1769; destroyed.
  (ii) Beauclerk Tower, 1776–7; extant though heightened.
  (iii) Range of offices in 'collegiate' style; designed 1777, execution planned 1778–80 but postponed till 1790, extant, but interior altered.
  (iv) Gothic bridge in garden; designed 1778, executed 1792; destroyed.

WESTMINSTER, London. Design for new choir and reredos in Westminster Abbey, 1773; rejected.

WIMPOLE, Cambridgeshire: Wimpole Hall, Construction of Gothic folly castle to general design of c.1750 by Sanderson Miller, 1768–70; extant.

WINCHESTER, Hampshire. Cathedral; survey of cathedral roof; 1773.
Further consultation on cathedral roof, 1782.
College; advice on repair of chapel tower, 1772; tower rebuilt, 1862–3.

7 THOMAS HOPPER

c.1806 CRAVEN COTTAGE, Fulham; alterations, burned down 1888.

1807 CARLTON HOUSE, London; conservatory and other works, dem. 1827–28.

1808 ROYAL SOCIETY OF MUSICIANS, 11–13, Lisle Street, London, dem. 1931.

1812 DROMOLAND CASTLE, Co Clare, Ireland; entrance lodge.

1813 MELFORD HALL, Suffolk; Library; staircase and other alterations.

1884 LEIGH COURT, near Bristol, Avon.

1818 PURLEY HALL, Berkshire; remodelling.
NORTH STONEHAM PARK, Hampshire, reconstructed 1831.

1820 ALSCOT PARK, Warwickshire; new porch.
ALTON TOWERS, Staffordshire: unspecified works.

GOSFORD CASTLE, Co Armagh, N. Ireland.
TERLING PLACE, Essex; alterations.
WILTSHIRE COUNTRY GAOL, Fisherton Anger.

1822 ESSEX COUNTY GAOL, Springfield, Chelmsford (altered 1845).

1823 WOOLVERSTONE HALL, Suffolk, additions.

1825 PENRHYN CASTLE, Gwynedd, Wales.
KENTWELL HALL, Suffolk; reconstructed interior.

1826 HATFIELD PEVEREL CHURCH, Essex; enlargement.

1827 ERDIGG PARK, Clwyd, Wales; new dining room.
BOREHAM HOUSE, Essex; additions.
ARTHUR'S CLUB, (now the CARLTON CLUB), St James's Street, London.

1828 DUNKELD HOUSE, Tayside, Scotland; new house, abandoned 1830.
LLANOVER HOUSE, Gwent.
ILFORD HOUSE OF CORRECTION, London.

1829 THE GUILDHALL, Salisbury, Wiltshire, enlargement.

1830 BERWICK PLACE, Hatfield Peverel, Essex.
MARGAM ABBEY, West Glamorgan, Wales.

1831 CRICHEL, Dorset; alterations.

1832 DANBURY PLACE, Essex.
WELFORD PARK, Berkshire; new dining room.

1834 AMESBURY HOUSE, Wiltshire; rebuilding.
ATLAS FIRE ASSURANCE BUILDING, 92, Cheapside, London.

1836 ROOD ASHTON HOUSE, Wiltshire; alterations.

1838 KIRTLINGTON PARK, Oxfordshire; alterations.
LEGAL & GENERAL LIFE ASSURANCE OFFICE, 10, Fleet Street, London, dem. 1885.
COUTTS BANK, 59, Strand; alterations dem. 1923.

1839 HOLY TRINITY CHURCH, Bromley Common, London; alterations; altered 1884.

1840 BUTTERTON HALL, Staffordshire.
STANSTED HOUSE, Sussex; alterations.

1841 ST JOHN'S CHURCH, Southend, Essex; additions.

1842 KINMEL PARK, Clwyd, Wales; additions.

1843 BIRCH HALL, Essex, dem. 1954.

1844 BUTTERTON CHURCH, Staffordshire.

1845 ST MARY'S HOSPITAL, Paddington.

1846 WIVENHOE PARK, Essex; remodelling.

1847 EASTON LODGE, nr Dunmow, Essex; rebuilding; reconstructed 1918.

1848 ST JOHN'S CHURCH, Epping, Essex; new porch.

8 SAMUEL SANDERS TEULON

A full catalogue containing precise references to sources has been donated to the RIBA Library and the Victorian Society and further copies can be obtained from the author c/o the publishers. For further details of ecclesiastical commissions, see the author's *The Churches of S S Teulon* 1982, The Ecclesiological Society, London. Major sources of information are: *Br, Eccl,* RA, RIBA obit. and

RIBA sketchbooks 1 & 2.

AGAR TOWN, London, N W 1, St Thomas.
  (a) School. Designed to serve temporarily as a church, fs May 21st 1857, cons. 19th November 1857.
  (b) First church. fs July 12th 1859 cost: £4,000 (excluding foundations).
  All buildings acquired 1860 for dem. in connection with St Pancras Station.
  (c) Second church. cons. June 18th 1863. Cost: £4,175. Also parsonage dem. c. 1960.

ALDERBURY, Wiltshire, St Mary. fs 9.5.1857, cons. 24.6.1858. Clients: 3rd Earl of Radnor, Longford Castle, Sir Frederick Harvey-Bathurst, Clarendon Park and George Fort, Alderbury House (chancel). Cost: £2,800.

AMPTON, Suffolk, St Peter. Restored 1848 for Calthorpe family.

ANGMERING West Sussex,
  (a) St Margaret: Rebuilt except for tower of 1506, sections of the chancel and the Gratwick Chapel. cons. Easter Day 1853. Stone carving by Phyffers & Forsyth. Glass by Gibbs.
  (b) School, schoolhouse, vestry hall, sexton's house and cottages. Vestry hall and sexton's house remodelled from existing building. School is now library.
  Client (for all structures): W G Kindleside-Gratwicke of Ham House, Angmering.

ARUN DEAN, Hampshire. 1861 for Mr Maberley of Hawkleyhurst.

BACONSTHORPE, Norfolk, St Mary. Restoration 1869.

BARKING, London, St Margaret. Restored 1854.

BATTERSEA PARK, Wrought-iron drinking fountain. 1860.

BENHILTON (Sutton), London, All Saints. 1863–65, N. aisle 1873. Cost: £24,000; £18,000 of which was given by Mr Thomas Alcock, MP, who also gave a site for the school and vicarage (dem). Roof destroyed in bombing 1944.

BENTLEY HEATH, Hertfordshire.
  (a) Holy Trinity. Private chapel. 1865. Cost: £860.
  (b) Nearby cottages, 1864.
  (c) Lodge to Wrotham Park and stone piers. Cost: £1,092. Client for all structures: 2nd Earl of Strafford.

BENWICK, Cambridgeshire, St Mary the Virgin. fs 12.6.1850. cons. 14.8.1851. Cost: £2,500. Client: Sir Henry Peyton and Rev A Peyton Spire rebuilt 1902 and dem. 1967. Remainder of church dem. 1983.

BERMONDSEY, Kipling Street (LB of Southwark).
  (a) St Paul. cons. 26.5.1848. Cost £5,350, Unexecuted designs of vicarage 1845. (dem. 1959–63).

  (b) School. Opened 1848, dem. 1963.

BESTWOOD, Nottinghamshire.
  (a) Bestwood Park. 1862–64. Client: 10th Duke of St Albans.
  (b) Alexandra Lodge gate. *Pevsner* says 1878 but could well be Teulon.
  (c) Emmanuel Church. 1868–69. W. porch redesigned 1870 as a memorial to Duchess who died March 31.

BILLINGSHURST, West Sussex. Vicarage. Cost: £900. 1859.

BILLINGTON, Bedfordshire. Parsonage. 1859.

BIRCH (Great), Essex.
  (a) S S Peter and Paul. 1850. Cost: just over £4,000.
  (b) Rectory. 1859. Cost £1,160.
  (c) Cottages in the village?
  Client for all buildings: Charles Gray Round (dem 1867) who chose Thomas Hopper to design his residence, in 1862, the now dem. Birch Hall.

BIRMINGHAM, Edgbaston, St James. 1851–52. Cost: £3,000. Client: Lord Calthorpe (dem 1851). Redundant.

BIRMINGHAM Edgbaston Hall. A proposed lodge to Edgbaston Hall and sketches of bookcases for the Hall itself.

BIRMINGHAM. Ladywood, St John the Evangelist, Monument Road. 1852–54. Client: Calthorpe family.
  (b) School and schoolmaster's house. 1856. Cost: £3,100.

BLENHEIM PALACE, Oxfordshire. Re-ordering of chapel including introduction of font, pulpit, reredos, double lectern, organ, stained glass by Clayton and a brass effigy of the 1st Duke. 1857–59 Chapel now cleared of Teulon fittings. Pulpit has been removed to Waddesdon Church, Bucks.

BLETSOE, Bedfordshire. Restored 1857. Client: Lord St John (cf. St. Leonards).

BLYTH HILL, Kent. House of Robert Espie 1843.

BOLTSHOPE, Northumberland. Row of cottages 1863.

BOTTESFORD, Humberside. St Peter's Chains. Restored 1857.

BRESSINGHAM, Norfolk. Rectory 1842.

BRETTENHAM, Norfolk.
  (a) St Andrew. Rebuilt 1852. Client: Sir Robert Buxton and the Dowager Lady Buxton of Shadwell Court. Small sections of medieval work retained. Cons. 24.2.1853. Cost: £2,000.
  (b) Several cottages in village.

BROCKLESBY, Lincolnshire. Rectory 1845.

BROUGHTON SULNEY, Nottinghamshire.
  (a) St Luke. Restored 1854.
  (b) The Rectory.

BURRINGHAM, Humberside. St John the Baptist. fs 18.6.1856. Cons. November 1857. Client: Mr Healey, Lord of the Manor. Cost: £1,270 excluding pulpit and font.

CANTERBURY, Kent. House for Col McQueen 1861.

CANTLEY, South Yorkshire. National schools 1847. Client: J W Childers, MP.

CHIPPING CAMPDEN, Gloucestershire. 1844 wing to Vicarage, dem.

CLEY-NEXT-THE-SEA, Norfolk, St Margaret. Restored 1848–49. Clients: Calthorpe family.

CLIFTON HAMPDEN, Oxfordshire, St Michael and All Angels. Lychgate.

COBHAM, Surrey. Two houses for Dr Finch and Mr Mackrell. 1861.

COLCHESTER, Essex, St James the Great, East Hill. Restored 1870–71. Cost: £5,000.

COMPTON, Berkshire. Vicarage and School 1854.

CONISCLIFFE, Durham.
(a) School. 1861.
(b) Extension to vicarage. 1859.

CROMHALL, Avon. Chapel of Tortworth Court. 1849–53. Client: 2nd Earl of Ducie.

CROYDON, London, Christchurch. Cons. 27.7.1852 Cost: £2,650 max. Client: Archbishop Sumner (of Canterbury). Faculty to dem. granted 1982.

CURRIDGE, Berkshire.
(a) Chapel-School. 1856. Clients: Mrs Stacpoole and Miss Wasey of Priors Court.
(b) Parsonage. 1857.
He also was responsible for a number of adjacent cottages.

DUDMASTON, Salop. Unexecuted scheme for large new porte-corchère for William Wolrych-Whitmore. House built c. 1690.

DUNSTABLE, Bedfordshire. Plans for new schools for the Ashton Charity. 1863.

EALING, London, St Mary. Recast 1863–74. Cost: Tender of £8,680 but final cost was £11,500 even though intended spire was abandoned.

EASTBOURNE, East Sussex.
(a) 'Proposed market'. 1852.
(b) Eastbourne, Designs for Trinity District Schools.

EASTERN GREEN, West Midlands.
(a) St Andrew's Church. Cons. 4.11.1875.
(b) Vicarage.
(c) School.
Joint cost: £6,300. £12,000 had been left to meet the cost of erection and endowment.

EAST TORRINGTON, Lincolnshire, St Michaels. 1848–50.

EBONY (Reading Street), Kent, St Mary. Resiting and restoration of a medieval chapel. August-November 1858. Cost: £270.

ELM, Cambridgeshire.
(a) All Saints. Restoration 1859.
(b) School Room. 1860.

ELVETHAM, Hampshire.
(a) School 1849.
(b) Cottages. 1849.

(c) Elvetham Hall. 1859–62 Substantial rebuilding. Client: Frederick Lord Calthorpe. Internal painted decorations by Fisher & Harland of London, fireplaces by Thomas Earp, metalwork by Skidmore. Cost: £70,000.
(d) Stables, bridge, water tower and engineer's residence 1862. In grounds of the Hall. Peter Allen also credits dovecote and clock tower at Home Farm on very plausible visual grounds.
(e) St Mary's Church. Teulon added angels and symbols of the Evangelists to the base and broaches of the spire which like the rest of the church is 1840–41 by Henry Roberts. Almost certainly responsible for internal refitting too, but much was lost on conversion into lecture hall in 1973.

ELY, Cambridgeshire.
(a) Ely Cathedral, Lady Chapel. Refitted 1860. New screen, stalls, heating and pavement intended. Nothing survives.
(b) School and schoolmaster's house, Broad Street. 1857.
(c) School, Silver Street, 1857.
(d) School, Gaol Street, 1857.
Clients for all four: Bishop, Dean and Chapter of Ely. All now demolished except for schoolmaster's house in Broad Street.

ENFIELD, London.
(a) School, Cockfosters. New half-timbered bedroom floor to schoolmaster's house.
(b) Trent Park. Additions for R C L Bevan (1809–90), cf Fosbury.

FOSBURY, Wiltshire.
(a) Christchurch. Cons. 30.9.1856. Client: R C L Bevan. Redundant. Privately owned since 1979. Plans of 1859 for spire unexecuted.
(b) Parsonage. 1855.
(c) School.

GREAT BEDWYN, Wiltshire. Cottages. 1858–59.

GREAT WARLEY, Essex, St Mary. Reconstruction and enlargement. 1858–60. Almost entirely dem.

GREENWICH, St Paul. Devonshire Drive, London SE10. 1865–66. Site given by George Blisset (cf. Wells). Rebuilt after bomb damage in 1950. Only shell remains. Cost: £7,000.

GREENWICH, Bridge Street
(a) St Peter. Cons. 20.11.1866. Site also free gift of Rev George Blisset. Cost: £6,000. Damaged 1941. Dem. 1955.
(b) Vicarage. 1866–67. Dem. 1955.
(c) School. 1866–67.

GRENDON, Northamptonshire. Rectory. 1850. RIBA (2).

GUILDFORD, Surrey, St Nicholas. Fs 2.4.1875. Cons. 20.4.1876. A design executed after his death by Ewan Christian. Client: Dr Monsell. Cost: £7,323.

HALL HYLE, Norfolk. RA 1845. For T E Wallace.

HAMMERWOOD PARK, near East Grinstead, West Sussex. 1792 by Benjamin Latrobe. Family diary of Oswald Augustus Smith who purchased house in 1864, said to contain reference to work commissioned from Teulon.

HAMPSTEAD, St Paul's, Avenue Road, London. Cons. February 1864. Cost: £2,800. (First scheme with tower and spire costed at £4,000). Bombed 1940, dem. 1958–59.

HAMPSTEAD, St Stephen, Rosslyn Hill, NW3. Fs 12.5.1869. Cons. 31.12.1869 (Aisles, porches, W. narthex, S. transept, organ chamber and vestry added 1870 and cap to tower 1871). Client: Rev Joshua Kirkman, Principal donors: Charles Henry Lardner Woodd and Reginald Heber Prance. Cost: £27,000. Carvings by Earp, mosaics by Salviati. Redundant since 1977.

HAMPSTEAD, Branch Hill Lodge, Branch Hill, London. Additions and gate lodge. 1868–70. Client: B W Smith.

HAMPSTEAD, Tensleys, The Green/Rosslyn Hill, London. Additions and alterations to the house Teulon bought for himself in 1846 and where he lived until his death. Dem.

HAMPTON WICK, London. Parsonage. 1854.

HANWORTH PARK, London, St George. Rebuilt 1865 retaining N. and S. nave walls from predecessor of 1812. Client: Algernon Perkins.

HARRINGTON, Lincolnshire.
(a) St Mary. Rebuilt 1854–55 retaining tower arch. RIBA (2).
(b) Rectory 1854.

HASTINGS, East Sussex.
(a) St Mary's Lodge, Priory Road. 1845. Client: Rev Thomas Vores, perpetual curate of St Mary-in-the-Castle. Now St Mary's Home.
(b) St Mary Magdalene Schools. 1856.
(c) Holy Trinity Church. Work began November 1856 on church, vicarage and schools in Cambridge Road (RIBA (2)) but site had to be switched to Robertson Street after land slip. Fs 22.7.1857. Client: Dr Thomas Crosse. Contractor: John Howell. Part Donor: Countess Waldegrave. Both designs at RA 1857, 1858. Tower unbuilt save for porch.
(d) Fountain in front of Holy Trinity formerly with statues of Our Lord and The Woman of Samaria. 'Opened' 24.5.1862.

HAWKLEY, Hampshire.
(a) SS Peter & Paul. Rebuilt 1865 in Neo-Norman.
(b) Hawkleyhurst. 1860–61. New house for James Maberley.

HISON (Hyson) Green, Nottinghamshire. St Paul's Parsonage, 1855.

HOLBORN, City of London.

(a) St Andrew's Church. Re-ordering of Wren interior. Re-opened 13.10.1872. Cost: new seating: £989, internal decoration: £1,176 (later reduced) by Stephen Phillips.
(b) Court House and new rectory, St Andrew's Street. 1868–71. Cost: Instructed Feb 1869 not to exceed £10,000. Client: Rev Henry George Scawen Blunt 1821–99, cousin of Wilfred Scawen Blunt, the poet. Extraordinary staircase.

HOLBORN, Queen's Square, London, WC1.
(a) St George the Martyr. 1706. Recast 1867–69. Re-opened 30.3.1869. New sanctuary fittings including pulpit and new external zinc-covered spirelet. Client: Rev John Backe. Carver: Mr Bromfield of Kennington Road.
(b) St George the Martyr Schools. 1864. Cost: £2,800.

HOLKHAM, Norfolk. Teulon was involved on the estate of the Earls of Leicester at Holkham in the late 1840s. RA Designs for 'Leicester Memorial' 1844, and 'Almshouse' 1848. Teulon prepared proposals to remodel the house itself including the vestibule of the N. hall and apparently terraces in the gardens. None of this was executed. The N. and S. lodges may be by Teulon but it seems that the stables are not.

HOLLESLEY, Suffolk. Rectory. 1845.

HOOLE, Cheshire. House for J Walker.

HOPTON, Suffolk, St Margaret. Rebuilding on new site given by Daniel Gurney of North Runcton Hall. Fs 5.9.1865. Cons. 27.9.1866. Cost: £3,300.

HORSHAM, West Sussex.
(a) St Mary the Virgin. Restoration and enlargement including new E. window. Teulon approached 1860. Re-opened 14.11.1865. Cost: £7,500. Client: The Rev James Fisher Hodgson.
(b) School, St Mark's, North Street. 1862.

HUDDINGTON, Hereford and Worcester. Lychgate.

HUMBERTON, North York. Cottages. 1861.

HUNSTANWORTH, Durham.
(a) St James the Less. Rebuilt 1862–63. Two-bay pulpit carved by McCulloch, a pupil of Earp.
(b) Vicarage. Converted from existing house 1863.
(c) Church School with adjoining house in adjacent hamlet of Townfield.
(d) Cottages. Teulon rebuilt virtually the whole of the village between 1863 and 1865, each cottage, or pair, being different. Client for all: Rev Daniel Capper of Newbiggin Hall (cf Huntley).

HUNTLEY, Gloucestershire.
(a) St John the Baptist. Built 1861–63 retaining medieval tower. Cons. 23.6.1863. Client: Rev Daniel Capper.

Lectern, pulpit and reredos by Earp.
(b) Huntley Manor. Extensive alterations
1862. Client: Henry Probyn, a friend of
the Earl of Ducie (cf Tortworth).
ICKLESHAM, East Sussex, All Saints. Restoration
1848–52. New font, porch and windows.
Unsigned watercolour in church may show
Teulon's intentions for the roof.
IPSWICH, Suffolk. Designs submitted to the
Corporation of Ipswich for County Hall and
Law Courts. Unexecuted.
ISLINGTON, ALMSHOUSE for Dyers' Company,
Balls Pond Road. Won in competition 1840.
Dem. 1939.
ISLINGTON, St Silas, Penton Street. Fs 19.7.1860.
Teulon dismissed. Built as Christchurch by
Loftus Brock, cons 1867 as St Silas.
KENNINGTON, Lambeth, St Mark. Recasting.
Begun 1863 but bulk of work 1871–73 at cost
of £2,000. Teulon's work destroyed in the
War.
KINGSCOTE, Gloucestershire, St John. Restoration
1851. Client: Rev A G Cornwall and Col
Kingscote.
KINGS LYNN, Norfolk. St Nicholas School, Pilot
Street. 1869. Cost: (Site and building) £1,300.
KINGSTON, London. Parsonage. 1856.
KIRMINGTON, Humberside, St Helen. Addition of
north aisle and organ chamber. 1859. Client:
Earl of Yarborough.
KNIGHTSBRIDGE, London, Holy Trinity 1860.
Competition design for new church to replace
Knightsbridge Chapel. Competition won by
Raphael Brandon.
LAKENHEATH, Suffolk. Vicarage. 1856.
LAMBETH, St Andrew, Coin Street, London SE1.
Fs 13.5.1855. Cons. 20.6.1856. Cost: £5,989
excluding heating. Stone carving by Forsyth.
Metalwork by Skidmore. Redecorated 1872.
Church bombed and dem. 1955. Teulon
almost certainly responsible for the church
school and adjacent minister's house (dated
1868) in Roupell Street.
LAMBETH, St Thomas, Westminster Bridge Road.
(a) St Thomas. Fs 24.11.1856. Cons.
24.6.1857. Cost: £4,375 Teulon also
designed temporary church in converted
builders' premises in Waterloo Road
1851–52.
(b) Vicarage, 1855–57. Cost £1,046.
Both church and school dem. 1961–62.
LAMBETH, Holy Trinity School, Carlisle Street.
(Paul Joyce)
LECKHAMPSTEAD, Berkshire, St James. Fs
3.5.1859. Cons. 30.10.1860. Cost: £1,745,
largely met by Rev John Robinson.
LEE, Kent. Projected baths, at RA, 1836.
.LEICESTER, Leicestershire.
(a) Holy Trinity Church. Recasting.
Commenced 7.1.1872. Re-opened
23.5.1872. Spire completed 24.10.1872.

Cost: £5,700. Radical internal alterations
1966.
(b) 'Westcotes', Westcotes Drive (now
hospital). For S Harris.
LETTON (Lyston) Court, Letton, Hereford and
Worcester. 1860–61, 1863 (Rev C J Robinson
'Mansions and Manors of Herefordshire'
1872). For Rev Henry Blisset (cf Greenwich
and Wells). House burned 1925.
LIMPSFIELD COMMON, Surrey, 'Tensleys' (formerly
Tinsley) for Thomas Teulon (1764–1844) and
Seymour Teulon, JP (1804–76).
LINCOLN, Lincolnshire, St Michael, Christ's
Hospital Terrace. First designs 1853. Cons.
16.9.1856. Client: Rev John Somerville
Gibney (1815–1875) who also founded the
North District School in Westgate, now
closed, which may be a work of Teulon.
Carving by Mowbray, gas fittings by
Skidmore, tiles by Minton.
LINCOLN, St Peter at Arches. Church of c.1720
recast 1854. Dem. 1936.
LITTLEPORT, Cambridgeshire.
(a) St George. New double north aisle,
seating, prayer desk and pulpit. Client:
Rev Edward Sparke, Canon of Ely.
(b) Adjacent schools and vicarage must be by
Teulon.
LONDON, City of, St Andrew by the Wardrobe by
Wren. Repairs 1838. Teulon left money to the
church in his will.
LONG NEWTON, Cleveland, St Mary. Proposals for
S. aisle, refitting and gabled mausoleum to the
Vane family. Unexecuted. Work entrusted to
P C Hardwick 1856–57.
MALVERN, Hereford and Worcester. Sketch for
large house in Old English style.
MANNINGTREE, Essex. Mechanics Institute. 1849.
MARLBOROUGH, Wiltshire. Cemetery Chapel.
Plans prepared 1859. For use by inmates of
workhouse. Cost not to exceed £475.
Unexecuted.
METHWOLD, Norfolk. Schools. 1855.
MIDDLETON STONEY, Oxfordshire.
(a) All Saints. Restoration and partial
rebuilding. 1856. Also restored by G E
Street.
(b) Schools. 1855.
MISTERTON, Leicestershire.
(a) St Leonard. Plans prepared for re-ordering
1858 but may have been unexecuted.
(b) School. 1857.
(c) New timber porch at Rectory, 1859.
MONK SOHAM, Suffolk. Rectory (former) 1846.
MOOR PARK, Hertfordshire. Plans for classical
conservatory dated July 1847. Client: Lord
Robert Grosvenor. William Burn carried out
alterations to house 1849.
NETHERFIELD, East Sussex.
(a) St John the Baptist. Cons. 26.8.1855.
Chancel arch capitals by Earp. 1859 plans

for spire unrealized.

(b) School and schoolmaster's house 1858–59.

(c) Parsonage — now Netherfield Court? Cost £1,470. 1859–60.

(d) Several three-bedroomed cottages in the village. Client (for all buildings): Sarah Lady Webster, widow of Sir Godfrey Webster 1815–1853 of Battle Abbey.

NETTLEWOLD. (No county given). School. 1856.

NEW BOLINGBROKE, Lincolnshire.

(a) St Peter. 1854. (RIBA (2) shows a modified design.)

(b) Vicarage. 1854.

NEWINGTON BAGPATH, Gloucestershire, St Bartholomew. Largely rebuilt 1858. Pressure from Eccl to add additional stage to tower resisted. Redundant and derelict.

NEWPORT, Essex, St Mary. New stone pulpit 1860 and 'restoration' of early medieval font with addition of serpentine columns.

NORTHAW, Hertfordshire. School. Cost: £750. 1851 Dem.

NORTH COCKERINGTON, Lincolnshire. Parsonage.

NORTH CREAKE, Norfolk.

(a) School. 1849. Built at expense of Earl Spencer and Rev G Keppel, brother of the Second Earl of Leicester (cf Holkham).

(b) Rectory. 1846.

NORTH ELKINGTON, Lincolnshire.

(a) St Helen. Rebuilding of Georgian church. Fs 14.7.1851. Cons. Aug 1852. Cost: £1,000. Now a house.

(b) Lodge 'at Elkington' with belvedere.

NORTH NIBLEY, Gloucestershire. The Tyndale Monument on Nibley Knoll. 1862–65. 120 ft high in style of campanile. In memory of William Tyndale, translator of Bible. Principal client: 2nd Earl of Ducie (cf Tortworth). Site presented by Lord Fitzhardinge. Enamel work by Salviati.

NORTH ORMSBY, Lincolnshire. St Helen. 1848 Client: Miss M Ansell. Now a house.

NORTH RAUCEBY, Lincolnshire, St Peter. Chancel rebuilt and sacristy added 1853.

NORTHWOOD, London.

(a) Holy Trinity 1852–54. Fs 12.10.1852 Cons. 5.1.1854. Site given by Lord Robert Grosvenor who is buried there.

(b) Parsonage, 1856. Site also given by Lord Grosvenor and Teulon almost certainly the architect.

NYMPSFIELD, Gloucestershire.

(a) St Bartholomew. Rebuilding. Cons. 23.7.1863. Cost: £3,000. 1470 tower retained. Massive stone lychgate.

(b) Schoolmaster's house. 1863.

OARE, Wiltshire, Holy Trinity. 1857–58. Romanesque style on instructions of client: Mrs Mary Goodman. Cost £1,900 (£1,000 from Mrs Goodman.)

OVER, Cheshire. St Chad. Restoration 1868–70.

(Chancel restored by Ewan Christian at same time).

OWLPEN, Gloucestershire. 'Large domestic work' near Uley for T A Stoughton.

OXENWOOD, Wiltshire. Construction of most of cottages in village 1861–62.

OXFORD, Oxfordshire. St Frideswide. Fs 13.12.1870. Cons. 10.4.1872. Client: Rev Thomas Chamberlain. Cost: £2,990. Tower incomplete.

PAGLESHAM, Essex. Rectory. 1861.

PAKENHAM, Suffolk.

(a) St Mary. Restored 1849, two new transepts. Client: Lord Calthorpe.

(b) Vicarage.

PENZANCE, Cornwall. Design for new Town Hall and Market Place jointly prepared with Sampson Kempthorne; submitted to the Corporation of Penzance. 1835. Unbuilt.

PERRY BAR, West Midlands. Perry Hall. Alterations and additions to 16th century house for Lord Calthorpe (Honourable Frederick Gough). Early 1850s. Dem. 1929.

POTTER'S BAR, Hertfordshire. Parsonage, St John.

POYNINGS, West Sussex. Schools. Designs prepared 1854, modified 1857 to reduce costs.

PRESTON, Northamptonshire. Repairs to house dem. 1872.

RAITHBY, Lincolnshire. Rectory.

RIBY, Lincolnshire.

(a) School and schoolhouse. 1849.

(b) Almshouses. 1848, dated 1851. Dem. Client (for both): Col G Tomline, MP, JP (of Riby Hall) whose uncle was Bishop of Lincoln (1787–1820).

(c) Some cottages in village could be by Teulon.

RISEHOLME, Lincolnshire.

(a) St Mary. Fs 4.4.1850. Cons. 7.8.1851. Client: Bishop Kaye of Lincoln. Cost: £1,306. Plans for tower and spire abandoned. Bellcote provided by Teulon 1853.

(b) Parsonage. 1856. Client: Rev William Frederick Kaye (cf South Carlton), son of the Bishop who by then was dead. Now offices. Altered 1873–74?.

ROADE, Northamptonshire. Parsonage client. Rev Alex Annand. RIBA (1).

RUSHFORD, Norfolk.

(a) St Mary. RIBA (2) has sketch of proposed rebuilding with exception of the tower. Unexecuted.

(b) Reconstruction of ruins of medieval Rushford College as vicarage. 1855. Clients: Buxton family (cf Shadwell).

RYDE, Isle of Wight. Woodlands. Extensive addition and alterations to older house. 1870–71. Client: Col the Hon Somerset J A Calthorpe.

RYE HARBOUR, East Sussex.
- (a) Church of Holy Spirit, Fs. 29.3.1849. Cons. 20.8.1849. Apse 1912.
- (b) School and schoolmaster's house. 1859. Now wholly in residential use.

ST LEONARD'S, East Sussex.
- (a) St John the Evangelist. 1856. Burned 1856 and replaced by Blomfield.
- (b) St Mary Magdalene School and schoolmaster's house. 1855–56. Benefactor: Dowager Lady St John. Cost: £2,300.

ST MARYLEBONE, London. Drinking fountain. Bryanston Square. 1860.

ST NEOTS, Cambridgeshire. School. Cost: just over £600.

ST PANCRAS, London. St Luke. Designs for new church 1855. Unexecuted.

SANDGATE, Kent.
- (a) St Paul. 1849. Sketch (fantasy design?) with campanile and spire and covered passageway from street.
- (b) Enbrook. 1853–55. Client: Hon J D Bligh, afterwards Earl of Darnley. Cost: £4,500. Only section of façade survives.

SANDRINGHAM, Norfolk.
- (a) St Mary Magdalen. Restoration including rebuilding of chancel and provision of lychgate, font and reredos. 1857–58. New choir stalls 1859. Client: Lady Harriette Cowper. Practically nothing remains.
- (b) Sandringham House. New two-storey E. porch and conservatory and other additions. Client: Honourable Spencer Cowper, Lord Palmerston's stepson. Estate purchased 1862 by H R H Prince of Wales. Some work survives.

SEAHAM, Durham. Seaham Hall. Plans prepared 1855–56 for alterations. Steward reports building work in progress March 1856. Vulliamy approached 1860–61.

SHADWELL, Norfolk. Extensive additions 1856–60. Client: Lady Buxton and Sir Robert Jacob Buxton, her son, then a minor. Clock tower at RA 1858 and tower 1859. Designs for fountain to cover St Chad's Well and cartoons for stained glass and fittings. 1859. Organ in hall by Gray and Davidson, metalwork by Skidmore, colour decoration by Fisher.

SHENFIELD, Essex, St Mary the Virgin. Restoration in 1858.

SIBTHORPE, Nottinghamshire. Rectory. 1854.

SIDMOUTH, Devon.
- (a) St Nicholas. New reredos. 1860.
- (b) All Saints School. 1867.

SILVERTOWN, London E16.
- (a) St Mark. Cons. 7.8.1862 replacing school-cum-chapel of 1857, both built for Rev H Douglas. Redundant 1974. Gutted by fire 1981. To be repaired.
- (b) Parsonage. 1860–63. Dem.

- (c) School. 1869. No definite attribution. Dem.

SKENDLEBY, Lincolnshire. Skendleby House. Additions 1848 for Sir Edward Brackenbury.

SLOUGH, Berkshire. St Lawrence. Designs for addition of chancel 1872. Unexecuted.

SOUTH CARLTON, Nottinghamshire. St John the Baptist. Addition of N. aisle 1851. Restoration 1859–60 — new roof, E. end, font and S. porch. Client: William Frederick John Kaye, Archdeacon of Lincoln from 1863 and son of Bishop Kaye (cf Riseholme).

SOUTH THORESBY, Lincolnshire. Rectory 1853–54.

SOUTHWARK, Christ Church, Blackfriars Road, London S E 1. Plans to rebuild church of 1738 prepared in 1853 abandoned. New brick apse and internal re-arranging 1857. Bombed, dem. and rebuilt.

SOUTHWARK, Manciple Street, London SE1.
- (a) St Stephen. Cons. 1850.
- (b) School 1848. Dem.
- Both buildings at RA 1848.

SOUTH WEALD, Essex.
- (a) St Peter. New nave, chancel, south aisle and upper portion of tower and internal fittings. 1867–68. Woodwork by Polley of Coggeshall, reredos and stone carving by Earp. Cost: £7,000.
- (b) Sir Anthony Browne's Almshouses, Wigley Bush Lane. 1854–55. Exhibited in 1856 Architectural Exhibition. Includes circular water pump shelter and chapel.
- (c) School, Wigley Bush Lane. Opened 1856. Client, as with church: Rev C A Belli. Angel Gabriel carved by Forsyth. Dem. 1968.

STANWELL, Surrey, St Mary. Restoration and addition of north aisle. 1863.

STAPLE, Kent, St James. Lychgate.

STAPLEFIELD, West Sussex, St Mark. Plans for re-ordering of E. end 1858.

STEEPLE BARTON, Oxfordshire.
- (a) Rectory. 1856. Cost £900 Hexagonal hall.
- (b) Barton Manor. RA 1859.

STIBBINGTON, Cambridgeshire.
- (a) St John the Baptist. Restoration 1847–48. Client: Duke of Bedford. Proposal for a new roof and floor, refitting, tower and spire. Duke asked for revisions but work went ahead.
- (b) Gatehouse, Stibbington Hall.

STOKE, Oxfordshire. School and Schoolmaster's house. 1858. Client: Sir H Peyton.

SUNBURY, Surrey, St Mary. Recasting of 1752 church. 1856–63 with new chancel and western porch (dem. 1972). Remodelling of tower unexecuted. Cost (increased accommodation); £1,200. Pulpit and sanctuary rails ejected 1972.

SUNK ISLAND, Humberside.
  (a) Holy Trinity. Church planned but unexecuted. Present building, 1877 by Ewan Christian.
  (b) School and schoolhouse. 1858.
  (c) Scattered cottages.
  Whole estate reclaimed from the sea by the Crown Office of Woods.

SUTTON, Cambridgeshire, St Andrew. Restoration by Jesus College, Cambridge. 1854.

TATHWELL, Lincolnshire. Vicarage for Rev John Waite. RIBA (1).

THEDDLETHORPE, Lincolnshire, St Helen. Rebuilt 1864–67.

THORNEY, Cambridgeshire. Teulon was involved for twenty years in improvements to the Thorney Estate of the Dukes of Bedford under two Stewards, Tyro Wing (d 1851) and his successor Robert Mein. (Beds CRO).
  (a) National School 1843–50.
  (b) A new wall for the churchyard 1848.
  (c) New farmhouse in French Drive (North Fen) at £1,001 9s 2d, 1848.
  (d) 15 cottages, Wisbech Road for £2,076. 1848–49
  (e) Post Office, also to double as Parish Constable's house and a room for the Relieving Officer. Plans prepared 1849.
  (f) New shops for the taylor, carpenter, wheelwright, fishmonger and cooper. Plans prepared 1849.
  (g) Water tower, carpenter's shop, sawmills, smithy and cottage off Station Road. Dated 1855 but plans noted at least as early as 1849.
  (h) School, Church Street (now Public Library).
  There seems no reason to doubt Teulon's authorship of a hundred or so other cottages in a variety of picturesque styles strung along the Wisbech Road, (4–28 dated 1856, 32–40 dated 1855, 82 dated 1849, 102–112 dated 1863, 27–35 dated 1861).

TORTWORTH COURT, Cromhall, Avon 1849–53. Client: 2nd Earl of Ducie. Cost: £45,000. RA 1855. RIBA (2) — design for Gothic glazed door and sketch probably of rejected design. Stained glass by Gibbs. Iron work by Baily. Also boathouse etc.

ULEY, Gloucestershire. St Giles (formerly St Matthew). Rebuilding 1857–58. Cost: £2,500.

UPSHIRE, Essex. Warlies Park House. Remodelling and extension for Sir Fowell Buxton in 1870's. RIBA obit.

VIRGINIA WATER, Surrey. Chinese Fishing Temple by Wyatville and Crace. Works of minor repair 1860.

WARLEY COMMON, Essex.
  (a) Christ Church. Fs 10.5.1853. Cons. 29.3.1855. Cost: £2,200.
  (b) Vicarage.
  (c) Chapel-school. 1855.

WATFORD, Hertfordshire, St Andrew. Fs Dec. 1853. Cons. 21.8.1857 (work suspended for two years). Spire completed late 1857. RIBA (2) and RA 1855.

WAVENDON, Buckinghamshire. Cottages 1861.

WELLS, Somerset.
  (a) St Thomas. Fs 6.3.1856. Cons. 2.12.1857. Client: Troth Jenkyns, widow of Richard, Dean of the Cathedral and former Master of Balliol whose idea the church had been but who died 1854. After her death 1857 completion by Rev Henry Blisset (cf Greenwich). Reredos and font 1857 by Forsyth. Altar rails by Skidmore, chancel windows by Wailes, south-west window by Clayton, the rest by Wilmshurst, reredos coloured by Fisher. S. aisle added 1864.
  (b) Vicarage. 1859.
  (c) Church school, 1859.
  (d) St Thomas's Terrace.

WELTON, Lincolnshire, St Martin. Restoration 1859.

WESTERHAM, Kent, St Mary the Virgin. Lychgate. Unexecuted.

WEST GRINSTEAD, West Sussex. Alterations 1863–66. Client: Sir Percy Burrell. New hall and porch tower.

WESTMINSTER, London
  (a) 14–16 Bedford Street? c.1863. (*Pevsner*).
  (b) St Michael's School, Pimlico 1847–48. Fs 14.7.1847. Opened September 1848. Dem. for Victoria Station.
  (c) St Luke, Berwick Street. Re-ordering 1863–64. Closed 1935, dem.
  (d) The Buxton Fountain, Victoria Tower Gardens. 1861–66. Client: Charles Buxton MP as a memorial to his father Sir T Fowell Buxton, MP and to mark the abolition of slavery. Buxton was himself an amateur architect and credited with design on tablet. Originally erected in Parliament Square. Stonework and sculpture by Thomas Earp, iron and enamelled roof by Skidmore (recently splendidly renewed by the Property Services Agency). Cost: £1,200

WETHERINGSETT, Suffolk. Rectory (now Manor House). RA 1844 and RIBA (1).

WIMBLEDON, London.
  (a) Christ Church, Copse Hill. 1857–60. Cost (including that of club): £3,425.
  (b) Club house. 1857–59 (for moral improvement of working classes).
  (c) Wimbledon College. Client: Rev J M Brackenbury. Cost: £9,000.
  (d) 47–73 Denmark Road, London SW19. Designed for the Cottage Improvement Society.

WINDSOR, Berkshire.
- (a) Queen's Terrace, Ascot Road, facing the Great Park. 1849. RA 1849.
- (b) Prince Consort Cottages off Alexandra Road. Built by Henry Roberts, extended in late 1850s by Teulon.
- (c) Workshops and cottages on Royal Estate.
- (d) Labourers' cottages.
- (e) Royal Lodge Chapel. Chancel rebuilt 1863. Nave by 1866 (jointly with Anthony Salvin).
- (f) St John the Baptist, Windsor's parish church. Rebuilding of chancel and nave roof 1869–73. Client: Canon H J Ellison, Queen Victoria's Chaplain in Ordinary. Intended construction for external narthex at W. front unexecuted.

Not a royal commission but the Queen gave £400 towards costs and fs of chancel was laid by Princess Christian.

WINSTON, Suffolk. Rectory (The Grange) 1843–44.

WOODCHESTER, Gloucestershire, St Mary. Fs 1862. Cons. 24.9.1863. Client: 2nd Earl of Ducie.

WOODSTOCK, Oxfordshire.
- (a) St Mary Magdalene, Recasting and extension. 1854–55. New W. front. Rebuilding of aisles to chancel. Raising of roof. Gothicisization of tower. Disappeared on reconstruction of church in 1878.
- (b) School. 1853–54.

WORDWELL, Suffolk, All Saints. Restoration 1857 with new bellcote and porch. Redundant. RIBA (2).

9 DAVID RHIND

Author's Note: This list is compiled without the benefit of access to either the archives of The Commercial Bank of Scotland or of Edinburgh Dean of Guild Court for the period. It seems likely that a substantial number of minor commissions are unnoticed.

Early 1830 BRANCH OF COMMERCIAL BANK OF SCOTLAND 138–40, High Street, Falkirk, Central. Love, *Antiquarian Notes & Queries* gives 1832 as date.

*c.*1833 RHIND FAMILY GRAVE, St Cuthbert's Churchyard, Edinburgh. Joint grave of David, McDuff & Robert Rhind families.

1835 Competition Design for new houses of parliament, London. The design was exhibited Edinburgh Architectural Association Exhibition, 1907.

*c.*1835 SUNLAWS HOUSE, Borders. (SRO GD224/508/1/57).

*c.*1837 BRANCH OF COMMERCIAL BANK OF SCOTLAND, Brown Street, Blairgowrie, Tayside. Information from DM Walker, SDD List.

1838 MONUMENT TO SIR WALTER SCOTT, George Square, Glasgow. National Gallery of Scotland Print Room D.2683.

1839 Competition Design for NORTH OF SCOTLAND BANK, Castle Street, Aberdeen. Part set of competition drawings with Clydesdale Bank, Castle Street Aberdeen. Copies in NMRS. ST. JOHN'S CHURCH, Leith, Lothian. Additions. SRO CH2/236/5.

*c.*1840 KNOCKDOLIAN CASTLE, Strathclyde. For Alexander Cathcart of Genoch & Knockdolian. James Paterson *History of Ayr & Wigton* Vol II.

1842 ACHNACARRY ESTATE, Highland, Stable block. SRO NRAS. Information from Elizabeth Beaton SDD.

1843–7 HEAD OFFICE OF COMMERCIAL BANK OF SCOTLAND, 14, George Street, Edinburgh. Working Drawings with Dick Peddie & McKay Architects, Edinburgh. James Wyatt's competition designs in RIBA Library. *ILN* 18th July 1846 *The Scotsman* 3rd April 1847. D R Hay *The Laws of Harmonious Colouring*, 1847 145. S H Jackson, 'The George Street Office, Edinburgh, of the Royal Bank of Scotland' in *The Three Banks Review* 92, Dec 1971.

*c.*1844–53 TRINITY COLLEGE CHURCH, Edinburgh. The demolition of this venerable medieval church to make way for the railway and the proposal to rebuild it on another site was the biggest 'preservation' scandal of 19th century Scotland. Rhind's services were retained to provide estimates for the rebuilding. In 1848 Rhind had the papers relating to his employment privately printed when the affair had come to litigation. See: David Rhind *Documents and Correspondence Relative to Trinity College Church*, 1848.

1844 FEUING PLAN FOR LONGCROFT, Linlithgow, Lothian. For Thomas Burns Esq SRO RHP 9191 Lithograph Plan. FEUING PLAN FOR MERCHISTON EAST & DOVECOTE PARKS, Edinburgh. For Governors of George Watson's Hospital. Lithograph plan & Ms report by Rhind of 23rd July at Merchant Company Hall.

1846 HEAD OFFICE OF CENTRAL BANK OF SCOTLAND, 48–50, St John Street, Perth, Tayside (& single storey shop development at 58, 60, St John Street). For Central Bank of Scotland founded 1834 (Merged with Bank of Scotland 1868). *AEB,* 1868 SDD List.

1848–67 WILLIAM HENRY MILLER MAUSOLEUM, Craigentinny, Edinburgh. For Samuel Christie MP under terms of W H Miller's will. *Br* 22nd Sept. 1860. John Christie-Miller *The Miller Inheritance* Unpublished Typescript May 1982.

1848–53 DANIEL STEWART'S HOSPITAL, Edinburgh. For Trustees of Daniel Stewart. Bound volume of working drawings at Merchant

Company Hall. 3 Sketch Designs RIBA Drawings Collection. *Br* 30th Nov 1850. *Civil Engineer & Architect's Journal* Vol XV, May 1852. J Thomson *A History of Daniel Stewart's College*. ND Irwin Campbell *Daniel Stewart's College*, unpublished undergraduate thesis University of Edinburgh, May 1971.

1849 CULGOWER FARM HOUSE, Sutherland Estates. NLS Dep 313/1178. James Loch to Duke of Sutherland: 'I enclose all the elevations, the smallest one was sent by Mr Rhind himself I think — it is ugly but if it had gables it would be cheaper, and in character with the place. The other two were drawn from sketches made by Mr Barry at Loch Inver'. Information from John Gifford.

1850 H I RAMSAY GARDENS, Edinburgh, Ragged schools. SDD List.

c. 1850 SHERIFF COURT, Jedburgh, Borders. Adaptation & Extension of former County Buildings. *AEB* 1868.

c. 1850 BRANCH OF COMMERCIAL BANK OF SCOTLAND Bank house, Buchan's Corner, Peebles, Borders. Information from D M Walker.

1851 OFFICE FOR LIFE ASSOCIATION OF SCOTLAND, 37, George Street, Edinburgh. Conversion of existing New Town House. Minute Book of Life Association of Scotland.

1851–55 CARLOWRIE CASTLE, Lothian. For Thomas Hutchison. Peter Hutchison *The Hutchisons of Carlowrie, A Sketch of a Lothian Family 1852–1982*, unpublished, typescript. John Small *Castles & Mansions of The Lothians*, 1883. Copies of surviving accounts in NMRS.

1852 CRAIGENTINNY HOUSE, Edinburgh. For Samuel Christie MP. Additions to existing house, stables & coach house. John Christie-Miller *The Miller Inheritance*, unpublished typescript, 1982. John Small *Castles & Mansions of the Lothians*, 1883.

BRANCH OF COMMERCIAL BANK OF SCOTLAND, Tower House, Hawick, Borders. SDD List.

1853 SUNLAWS HOUSE, Borders. Additions. Plans in NMRS.

1854–6 BRANCH OFFICE OF COMMERCIAL BANK OF SCOTLAND, Gordon Street, Glasgow. Design exhibited Royal Scottish Academy 1859 No. 627 & Edinburgh Architectural Association Exhibition 1907. *Building Chronicle* 1st Feb & 1st Dec 1855 *Civil Engineer & Architect's Journal* Vol 19, 1856. *A Series of Executed Examples of Ecclesiastical and Domestic Structures,* by GG Scott & Others, 1858.

1855–59 HEAD OFFICE OF LIFE ASSOCIATION OF SCOTLAND, 82, Princes Street, Edinburgh. Jointly with Sir Charles Barry. Minute Book of Life Association of Scotland (transcript of architectural references in NMRS). *Building Chronicle* 1st Feb, 1st May, 1st Aug 1856. *Br* 1st Jan 1859.

1855 ST LUKE'S EPISCOPAL CHURCH, Dumbarton, Strathclyde. *Dumbarton Herald* 28th June 1855. Note of laying of foundation stone '... to be by David Rhind of Edinburgh' (Information from Aonghus MacKechnie)

1856 SHERIFF COURT HOUSE, Oban, Strathclyde. SRO GD 112/49/5/1–8 Correspondence, alternative plans etc.

1857 COMPETITION DESIGN FOR GOVERNMENT OFFICES, London. Design Exhibited Edinburgh Architectural Association Exhibition, 1907.

1858 BRANCH OF THE COMMERCIAL BANK OF SCOTLAND, 38, South Street, Perth, Tayside. *Br* 28th March 1857.

1859 SELKIRK PARISH CHURCH, Borders. SRO GD157/587. Rhind supplied plans for new Parish Church.

BRANCH OF COMMERCIAL BANK OF SCOTLAND, Linlithgow, Lothian. Signed 'DR' and dated 1859. (Information from D M Walker).

1860 LODGES to Head Office of Commercial Bank of Scotland, Edinburgh. Edinburgh Dean of Guild (Information from DM Walker).

1860 PULPIT, Kirkliston Parish Church, Lothian. For Hutchisons of Carlowrie Colin McWilliam *Lothian* (The Buildings of Scotland, 1978.)

c. 1860 LIFE ASSOCIATION BUILDINGS GLASGOW, (?123 St Vincent Street). For The Life Association of Scotland. Design exhibited Edinburgh Architectural Association Exhibition, 1907.

1862 COMPETITION ENTRY FOR EDINBURGH MEMORIAL TO PRINCE CONSORT. Description of design in *Br* Obituary.

SHERIFF COURT, Buccleuch Street, Dumfries, Dumfries and Galloway. *AEB*, 1868. *Br* 2nd Aug 1862, 10th Aug & 5th Sep 1863, 10th Nov 1866.

HOPEKIRK PARISH CHURCH, Borders. SRO RHP 7684–5 Parts etc. of Contract Drawings.

LINLITHGOW MANSE, Lothian. Additions SRO RHP 12443.

1862–66 SHERIFF COURT, Wick, Highland. *AEB*, 1868.

1863 ROBERTON PARISH CHURCH, Strathclyde. *Br* 17th Dec 1864.

FEUING PLAN FOR BOROUGHMUIRHEAD with revised Feuing Plan for Merchiston Parks, Edinburgh. For George Watson's Hospital. Lithograph Plan incorporating elevations 26th Jan 1863 at Merchants Company Hall. (After a dispute over Merchiston Terrace Rhind was dismissed in 1867 when David McGibbon was appointed Hospital architect.) The plans for 12 Merchiston Place approved by Rhind in 1865 are in NMRS.

ILLUMINATIONS TO CELEBRATE MARRIAGE OF PRINCE & PRINCESS OF WALES, Edinburgh. March 11th. For private subscribers *Scotsman* Obituary. *The Scotsman* 11th March 1863. Edinburgh Town Council Minutes.

DESIGN FOR EDINBURGH IMPROVEMENTS, Town Hall etc. *Br* 16th May, 1863. SRO RHP 6514/1 Lithograph Plan.

1865 BRANCH OF COMMERCIAL BANK OF SCOTLAND, 28 Broad Street, Peterhead, Grampian. *Br* 25th March, 1865.

SHERIFF COURT, Selkirk. Borders *AEB*, 1868.

1866 CHURCH OF SCOTLAND ASSEMBLY HALL, Edinburgh. Additions (now Tolbooth St John's Church) *Br* Obituary, SRO MW/5/187.

1868 SHERIFF COURT, Kirkcudbright Dumfries and Galloway. *AEB*, 1868.

1869 BRANCH OF COMMERCIAL BANK OF SCOTLAND, St Andrew's, Fife. SDD List (now Burgh Offices.)

FEUING PLAN FOR LIVILANDS PARK, Stirling Central. SRO RHP 24837 Photostat of Lithograph feuing plan.

c.1870 ETTRICK LODGE, Selkirk, Borders. For T Craig-Brown. Additions to existing house. Information from DM Walker. Billiard Room dated 1870. Photocopy of Craig-Brown's notes on the house with description of Cuadros's paintings in Billiard Room (now missing) in NMRS.

c.1870 BRANCH OF COMMERCIAL BANK OF SCOTLAND, Girvan, Strathclyde. Scottish Civic Trust *Historic Building at Work,* 1983.

1872–4 WATT INSTITUTION AND SCHOOL OF ARTS, Chambers Street, Edinburgh. Elevation conforms to David Cousin's design for the street. Robert Strathearn Lindsay *History of the Masons Lodge of Holyrood, St Lukes,* 1935.

1872 BRANCH OF COMMERCIAL BANK OF SCOTLAND, Murray Place. Stirling *CL* Aug 28th 1969, 503.

1875 SHERIFF COURT, Lerwick, Shetland. Scottish Civic Trust *Historic Buildings at Work,* 1983.

1878 BRANCH OF THE COMMERCIAL BANK OF SCOTLAND, Commercial Street, Dundee, Tayside. Plans in NMRS.

1878 'CAMPO VERDE', 9 Tipperlin Road, Edinburgh. Villa for Dr Kalley. George Watson's Hospital Property Minutes (Information from Maurice Berrill).

1878–9 NORMAL COLLEGE, Chambers Street, Edinburgh. For Church of Scotland. Elevation conforms to David Cousin's design for the street. *Scotsman* Obituary.

1879 NORTH LEITH PARISH CHURCH, Lothian. Re-arrangement of interior seating, pulpit etc. SRO RHP 7307–7310.

c.1879 ST STEPHEN'S CHURCH, Edinburgh. Alterations & installation of organ. Documents in possession of St Stephen's Church.

1880 TWEEDDALE MONUMENT, HADDINGTON, Lothian. Replica of Pinkie fountain, sheltering marble bust of 8th Marquess of Tweeddale by G B Amendola. *Groome's Gazeteer.*

1880 HAWTHORNDEN, Lothian. Feuing plan for land round Gorton House. SRO RHP 13697 Plan signed David Rhind, 3rd Nov 1880 ex

GD/230/491.

10 ERNEST NEWTON

Newton was extraordinarily prolific, designing literally hundreds of buildings. This selection gives his more important projects.

1879 Development at GROVE PARK, Lewisham, London, for the Earl of Northbrook, mostly demolished though the Baring Hall Hotel survives altered.

1880 BAILLIFF'S COTTAGE, West Stratton, Hampshire.

1881 CHURCH OF THE GOOD SHEPHERD, Handen Road, Lee, Lewisham, London, designed c.1881, destroyed 1939–45.

1883 HOUSE OF RETREAT and school, Lloyd Square, Clerkenwell, Islington, London, for the Sisters of Bethany.

124–128, BROMLEY ROAD, Beckenham, Bromley, London, (originally one house).

LYNDHURST, 8, Bird-in-Hand Lane, Bickley, Bromley, London, for himself.

1884 RAMMELS HOUSE, The Hill, Cranbrook, Kent, (with William West Neve).

1885 RED HOUSE, 5, Hawthorne Road, Bickley, Bromley, London.

BEECHCROFT 19, Bickley Road, Bickley, Bromley, London.

1886 CHURCH OF ST GEORGE, Bickley, Bromley, vestry addition.

c.1887, 7 THE GRANGE. Wimbledon, London.

1888 BULLER'S WOOD, St Nicholas Lane, Bickley, Bromley, London, remodelled, (now school).

1889 WESTWOOD 6, Bird-in-Hand Lane, Bickley, Bromley, London.

1890 CHURCH OF ST SWITHUN, Hither Green Lane, Hither Green, Lewisham, (c.1890–95).

FARRANTS, Bickley Park Road, Bickley, Bromley, extensions, (and 1898).

1891 BANSTEAD HALL, Surrey, alterations, (also 1905).

BICKLEY HALL, stables, Bickley, Bromley, London.

HOUSE OF RETREAT, CHAPEL, Lloyd Square, Clerkenwell, Islington, London.

ST LUKE'S INSTITUTE, Southlands Road, Bromley. BEECHCROFT, 19, Bickley Road, Bickley, Bromley, London (now house).

1893 PRESTBURY, VICARAGE, Cheshire.

THE CEDARS, Camden Park Road, Chislehurst, Bromley.

3 and 5, (formerly stables), GRASMERE ROAD, Bromley.

1894 REDCOURT, Haslemere, Surrey.

HOUSE, Sutton Coldfield, West Midlands.

1895 BROOME HALL, Surrey, service wing.

1896 HIGH LANDS, Burley-in-Wharfedale, West Yorkshire.

181, MARTIN'S BANK AND BELL INN, High Street, Bromley.

FRENSHAM VICARAGE, Surrey.

1897, 67–79, Bebington Road, Port Sunlight, Merseyside, c.1897.

GLEBELANDS, Wokingham, Berkshire.

1898 VICARAGE, Shrigley Road Bollington, Cheshire.

COTTAGE, Hazeley Heath, Hampshire, (remodelled for himself).

ELM BANK, Camden Park Road, Chislehurst, Bromley, late 1890s.

BONCHESTER HOUSE, Camden Park Road, Chislehurst, Bromley, late 1890s.

1899 WAREHOUSE, Corsham Street, Hoxton, Hackney, London.

HAYES GROVE, Preston Road, Hayes, Bromley, London c.1899.

THE LODGE, Overbury, Hereford and Worcester.

MOLESCROFT, Hill Brow, Bickley, Bromley, London.

DERWENT HOUSE, Camden Park Road, Chislehurst, Bromley, London.

c.1900 FREMINGTON HOUSE, Devon,

STEEP HILL, Jersey, (designed 1899).

1902 NEWBIES, Baughurst, Hampshire.

107, PLAISTOW LANE, Bromley, London.

FOUR ACRE, West Green, Hampshire, (c.1902).

DORMAY COTTAGES, Overbury, Hereford and Worcester.

21 AND 23, PAGE HEATH LANE, Bickley, Bromley, London, altered.

LITTLE ORCHARD, Page Heath Lane, Bickley, Bromley, London.

1903 SHAVINGTON HALL, Cheshire, alterations, dem.

ALLIANCE ASSURANCE BUILDING, 88, St James's Street, London, (with Shaw).

FAIRACRE, Camden Park Road, Chislehurst, Bromley, London.

ENNORE, Chislehurst Road, Bickley, Bromley, London.

1904 23, GARDEN ROAD, Sundridge Park, Bromley, London.

BICKLEY COURT, Chislehurst Road, Bickley, Bromley, London.

CROSS HAND, Chislehurst Road, Bickley, Bromley, London.

COPLEY DENE, Wilderness Road, Chislehurst, Bromley, London.

TRISCOMBE HOUSE, Somerset, remodelled.

1905 FIELD HOUSE, Begbroke, Oxfordshire, (now convent), alterations.

SPIRE and tower, Church of St George, Bickley, Bromley, London.

CLYFFE HALL, Market Lavington, Wiltshire, alterations.

HOUSE, Reigate, Surrey, c.1905.

13, DENBRIDGE ROAD, Bickley, Bromley, London.

1906 ARDENRUN PLACE, Crowhurst, Surrey, (mostly dem).

MOOR PLACE, Much Hadham, Hertfordshire, wing.

LUCKLEY, Wokingham, Berkshire.

1907 SCHOOLMASTER'S HOUSE, Overbury, Hereford and Worcester.

LUDWICK CORNER, Cole Green Lane, Welwyn Garden City, Herts.

UPTON GREY MANOR HOUSE, Hampshire, remodelled, for Charles Holme, Editor of *The Studio*.

DAWN HOUSE, Romsey Road, Winchester, Hampshire.

18, EDWARD ROAD, Sundridge Park, Bromley, altered.

1908 SCOTSMAN'S FIELD, Church Stretton, Salop.

PARISH HALL, Church of the Holy Trinity, Lee, Lewisham, London.

1909 OVERBURY COURT, Hereford and Worcester, alterations, 1909–11.

CONDERTON COTTAGES, Overbury, Hereford and Worcester.

1910 BRAND LODGE, Colwall, Hereford and Worcester.

FEATHERCOMBE, Hambledon, Surrey.

APPSLEY PADDOX, Oxford, alterations.

THE GREENWAY, Shurdington, Gloucestershire, alterations.

AVONHURST, Camden Park Road, Chislehurst, Bromley.

1911, 1, RECTORY PLACE, Guildford, Surrey, alterations and additions.

R. C. CHAPEL OF SS GREGORY AND AUGUSTINE, Woodstock Road, Oxford.

LUKYNS, Ewhurst, Surrey.

GLEBE HOUSE, Kettleshulme, Cheshire.

1912 GREAT BURGH, Burgh Heath, Surrey.

OLDCASTLE, Dallington, East Sussex, alterations and additions.

KINGSWOOD HOUSE, Kingswood, Surrey.

EAST AVENUE, Whiteley Village, Cobham, Surrey, (altered).

1913 ABBOTSBURY CASTLE, Dorset.

LOGMORE, Westcott, Surrey.

FLINT HOUSE, Goring Heath, Oxfordshire.

JOUY-EN-JOUAS: HOUSE, Eure-et-Loire, France, (c.1913, unfinished).

TOMB OF RICHARD NORMAN SHAW, Churchyard of St John, Hampstead, London.

NINDFIELD, Overbury, Hereford and Worcester, additions.

1914 COGBILL'S COTTAGE, Overbury, Hereford and Worcester.

1919 NORSBURY HOUSE, Sutton Scotney, Hampshire, remodelled.

PENCARROW, Cornwall, alterations.

MEMORIAL SHRINE AND HALL, Uppingham, Leicestershire.

FARMHOUSE, Elmbridge Green, Oxfordshire.

RECTORY OF ST NICHOLAS, Stevenage, Hertfordshire, dem.

1920 CARMELITE CONVENT, Caen, Normandy, France, (with William Nicholls, unfinished).

INCE CASTLE, Cornwall, additions.

LIST OF ILLUSTRATIONS

PHOTOGRAPHIC ACKNOWLEDGEMENTS

The Publishers wish to thank the following for their kind permission to reproduce material in this volume.

BLACK AND WHITE ILLUSTRATIONS

By gracious permission of Her Majesty The Queen, 59,

E.R.M. Pratt 1, 11; The Royal Commission on Historical Monuments (England) 2, 5, 7, 12, 13, 21, 27, 41, 42, 58, 68, 71, 72, 74, 75, 80, 81, 82, 83, 84, 85, 86, 91, 92, 97, 99, 103, 104, 105, 106, 111, 113, 114, 115, 116, 117, 119, 120, 122, 124, 125, 142, 144, 145, 147, 148, 150, 151, 152, 153, 154, 155, 156; The Syndics of Cambridge University Library 3, 8, 9, 10, 24, 25, 28, 29, 30, 32, 33, 43, 44, 63, 87; B.T. Batsford Ltd 4; The National Trust 6 (Bankes Collection, Kingston Lacy), 15, 102; Lord Skelmersdale 14; R. Fleetwood-Hesketh 16; The Earl of Wharncliffe/The Director of Libraries and Information Services, Sheffield City Libraries 17; Edizione d'Arte di Carlo E. Bestetti and C. S.A.S. 18, 20; The Rt. Hon. Lord Petrie/Essex Records Office 19; The Rt. Hon. The Lady Lucas/The Wrest Park Papers, Bedfordshire Records Office 22; The Warden and Fellows of Worcester College, Oxford 23; The British Architectural Library, RIBA, London 26, 29, 45, 46, 55, 56, 107, 108, 109, 126, 139, 143, 146; The Trustees of the Ecton Estate/Northamptonshire Records Office 47; Christie's 49; The Board and Trustees of the Victoria and Albert Museum 51, 62, 66, 67, 73; The Greater London Council, Print Collection 52; The R.A.C. Country Club 53; The British Library 54, 65, 88, 89; The Society of Antiquaries 57; Lord Camrose 60; Country Life 64, 95, 149; Christopher Lyster 70; The Master and Fellows of Downing College, Cambridge 79; The Guildhall Library, City of London 93; South Glamorgan County Library 98, 100; The Northern Ireland Archaeological Survey 101; Peter Reid 110; The Royal Commission on the Ancient and Historical Monuments of Scotland 127, 132, 134, 135, 136; The Clydesdale Bank 128; The National Galleries of Scotland, Edinburgh 129, 130; Aonghus Mackechnie 133; The Royal Incorporation of Architects in Scotland 137; City of Edinburgh Museums and Art Galleries 138; A.F. Kersting 157.
Others by the authors

COLOUR PLATES

Tim Mowl i, xviii; Nigel Silcox-Crowe ii; The National Trust iii, iv; Woodmansterne (Courtesy of The National Trust) photo: Nicholas Servian v, photo: Clive Friend xxiv, xxv, xxvi, xxvii; Tom Owen Edmunds vi, xxviii, xxix; Andor Gomme vii, viii, ix, x; Westminster City Libraries xi; The Yale Center for British Art, Paul Mellon Fund xii; Sir John Soane's Museum xiii; Roger White xiv; The

GLOSSARY

ABACUS: The flat top of the CAPITAL of a column, supporting an ENTABLATURE.

ACANTHUS: A fleshy leaved plant conventionalized in the decoration of classical capitals.

AEDICULE: A small, PEDIMENTED structure originally a shrine; hence frame for a niche.

ANTAE: Flat PILASTERS at either end of a row of columns.

ANTHEMION: Ornament in Greek architecture resembling honeysuckle often incorporated with ACANTHUS.

APSE: Semi-circular or polygonal recess usually at end of presbytery, choir or aisle of church.

ARCHITRAVE: 1. Lowest member of the ENTABLATURE resting directly upon capitals of supporting columns.
2. Moulding surrounding door or window.

ARTISAN MANNERISM: A non-courtly style of architecture of the seventeenth century in which elements of Elizabethan, Jacobean, Mannerist and Classical styles are used indiscriminately.

ARTS AND CRAFTS: Movement in the late nineteenth century inspired by the teaching of William Morris and Ruskin, to revive handicrafts and improve standards of design.

ASHLAR: Masonry walling made of large, smooth, even blocks.

ASTYLAR: Term describing a facade without PILASTERS or columns.

ATTIC STOREY: 1. A stage above the principal ENTABLATURE of a classical building.
2. The 'attic' in modern speech, space used loosely to mean garrett.

BALL FINIAL: see FINIAL.

BALUSTER: Individual element of a balustrade; short post or pillar supporting a handrail or COPING.

BAROQUE: Movement of the seventeenth and early eighteenth centuries. Architecture characterised by exuberant decoration and massing and complex composition.

BARONIAL: Scottish Revivalist style of the nineteenth century inspired by Scottish fortified architecture.

BARREL VAULT: See VAULT.

BATTER: A slight tilt of a wall from its base upwards.

BAY: Compartment or section in a building marked on the outside by windows, inside by columns, PILASTERS etc.

BEAUX ARTS: Rich classical style favoured by the École de Beaux Arts in late nineteenth-century France.

BELVEDERE: Small structure of Italian derivation erected on the roof to give a good view.

BREASTSUMMER: A massive horizontal beam sparring a wide opening such as a fireplace or a projecting gable.

BUCRANE/BUCRANIUM: A carved ox head or skull, usually garlanded, used decoratively in classical architecture.

CAPITAL: The moulded or carved top of a column, the type of ornament depending on the ORDER.

CARYATID: Sculptured female figure used in Greek architecture instead of a column to support an ENTABLATURE. Loosely, columns and pilasters, carved wholly or partly in human form.

CHAMFERED: An angle or edge of stone or wood block cut off diagonally.

CLERESTORY: Storey of aisled basilica or church above the range of arches or columns, pierced by windows. Applicable to domestic buildings.

CLUNCH: A type of chalk, strong enough to be used as building stone.

COADE STONE: Artificial stone resembling terracotta manufactured in London from 1769 onwards.

COMPOSITE: See ORDERS.

COPING: The uppermost course of masonry or brickwork in a wall, usually sloping, to throw off rain.

CORINTHIAN: See ORDERS.

CORNICE: Projecting horizontal section at top of ENTABLATURE, also any projecting ornamental moulding crowning an external façade or internally at junction of wall and ceiling.

COVE: Large concave moulding especially that produced by the arched junction of wall and ceiling.

CROCKET: A GOTHIC decorative feature, based on foliage projecting at regular intervals from spires, pinnacles, canopies, GABLES, etc.

CROW-STEPPED GABLE: See GABLE.

CUPOLA: A small dome on a circular or polygonal base crowning a roof or turret, frequently used to light a staircase.

CURVILINEAR: See TRACERY.

CUSP: Projecting barb-like motif formed by the junction of foils. Used to ornament GOTHIC tracery.

CYCLOPEAN MASONRY: irregular blocks of stone; has come to mean any polygonal masonry of a very large size.

DADO: Usually the finishing of the lower part of an interior wall from floor to waist height, often decorated with a frieze or similar device.

DECORATED: English GOTHIC architectural style *c*.1290–1350 characterised by foliage carving and complex window tracery. Much use of the OGEE ARCH.

DENTIL: A small square block used in series in

IONIC, CORINTHIAN, COMPOSITE, and more rarely, DORIC cornices.

DIAPERWORK: Surface decoration or a small repeated geometric pattern prevalent in the later middle ages.

DOGTOOTH: A four-armed star-shaped motif prevalent in Early GOTHIC architecture.

DORIC: See ORDERS.

DORMER WINDOWS: A window placed vertically in a sloping roof and with a roof of its own.

DOSSERET: French term for an additional high block or slabs on top of an ABACUS.

DOUBLE PILE: A type of house plan popularised by Sir Roger Pratt in the seventeenth century in which the house is two rooms deep, the series of rooms separated by a longitudinal corridor.

DRIP MOULD: A projecting moulding to throw off the rain, on the face of the wall above a window.

EARLY ENGLISH: The earliest form of GOTHIC architecture in England c.1180–1260.

ELEVATION: The external faces of a building; also used to mean a drawing made in projection on a vertical plane to show any one face of a building.

ENTABLATURE: Upper part of an ORDER consisting of ARCHITRAVE, FRIEZE and CORNICE.

EXEDRA: Small apse-like termination to a room or hall.

FAN VAULT: See VAULTING.

FINIAL: Ornamental feature, generally stone, placed on top of pinnacle or apex and base of gable. BALL FINIAL — a finial terminated by a small stone sphere.

FOLLY: A deliberately functionless building or ruined structure, popular in the eighteenth century to add an element of the picturesque to the landscape.

FRETTING: Geometrical ornament of horizontal and vertical straight lines repeated to form a band.

FRIEZE: Middle division of an ENTABLATURE, between the ARCHITRAVE and the CORNICE, usually decorated but may be plain.

GABLE: The vertical, triangular portion of a wall at the end of a ridged roof, from the eaves level to the apex. A CROW-STEPPED GABLE has stepped sides.

GIANT ORDER: See ORDER.

GIBBS SURROUND: The surround of a doorway or window made up of alternately large and small blocks of stone, named after the architect James Gibbs.

GOTHIC: Style of architecture prevalent in Europe c.1130–1550. Salient features are the use of the RIB-VAULT, the flying buttress and the pointed arch, and, in its most refined forms, a structural unity and a dissolution of walling to gain large windows.

GOTHICK: Eighteenth-century use of GOTHIC forms to create a Romantic mood in a building without recourse to GOTHIC precepts of design.

GOTHIC REVIVAL: movement to revive the GOTHIC style belonging chiefly to the eighteenth and nineteenth centuries. Distinguished from GOTHICK by a more correct archaeological use of motifs.

GROIN VAULTS: See VAULTING.

GROTTO: Man-made and highly stylized cave, popular in the eighteenth century as a feature in the gardens of country houses.

HEXASTYLE: See PORTICO.

HIPPED/HIP: The external angle formed by the meeting of two floating roof surfaces.

IN ANTIS: See PORTICO.

INTERSTICES: Intervening spaces between members of e.g. a vault.

ITALIANATE: Nineteenth-century revivalist style of architecture evoking Renaissance Italy.

JETTIED CONSTRUCTION: The projection of an upper storey beyond the storey below, found in timber framed buildings. On their outer ends is placed the sill of the walling for the storey above.

KEYSTONE: The central stone of an arch or rib vault.

LIGHTS: Openings between the MULLIONS of a window.

LINTEL: A piece of stone or timber laid horizontally across a doorway or window opening.

LOGGIA: A gallery open on one or more sides, sometimes pillared; it may also be a separate structure, usually in a garden.

MACHICOLATION: A projecting parapet built on the outside of fortified buildings with openings in the floor through which to drop lead etc. onto assailants.

MANNERISM: The style current in Italy from Michelangelo to the end of the sixteenth century when strict canons of classical design were being relaxed or reversed.

MANSARD ROOF: Roof made up of two planes, the lower being longer and steeper than the upper.

METOPE: A square panel between the TRIGLYPHS as the frieze of the DORIC ORDER.

MULLION: Vertical strip, usually of masonry dividing a window into two or more LIGHTS.

NEO-CLASSICAL: A term describing the architecture of a movement which began in the 1750s as a return to the principles of Greek or Roman Art and Architecture.

NEO-GEORGIAN: A late nineteenth and twentieth-century revival of the principles of Georgian house design, i.e. a domestic architecture of restraint and symmetry decorated with classical details especially round doorways.

OCULUS: A round opening in a wall, often used as window.

OEIL-DE-BOEUF WINDOW: A round or oval window.

OGEE ARCH: A pointed arch made up of two curves each of which is made up of a convex and concave part.

ORDERS: In classical architecture, a system of architectural design comprising a column with base, shaft, and CAPITAL supporting an ENTABLATURE. The whole ornamental according to five ordained styles: DORIC, TUSCAN, IONIC, CORINTHIAN or COMPOSITE (see illustration).

COMPOSITO CORINTHO IONICO DORICO TOSCANO

The Orders; plate III from *Regola delli Cinque Ordini d'architettura* by Jacomo Barrozzio da Vignola.
Reproduced by kind permission of the Architectural Association.

GIANT ORDER — an order where the columns rise from the ground through two or more storeys.

PALLADIAN: In English architecture, the classical style of the Italian architect Andrea Palladio introduced by Inigo Jones in the early seventeenth century, and later made popular by Lord Burlington and his followers.

PALMETTE: A fan-like ornamental motif composed of a number of thin strips coming together at the base, in the manner of a palm frond. Mainly used as a frieze decoration.

PARGETTING: The covering of buildings, usually timber-framed, with a durable plaster of lime, the surface of which is often decorated with ornate patterns.

PATERA: A circular ornament sunk into a wall, decorated with stylized foliage or petals.

PEDIMENT: Originally a low pitched triangular GABLE over a PORTICO used in classical architecture and frequently used later to decorate doorways and windows.
BROKEN PEDIMENT — one in which the apex of the triangle is removed, leaving a roughly arc-like shape though other shapes are possible. OPEN PEDIMENT — one in which a section of the base of the triangle is removed. SEGMENTAL PEDIMENT — one made of an arc of a circle, almost always used over doors or windows.

PERRON: A platform in front of a house, church or civic building, reached by a flight of steps.

PERPENDICULAR: A late GOTHIC architectural style, unique to England. It evolved around 1330 and was general until *c.* 1540. Characterised by windows dominated by vertical lines hitting the arch, so as to give a grid-iron appearance.

PIANO NOBILE: An Italian Renaissance term, signifying the principal floor of a house containing the reception rooms, the whole raised on a basement storey.

PILASTER: A flat column set against the surface of a building built into it and projecting not more than one third of its surface breadth.

POLYCHROMY: The use of several colours of brick or stone to decorate the surface of a building.

PORTICO: A roofed structure supported by columns, attached to a building normally as an entrance feature. PORTICO IN ANTIS — one in which the columns are in a plane with the walls of the building i.e. the PORTICO does not project beyond the building. A HEXASTYLE portico is one with six columns. A TETRASTYLE portico is one with four columns.

PYLON: Originally the pyramidal, truncated, rectangular towers used to flank an entrance in Egyptian architecture; often used now to mean any large isolated structure.

QUATREFOIL: A four-lobed ornament used mainly in GOTHIC architecture, as a surface decoration also found in window tracery.

QUEEN ANNE: English domestic architecture of the early eighteenth century, admired for its simple grace by Norman Shaw and revived by his office in the late nineteenth century.

QUOINS: Dressed stones at the corner of a building, sometimes imitated by groups of brick in wholly brick buildings.

REGENCY: The style of architecture prevalent under George IV as King 1820–1830, or as Prince Regent 1811–1820, epitomised by the works of John Nash.

REPOUSSÉ: Metalwork beaten into relief by hammering from the reverse side, used, for example, in ornamental lead troughs.

RIB VAULT: See VAULT.

ROCOCO: A very ornate, light, mid-eighteenth-century style of art and architecture, following the more weighty BAROQUE. In England it was mainly confined to interior design, plasterwork and furniture, while a stripped down PALLADIAN style was almost exclusively used for the exterior of major buildings.

RUSTICATION: The use of massive elements of masonry mainly in the basement storey of a building, to give an impression of strength. Originally the blocks were rough hewn; in later styles, the surface would be smooth with artificially large courses cut between the blocks. VERMICULATED RUSTICATION — the surface of the rusticated blocks are heavily channelled with curved, irregular grooves, giving an impression of the surface being riddled with worms.

SASH WINDOW: One made of sashes i.e. sliding wooden panels of glass set in grooves.

STRAINER ARCH: An arch inserted across the width of the building to support a weight above, often used in medieval churches e.g. Salisbury, to support the central tower.

STRAPWORK: Elizabethan and Jacobean surface ornament composed of interlacing strips giving the impression of punched and studded leatherwork, sometimes used to create an ornate skyline.

STRING COURSE: A projecting course of stone or brick running horizontally across a building.

SWAG: A carved representation of drapery and/or foliage hanging from two level points.

TETRASTYLE: See PORTICO.

THERMAL WINDOW: A semi-circular window divided by two MULLIONS derived from classical baths.

TRACERY: The ornamental pattern filling the head of a GOTHIC window of two or more LIGHTS; also applied to the surface of buildings as decoration.

TRANSOM: A horizontal strip of masonry dividing up a window.

TREFOIL: A three-lobed figure in TRACERY or a three-lobed carved leaf.

TRIGLYPH: A slightly projecting block having three grooves on its face in the FRIEZE of the Greek DORIC ORDER.
Elements in a DORIC FRIEZE, which separate the METOPES.

TUDORBETHAN: An imprecise nineteenth-century revival of sixteenth and seventeenth-century styles, mixing Tudor, Elizabethan, and Jacobean motifs.

TUSCAN ORDER: See ORDERS.

TYMPANUM: The triangular rounded area within a pediment and the area above a doorway enclosed by the LINTEL and the surrounding arch.

VAULT: a. Barrel or tunnel vault: vault in continuous semi-circular or more rarely, pointed sections.
b. Groin vault: composed of the intersection of two tunnel vaults at right angles, giving four compartments.
c. Rib vault: vault with stone ribs projecting from the groins i.e. the intersecting planes of the vault.
d. Fan vault: complex late medieval vault in which all ribs are of the same length and the same distance apart, and of the same curvature. Sometimes the interstices or panels between the fans are decorated with pendants i.e. projecting ornamental features.

VENETIAN WINDOW: A classical window made up of three parts, the central part wider and taller than the other two and arched. Also used for doorways.

VERMICULATED RUSTICATION: See RUSTICATION.

VITRUVIAN SCROLL: A repeated classical motif made up of features reminiscent of waves terminated by scrolls.

VOLUTE: A spiral scroll used in the IONIC CAPITAL as a linking motif in classical architecture.

WEATHERBOARDING: Overlapping strips of wood, cladding a building.

INDEX

Sketches for Country Residents (Newton) 174
Skidmore (metalworker) 145
Slater, James 40
Sleter, Francesco 24, 25, 39, 41
Slingsby, Henry 16
Smeaton Manor, North Yorkshire 173
Smirke, Sir Robert 126
Smith, Edmund 12
Smith, Francis and William 45–7, 54, 60
Smith, George 154
Smith, Richard 46
Soane, Sir John 114, 134
Soldi, Andrea 25
Some Designs by Mr Inigo Jones and Mr William Kent (Vardy) 65
Sompting Church, West Sussex 147
South Carlton Church, Lincolnshire 146
Sowersby, Mr 15
Sparke, Robert 40
Specimens of Gothic Architecture (Willson) 113
Spelsbury Church, Oxfordshire 96, 97, Pl. XVIII
Spencer, Lord John 77–8
Springfield Gaol, Essex 122
Stamford, Lord 84
Standen House, East Sussex 174
Stanford Hall, Leicestershire 19, 46
Stanhope, General 38, 43
Steep Hill, Jersey 179, 180, 181, Ill. 146
Stepleton House, Dorset 19
Stibbington Church, Cambridgeshire 146
Stivichall House, West Midlands 48–9, 52
Stone, Nicholas, the younger 1
Stoneleigh Abbey, Warwickshire 46, 48–9
Stowe, Cornwall 19
Stratford, Holy Trinity Church, Warwickshire 59
Street, G. E. 134, 145, 152, 173, 175
Streeter, Robert 15
Strutt, Colonel 123
Stuart, James Athenian 76, 78, 80, 101
Studley Royal, North Yorkshire 37
Sudbrook House, Surrey 34
Sudbury Hall, Derbyshire 10
Summerson, Sir John 22, 45, 114
Sumner, Archbishop of Canterbury 137
Sunbury Church, Surrey 140
Sunlaws House, Borders 156, 157, Ill. 127
Switzer (mason), 15
Symonds, Ralph 1

Tabley House, Cheshire 55
Tait, Bishop Archibald C. 150
Talbot, Christopher M. 124
Talman, John 27
Taylor (carpenter) 12
Taylor (furniture-maker) 159
Taylor, Sir Robert 83–4, 91
Tenchleys, Surrey 132
Tensley Villa, Limpsfield, Surrey 134

Terling Place, Essex 123–4
Teulon, Samuel Sanders (1812–73) 132–52 portrait 133, Ill. 107
Teulon family 132–3, 135, 151
Thomas, John 162, 170
Thorndon Hall, Essex 23–5, 27, 28, 30, Ill. 19
Thorney Abbey, Cambridgeshire 8
Thorney, Post Office and Constable's House, Cambridgeshire 134, 140, 145, 149, Ill. 123
Thornhill, James 34
Thorpe Hall, Peterborough 3, 7, 9, 16
Tirali, Andrea 31
Tite, Sir William 134
Tong Castle, Shropshire 97
Tortworth Court, Avon 138, 143, Ill. 110
Tredegar Park, Gwent 18
Tregothnan House, Cornwall 124
Triscombe House, Somerset 181
Tuddenham Hall, Suffolk 6
Tufnell, George 68
Tynte, Sir Charles Kemys 82
Tyson, Michael 98, 107–8, 111–13

Uppingham School, Leicestershire 186, 188, Ill. 157
Upton Grey House, Hampshire 185

Vanbrugh, Sir John 34, 63, 130
Vardy, John (1718–65) 63–81 writings by 65
Venice
— San Salvatore 31
— San Stae 31
— Santa Maria del Rosario 31
— Scuola Grande della Misericordia 31
Verney, Sir Ralph 1
Views of Seats (Neale) 124
Villa Arsiero 34
Villa Badoer, Fratta Polesine 34
Villa Barbarigo Rezzonico, Vicenza 29, Ill. 20
Villa Barbaro Maser 37
Villa da Porto 31
Villa Emo, Fanzolo 34
Villa Garzoni Pontecasale 28, Ill. 18
Villa Thiene, Quinto Vicentino 37
Villa Valmarana 21, 38, 42, Ill. 31
Vitruvius Britannicus (Campbell) 7, 33, 36–40, 56–7, 130
Voyage dans l'Egypte (Denon) 116
Vuilliamy 71

Walpole, Horace 64, 74, 98, 106, 108, 110, 112
Walpole, Sir Robert 38
Wanstead House, Essex 38
Ware, Isaac 21, 27, 55, 63, 66, 75 writings 75
Warwick, St Mary's Church 61
Warwick, Sir Philip 18

Warwick, Guy's Cliffe House 50
Warwick, Shire Hall 45, 48–9, 60
Watford, St Andrew's Church, Hertfordshire 134
Watson, Henry 34
Webb, John 6, 31, 34–6, 79, 126, 129–130
Webb, Philip 173, 187, 188
Wentworth Woodhouse, South Yorkshire 34
Wetheringsett Rectory, Suffolk 135, 136, Ill. 109
Whiffen, Marcus 53, 54
Wilkins, William 114, 122, 124
Willett, William 179
Willis R. & Clark, J.W. 113
Willson, E.J. 113
Wilton House, Wiltshire 4, 37, 70
Wimborne St Giles, Dorset 3
Wimpole Hall, Cambridgeshire 4, 19, 86
Winchester Cathedral and College 110
Winchester Palace 30
Winde, William 3, 19
Windsor Great Park, Berkshire 75, Ill. 59
Windsor Royal Estate 136
Wing, Tyro 135
Wisbech Castle, Cambridgeshire 3, 4, 9
Witham House 34
Wittkower, Rudolf 21
Wivenhoe Park, Essex 131
Wolfe, L.J. 155
Wolverley House, Hereford and Worcester 49, 52–3, Ill. 39, 40
Wood, Anthony 45
Woodchester Church, Gloucestershire 138
Woodcote Park, Surrey 70, 71, Ill. 53
Woodlands Vale, Isle of Wight 134, 141
Woodyer, Henry 141
Woolverstone Hall, Suffolk 117, 119, Ill. 94
Worcester, Bishop of 87
Worcester Castle 86
Worksop Manor, Nottinghamshire 9
Worsley, Henry 27
Wortley Hall, West Yorkshire 23–4, 25, 26, Ill. 17
Wortley-Montagu, Edward 25, 26
Wren, Sir Christopher 16, 22, 72 influence of 89, 99–101, 130, 150, 179
Wrest Park, Bedfordshire 24, 27, 34, Ill. 22
Wright, Stephen 99
Wrotham Park, London 55
Wyatt, James 23, 96, 110, 114, 126 influence of 120, 126
Wyatt, Lewis 76
Wyatt, Sir Mathew Digby 152
Wyatt, Samuel 76
Wycombe House, Buckinghamshire 23–4, 26

York Minster 65, 74